GOOD IDEAS
AND
POWER MOVES

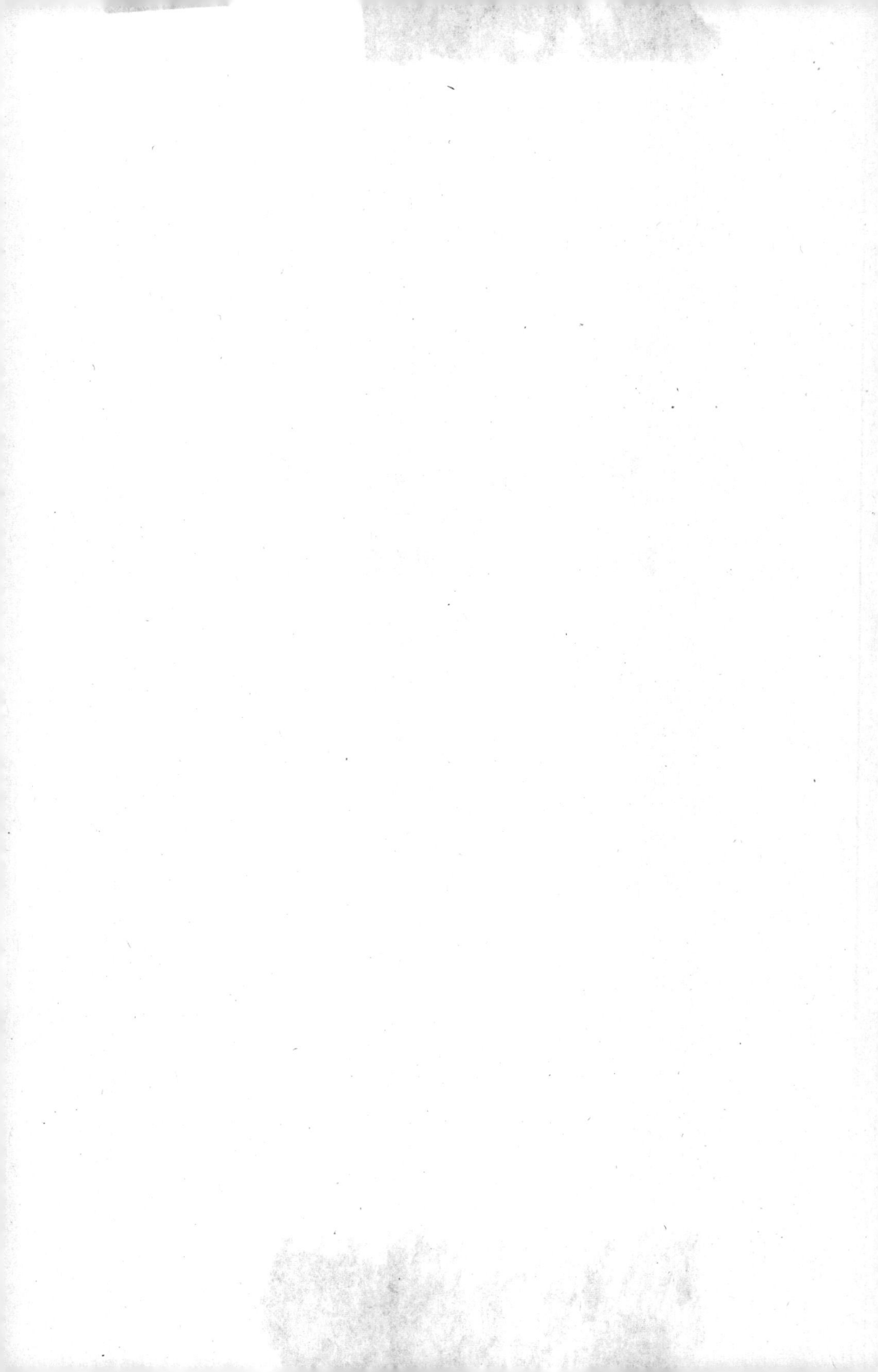

GOOD IDEAS
AND
POWER MOVES

TEN LESSONS
FOR SUCCESS
FROM
TAYLOR SWIFT

SINÉAD O'SULLIVAN

EBURY EDGE

UK | USA | Canada | Ireland | Australia
India | New Zealand | South Africa

Ebury Edge is part of the Penguin Random House group of companies
whose addresses can be found at global.penguinrandomhouse.com

Penguin Random House UK
One Embassy Gardens, 8 Viaduct Gardens, London SW11 7BW

penguin.co.uk
global.penguinrandomhouse.com

Penguin
Random House
UK

First published in the United States by Viking in 2025
First published in the United Kingdom by Ebury Edge in 2025
1

This edition published by arrangement with Viking, an imprint of
Penguin Publishing Group, division of Penguin Random House LLC.

Printed and bound in Great Britain by Clays Ltd, Elcograf S.p.A.

The authorised representative in the EEA is Penguin Random House Ireland,
Morrison Chambers, 32 Nassau Street, Dublin D02 YH68

A CIP catalogue record for this book is available from the British Library

ISBN 9781529146882

Book design by Daniel Lagin

Penguin Random House is committed to a sustainable future
for our business, our readers and our planet. This book is made
from Forest Stewardship Council® certified paper.

MIX
Paper | Supporting
responsible forestry
FSC
www.fsc.org   FSC® C018179

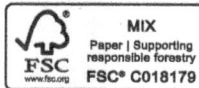

I can dedicate this book to none other than the immeasurable number of Swifties who have changed my life by constantly and consistently espousing the Power Moves I discuss henceforth.

In the words of Taylor Alison Swift:

This one is about you,
you know who you are.
I love you.

If you're lucky enough to be different,
don't ever change.

Taylor Swift

CONTENTS

GOOD IDEAS AND
POWER MOVES

INTRODUCTION

T HIS IS A BOOK ABOUT TAYLOR SWIFT, OF COURSE. BUT TO *really* understand what I've written in this book, there are a couple of other things you need to understand first . . .

YOU (YES, YOU!) CAN WORK AT NASA

When I was a fifteen-year-old high schooler, I was given the opportunity to travel from Northern Ireland to Houston's Mission Control on the trip of a lifetime: to Space Camp. I had always had an indiscriminate love for all things in the sky: planes, black holes, Mars rovers, astronomy, and more, so when I heard about the opportunity, I applied straightaway and, to my surprise, made it through the interviews to get a coveted place.

It was next-level *amazing*!

When I arrived in Houston, I was picked up at the airport by my host family of NASA engineers who happened to live next door to the Johnson Space Center. In fact, and rather unsurprisingly, during my time at Space Camp I met person after person who worked at NASA.

Like the guy who did the thermal engineering on the astronaut's space-walk glove. The guy who worked on the new ion-thruster propulsion system. The scuba-diving woman who trained astronauts in the massive underwater mock-up of the International Space Station. I got to sit in the Mission Control Center and talk to the flight director once he was finished speaking to the astronauts aboard the space station. One of my more daring Space Camp pals managed to bum a cigarette off the college intern who was working on orbital trajectory.

In the evenings, we hung out with the kids of the NASA employees and went around to friends of my host family's houses for dinner. One of them had a swimming pool, and we had a pool party. Me? In America? Having a *pool party*? I felt like I was in a TV show!

Once Space Camp sadly concluded, after weeks of sweating in a type of heat and humidity that I had never experienced before, I went back to my home in Northern Ireland just in time to start back at school.

A few months later, the time came to start college applications. For me, deciding what to study was the easiest decision I had ever made. I was going to study aerospace engineering so that I could one day work at NASA. So naturally, when my teachers and friends and even friends of my parents asked me what I wanted to do, I told them as much.

Their reaction?

"Oh. Ummm . . . Sure? Okay."

I could see in their eyes that what they were *really* thinking was: "This poor, delusional girl." I may as well have told them that I wanted to grow up to be the Princess of Genovia. My teachers told me to "apply for something else as well . . . you know . . . *just in case*." My friends sometimes asked me, "But what do you *actually* want to do?" And my parents assumed I'd "grow out of it" at some stage.

Anyway, that was a million years ago now.

I did, in fact, study aerospace engineering in Northern Ireland. And then I moved to the United States to study more aerospace engineering at grad school. I specialized in human spaceflight and got to work with astronauts and mission controllers, and, yes, I got to work on designing space missions for NASA. My good friends became the men and women who designed rovers for other planets, and I even got to be in the Mission Control Center at the Jet Propulsion Laboratory when the Mars Curiosity rover touched down on a planet 200 million kilometers away. My friends would talk about their rocket testing in the same way that other people may talk about football results.

The reason I bring this story up in a book about Taylor Swift is simple.

This book is fundamentally about looking at what Taylor has done (and continues to do), and then saying: You, too, can do this.

Which in theory, and at least to me, sounds perfectly normal.

But over the years I've come to realize that, to so many people, this is something that sounds *totally* batshit crazy.

"You think *you* can be like Taylor Swift?"

"You think *you* can work at NASA?"

Unfortunately, a lot of people are absolutely convinced that these types of achievements are beyond the realm of what is possible for mere mortals to achieve.

But what if I told you that the people achieving such things *are* only mere mortals?

You see, what I was so incredibly lucky to learn and internalize when I was fifteen, and the one thing that ultimately had more impact on my life than anything else, can be summarized by one word: *agency.*

It's the idea that we do have control over the outcomes of our life, and in fact, far more control than you may even realize. Agency is the premise that if you want to do something, you can actually just go right ahead and do it without seeking permission or waiting for it to happen to you.

If *anybody* can do *anything*, then why not *me*? Or why not *you*?

My preconceptions of NASA were probably similar to what most people think of the place: secretive, full of the world's smartest people and famous astronauts, and totally, 100 percent unachievable as a career choice.

But when I actually spent time there as a student, I realized this couldn't have been further from the reality.

Sure, everybody was really smart. But aside from the one in every few hundred people who were modern-day Einsteins, most people had gone to college, studied engineering or science, achieved average to good grades, and worked their way into NASA in the same way that you might work your way into any other engineering job.

What separated those who worked on space missions instead of designing bridges was not their intelligence but simply their *interest* in space missions instead of bridges.

NASA engineers were just normal people. They got up in the morning after hitting the snooze button too many times, rolled into work, did some really cool stuff, and then went home again for dinner with the family. If anything, I was slightly disappointed by just how normal (mundane?) even the astronauts' lives were.

During a recent podcast interview, I was asked the following question: "What is it that really separates NASA engineers from normal engineers?"

My response: NASA engineers *are* normal engineers; they just work on slightly different things.

Astronauts are just regular people, it turns out, with a government job (albeit an extremely cool and prestigious one). And when I shyly told these astronauts to their faces that I, too, would like to be an astronaut, you know what they said?

"Great! So here's what you need to do. Let me know if you need any help along the way."

Once I got home from Space Camp, I felt like my life had permanently changed. I also felt like I had been lied to my whole life: People pretended that becoming an astronaut was impossible, but it's clearly not. I had met real-life astronauts, and they had told me how I could become one too.

What other things were people lying about being impossible to do?

ON BEING FEARLESS

Two weeks after I started my undergraduate engineering course in Northern Ireland, Taylor Swift released her second studio album, *Fearless*. I sang "Love Story" with my best friend, Kirsty, when we won our first-year Aircraft Design competition. Taylor then released *Red* when I started learning how to drive, the CD of which was the only one I had in my car as I drove (quite badly!) between Belfast and Dublin to visit my first serious boyfriend.

My move to the United States coincided with her release of the "Welcome to New York" anthem on her *1989* album, and I wrote at least fifty thousand words of my grad school dissertation on spaceflight listening to "Blank Space." I fell in love with a new boyfriend over "You Are in Love."

In the midst of "Wildest Dreams," I emailed the CEO of a large spaceflight company one day out of the blue to ask her how I could, one day, get her job, and I finally got a response: "You need to go and get an MBA." And so, after quickly googling what an MBA was (a master's in business administration, it turned out), I moved to Boston to start a new era at Harvard Business School.

Once there, I parted ways with my previously mentioned boyfriend, rather fittingly, to the *Reputation* soundtrack.

However, around that time, I happened to fall in love in my professional life, unexpectedly, with something new: business and finance. I decided *not* to return to spaceflight at NASA after my MBA but to remain in Boston at Harvard, researching innovation, ideas, finance, and strategy.

As with most of her fans, Taylor Swift has been a massive part of my personal story for as long as I can remember. This boyfriend; that album. This place; that song. Nearly every Swiftie I've ever met is able to write their personal story through Taylor Swift's discography, just like I've done.

At Harvard Business School, however, I started to think about Taylor Swift's journey through a professional lens too. Over time, I had become more and more obsessed with the thing I learned when I was fifteen: How do seemingly normal people do extraordinary things? It was a question that consistently reared its head when I thought about my hobbies, my interests, my research on economics and innovation, and even when I listened to my favorite musician— Taylor Swift.

I started cold-calling people who were at the top of their field and asking them basic questions about their lives. Why do you do the same training, over and over again, every day? Don't you get bored of running? Why did you choose to work on this album instead of that one? Did you know that this start-up was going to be successful when you invested millions of dollars into it? And most important: *How* did you become so successful?

As this happened, I noticed three key things.

The first is that when you reach out to people when you're genuinely trying to learn about them and their decision-making process, it's kind of wild how often they will actually respond to you in a very positive way. In my experience, most people have replied to me, which initially came as a shock (so yes, send that email or make that call!).

The second thing is that nearly every one of these people told me the same thing, regardless of whether they were an athlete, a performing artist, a chef, an investor, or in some other niche. And that thing was:

"Doing what I do is not at all *impossible*. It's actually not even complicated. But it does take a *lot* of hard work."

The hunch I had as a fifteen-year-old was correct—you can literally do *anything* that you put your mind to, especially if somebody shows you which path to take and you work harder than most other people.

The third thing I noticed was that around this time Taylor Swift was becoming an increasingly large part of my thinking around the *hows* and the *whys* of outsize success. And this coincided, in particular, with a period of my professional life when I was looking, nearly in desperation, for guidance from a role model who espoused my values and whose story I could connect with.

When I wanted to attempt new, risky projects or take a different, more creative approach with my work, there were a million people I could have spoken to who would have told me to "wait until you're more established," or said it was a "great idea, but why not do it the conventional way first."

And every single time I was on the fence about trying something bigger or riskier, I would look at Taylor Swift and think, *Fuck it.*

There's an expression that gets thrown around a lot, especially about women in their careers: "If you can't see it, you can't be it." As much as people tend to use this expression offhandedly, I want to double down on how true it actually is for a moment.

It was only after I met NASA engineers that I realized I, too, could be one; it was only after I spoke to several writers that I realized I, too, could one day write a book; and it was only because I watched Taylor Swift for more than a decade as I was making my own career-defining decisions that I realized that there's more than one way for me to do this whole career thing successfully.

As someone who internalized at a young age that I could replicate other people's success by understanding their actions and decisions and then copying them, I became fixated on watching and learning from other people. And for an absurdly long amount of time, one of those people was and continues to be Taylor Swift. For both personal and professional guidance.

I like to think that it's not a coincidence that Taylor released *Fearless* at the same time that I entered into my career and my adulthood, because, thanks to her, this is how I've consistently tried to act in both: fearlessly.

*   *   *

I have spent the majority of my professional life at Harvard Business School, thinking deeply about business, economics, and strategy across an unimaginable number of industries and business types and working with the superstar CEOs who impact and influence our lives. Working alongside the most famous economists and strategists, I've spent more than a decade analyzing products, companies, and economies. Creating financial, operational, and corporate strategy with the leaders, politicians, and CEOs who head them up has formed most of my research.

Through that research, I'll try to answer certain questions, like: Is this investment likely to return capital to investors? Is this CEO the right person for the job? Is this industry about to get disrupted? Should the company release a new product this year or next year?

I've been extremely lucky that through this work I've been able to gain valuable experience from the largest and most impressive businesses in the coolest industries and gotten to meet some of the most infamous and outstanding investors and business executives.

Unsurprisingly, all these industries, businesses, executives, and investors have been written about. A *lot*. Some even have whole textbooks outlining what they're doing and why.

And then I think about one of the most, if not *the* most, consequential businessperson of my era: Taylor Swift, the CEO.

As an asset, this pop star has higher returns than 99.9 percent of hedge funds. She is a better strategist than most successful corporate CEOs, and she is the only person that the US Federal Reserve and European Central Bank track with precision because she can move financial markets faster than high-frequency traders. Just this morning, I read an article in the *Financial Times* about how investors in electric vehicles are closely analyzing Taylor in an attempt to hedge their investments. There is no economy or industry that, regardless of how distant it seems from pop music, is not impacted by her.

I wrote this book because she is somebody it is clearly very important to understand.

However, mostly I wrote it because I know people can learn as much as I do from Taylor Swift as both a CEO and a leader, and as a business and a brand that has grown into a multibillion-dollar global enterprise.

In this book I have outlined not only how Taylor operates but, more important, how she has used this operational strategy to usher in more success than nearly every other executive today.

In the same way that the astronauts told the fifteen-year-old me, "This is what you need to do to become an astronaut," I've outlined the lessons that I've spent nearly a decade reverse-engineering by carefully analyzing Taylor and her business from afar. These are the lessons I use when I think about my own life—personal and professional—since I became fearless more than two decades ago. It's the book I wish had existed during the many ups and downs and inside-outs of my own path.

In her song "The Man," Taylor herself compels her fans to wonder: Would she ever, despite the crazy and unique business and leadership path that she has forged, be talked about for more than what she wore, who she was dating, and whether she deserved any of her success?

Could any of that be *"separated from my good ideas and power moves"*?

Well, this book does just that. I am convinced that in dissecting her good ideas and power moves, you will learn just as much as I did about how to live fearlessly, personally and professionally.

People pretend that it's impossible to do extraordinary things, but that's simply not true. I know this because I've met the normal people who break world records, produce chart-topping music, win Nobel Prizes, and more.

Everybody, it turns out, can be like Taylor Swift. You just need to know how . . .

POWER MOVE ONE

BE A UNICORN

BEING LIKE TAYLOR SWIFT IS NOT IMPOSSIBLE. HOWEVER, IT TURNS out that it's not exactly easy.

"But what happens if you get sick?" I asked my friend, a chef of a two-Michelin-star restaurant, over dinner.

It's a fascinating question, because it really highlighted the difference between our lives. If I were to get sick, I would send a few emails to postpone meetings, and when I'm feeling a bit better, I might even attempt to do some work from bed. This is the ultimate luxury of being a white-collar, work-from-anywhere worker.

My sister, who works in a hospital where she must be physically present to do her job, can even phone in sick and have someone cover her shift. Is it ideal? No. But is it catastrophic? Also no.

A two-Michelin-star restaurant, however, is slightly different.

Six-month waiting lists, for both lunch and dinner, and a small, ninja-like team of the most skilled chefs in the world performing what is essentially microsurgery on food to produce an extremely complex menu at high speed.

When your customers are spending hundreds of dollars per

meal, at a minimum, the lowest acceptable outcome is complete *perfection.*

"Sick? You don't get sick. I haven't had a sick day in years," the chef tells me, baffled by the question in the first place. "It's not an option."

Of the estimated 15 million restaurants in the world, only 0.018 percent of them hold one or more Michelin stars. Of that, only 650 two- or three-Michelin-star restaurants exist today, putting my friend in the top 0.004 percent of chefs in the world.

I thought about a trip I took last winter, a four-hour flight each way with a three-day vacation in between. And afterward, a five-week battle with a chest and sinus infection that I definitely caught at the airport. If I were a chef, would I have not traveled so that I didn't get sick? Or would I have ignored being sick?

Then I thought about Taylor Swift's eighteen-month-long Eras Tour across five continents, consisting of 149 shows in some of the most extreme weather conditions on earth. What the hell? Just *how?*

I'm pretty sure I read that somewhere in the middle of her Brazilian shows, she performed her three-and-a-half-hour, ten-thousand-calories-burning show, boarded her plane still in her show attire, flew for ten hours to New York, and was papped the next day up to her usual shenanigans of recording a new album, hanging out with celebrity friends, and being the ultimate woman-about-town.

I say this as someone who is exactly the same age as Taylor Swift and would love going to the pub in pajamas to be normalized: *How* does she do it?

How does she not get sick? How does she have the energy? Has anybody actually verified that she *doesn't* have a twin?

To put this into the context of where I, part of the Taylor-aged cohort, am, one of my friends texted me yesterday asking me to congratulate her for wearing a bra for the first time in a week.

"I know I'm going on that stage whether I'm sick, injured, heart-broken, uncomfortable, or stressed. That's part of my identity as a human being now. If someone buys a ticket to my show, I'm going to play it unless we have some sort of force majeure," Taylor said in a mid–Eras Tour interview.

I'm not entirely sure what the correct single metric for trying to measure Taylor's success as a singer-songwriter would be, and it's likely that the topic could be a long book on its own, but consider that in 2022, thirty-six million songs were released to the public. Figuring out which artist is best among those releasing these millions of songs is complex, but just bear with me when I make the assumption that across these releases, Taylor comes up top.

That means she is 1/36,000,000. Which means she is in the top 0.0000028 percent of artists releasing music. And that is just *wild*.

So yeah, we live in a world where there are two types of people: the normal people who try their best to wear bras to work and the Taylor Swifts. The chefs of two-Michelin-star restaurants. The prima ballerinas. The Navy SEALs. The Nobel Prize winners. The statistical outliers.

The Unicorns.

BUT . . . UNICORNS ARE NORMAL PEOPLE TOO

There is a huge paradox regarding people who do extraordinary things.

In one way, they are just ordinary people like you and me who just so *happen* to be doing extraordinary things. Sometimes I like to think that even someone as powerful as the president of the United

States puts on his pajamas, gets into bed at night, and thinks, "Thank god. Another day at the office done," before watching cat videos on an anonymous account on Twitter.

I happen to be writing this book from a little village in Ireland that houses a beautiful castle, where celebrities sometimes visit. One day, I walked into the tiny corner pub only to be told that I had just missed a global music superstar. "I don't see the big deal," the bar lady retorted across the pub. "He's just another man who sits on the toilet every day, bored like the rest of us."

In fact, some people have not subscribed to the celebrity-culture obsession that has permeated our lives, including most of my friends and family, who are blissfully unaware of any "famous" people and are unable to see Unicorns as anything *but* ordinary people. The "extraordinary" things they do are seen as nothing more than part of their job, no different from being a builder or an accountant.

And this is, in fact, probably a good way to think about them.

I've had the benefit of meeting, working with, and even befriending many Unicorns, and they are indeed normal people in the ways that make people *human*. They are insecure. They are scared. They worry about people not liking them. They also find it hard to get dates (I know!). They, too, will stare at their phones wondering if the person they like will ever text them back. They have complex friends and families. They start their day by waking up, jumping in the shower, and wondering whether or not they can get away with using dry shampoo instead of the real stuff.

And this is largely who we think about when we think about Taylor Swift. Or at least this is the way most people have been thinking about her for the last twentyish years. Because she is the ultimate girl next door.

She is a beautiful, ultratalented, successful, fun, witty billionaire that everybody wants to date. But is there anything more relatable than the fact that she *still* happens to get ghosted by her dates like the rest of us?

The depths of her perceived—and, to a large degree her *real*—normalcy will be a central theme in later discussions in this book on her strategy, her engagement, and why we all still seem to love her so much despite her success (yes, we typically dislike successful people, and greatly despise successful women).

I mean, being "normal" is her *thing*. Normality is her multibillion-dollar business. There's nobody who does "normal" better than the most famous and influential billionaire alive, even with her private jets.

But before we get into the specifics of her normalcy, I want to take a chapter, just one, to talk about the ways in which the *ordinary* people who do extraordinary things are actually pretty damn *extraordinary*.

Because until you have a good sense of what makes a Unicorn extraordinary, and until you really understand their superpower, it's going to be hard to contextualize just how insanely talented and special they are, and how downright difficult everything they do is.

Or learn how to actually do extraordinary things yourself, as an ordinary person.

You see, all the things that Taylor manages to do, and all her Power Moves and good ideas and superstardom and cunning cleverness, come from the little bit of "extraordinary" that lives within her.

People simply don't know how to identify Unicorns or to understand what makes them special, and the reason that ordinary people find it so hard to become Unicorns is that they don't know *how* to. I mean, how is Taylor Swift able to do the frankly insane things she does? It feels like a question that is too large to answer, and throughout this book I'll try to explain.

But when you step back and really look at, spend time with, and study the very ordinary people who do extraordinary things, the statistical outliers, you realize that they all share common traits, characteristics, and beliefs that allow them to transcend ordinariness to achieve Unicornness.

I call them common traits for the simple reason that you or I could, if we really *wanted*, achieve them too.

One of the most dangerous beliefs in the world is one that I hear constantly from many people, including the students I teach, and is something that I catch myself sometimes repeating inwardly and outwardly: *I can't be a Unicorn.*

You'd be amazed to learn that the only real difference between someone wondering whether they'll wear a bra this week and Taylor Swift performing sellout shows around the globe is that Taylor figured out how to be a Unicorn, whereas others didn't.

Now, I'm not saying that what Taylor is doing is easy—quite the opposite.

But to the extent that all of us have enormous potential to change the world in little or large ways, we're also all guilty of leaving immense amounts of that potential unfulfilled. Even Taylor Swift knows this: When she got the news that *Reputation* was not being nominated for any Grammys, she said, with tears in her eyes, "I just need to make a better record."

And even after more than thirty years as one of the best chefs in the world, my friend tells me that "every day it's about just trying to make one small thing better, because there's still a very long way to go."

But looking at what Unicorns do in order to reach the extraordinary outcomes they achieve is, if nothing else, helpful for guiding us closer to being extraordinary.

ACHIEVING UNICORN STATUS

There is a myth that extraordinary people are born as extraordinary people. That there's no point in trying to be the next Clara Bow—the world's original and most famous "It Girl"—because, well, Clara Bow came out of the womb absolutely and divinely fabulous. That Taylor Swift has some freakish brain wiring that nobody else does. That Nobel Prize ideas are contained in a person's mind at birth.

Well, this is not exactly how it goes.

According to William Shakespeare (and popularly believed to be true) there are three ways to achieve Unicorn status: "Some are born great, some achieve greatness, and some have greatness thrust upon them."

Let's start with being born great. There is no doubt that some people are born with unnaturally huge advantages that enable them to do extraordinary things. The swimmer Michael Phelps, for example, a physiological Eighth Wonder of the World, won eighty-two medals in major international swimming competitions over his career, no doubt aided by his genetically predisposed body.

Then you have people who were born into Unicorn status simply because of who they are. Think of nepo children of family-run conglomerates, who will ultimately have power and prestige transferred to them upon succession, as their last name is a stronger indicator of likely future leadership than a proven track record. Here, Unicorn status is achieved merely because of who you are, not something you've done.

And then you have the Unicorns who have had greatness thrust upon them. The one example that lives in my brain constantly is that of a former actor, voice of Paddington Bear, and comedian whose move into politics was largely predicated on his viral comedy platform. After using humor and social media sketches to win his way into the presidency, the invasion of his country became one of the most geopolitically, economically, and security-significant events of our century. I am, of course, talking about Volodymyr Zelensky, the president of Ukraine, who had greatness inadvertently thrust upon him, and who has risen to the occasion of being one of the most important political figures of this and the last decade.

No doubt you can also think of or have already come across many people who have had greatness given willingly and freely to them for, well, unknown reasons—the people who have seemed to "fail upward," of whom we all annoyingly know many. Yes, it is excruciatingly infuriating to see.

But I guess some people who have greatness bestowed upon them do deserve it. There's also a category of people who are extremely talented, yet because of the dynamics of the industry they're in, will still rely on the powers that be to "anoint" them. Just look at *American Idol*, the TV show in which thousands of similarly talented people hope to become "the chosen one." The world of celebrity endorsements and partnerships doesn't feel too far removed from this, as executives at huge brands decide which model to turn into the next "It Girl." The next Clara Bow.

So yeah, both the "born great" and "had greatness thrust upon them" are two very real ways in which people move from being ordinary to extraordinary and achieve Unicorn status. I mean, after all my years at Harvard University, it's hard to ignore the fact that an overwhelming percentage of the student population is there because of their triple-barreled last names. I've met enough athletes standing at over seven feet tall to know there was one reason they'd been handed scholarships. And I've certainly been in enough meetings to know that, behind closed doors, the "winners" aren't always chosen based on merit. I've just seen too much not to be cynical about how opportunities are distributed.

But here's the thing—only a very, very small number of people become Unicorns in these ways.

Meaning that the overwhelming majority of extraordinary people, of Unicorns, who achieve statistically nearly impossible outcomes, are much more like you and me than you may think. They are the people who have had to achieve greatness themselves, in their short lives. They are the *most ordinary* of the ordinary people who do extraordinary things.

Which, you know, is great news. Because it means that if most of the Unicorns in the world are actually normal people who were able to achieve greatness on their own terms and not because of some external, impossible-to-replicate situation—like who their parents are, or exceptional biological advantage—then we, too, can achieve greatness.

CAN YOU TEACH GREATNESS?

Most people assume that Unicorns are born into greatness because of the fact that by the time you witness a Unicorn's talent, it's so great that it seems to be a natural extension of the person and, therefore, that they were born with it.

One of my favorite videos of Taylor Swift is the one of when she was fourteen, singing a song called "Lucky You" for the first time after writing it the day before. The song is actually surprisingly good, and watching such a young teenager—practically still a child—singing it really makes you think: Wow, I couldn't write that at the age of thirty-five, never mind fourteen. She's so naturally gifted!

As it so happens, lyrics from the first chorus include: "*Live forever, never say never* / You can do better, *that's what she says.*" (The emphasis is mine.)

Even back then, Taylor knew you could always do better. Long before she was an adult, she had internalized the need for constant improvement.

It turns out that humans make the mistake of assuming talent is something we simply have or don't: We take something that we do not understand, like the process of songwriting, and assume that because we cannot currently do it ourselves, it must be *too hard.*

The reality is that even if things are *hard*, they're rarely *too hard.* Instead, they're simply a thing that we haven't learned yet. And the fact that we don't know when or how someone has learned something that we haven't means we often assume they were born with that knowledge or skill.

Once you understand this, and have seen it many times, you start to see it *everywhere.* Which kind of sucks, because you soon realize that the people you used to think were total geniuses are not. But it is also kind of great because it means that you, too, could probably do that thing if you tried.

The first time I saw this up close, in my previous life as an aerospace engineer, has stuck with me permanently. When I first started a project at NASA many years ago, I struggled enormously to come to terms with the fact that everybody else was just so much *smarter* than me. I would watch them write computer code in seconds and solve complex math problems as easily as they brushed their teeth. I would ask them a question, to which they would respond in what felt like a language I couldn't understand.

One day, I had had enough. Exasperated and in tears, I told my colleague that I was thinking about quitting. "I have no idea how you just *know* these things. Like how could it ever possibly occur to you to solve this problem in this extremely, seemingly random way? I'm never going to be good enough to contribute here!"

There was no point, I thought, in trying to compete with people who were born with supernatural intelligence.

To which my colleague, looking me dead in the eyes, replied, "I literally learned how to do this exact thing in the last year of my undergrad. We all did. We all took the same classes."

It stunned me. Just a couple of years prior, they didn't know this stuff either. Instead of having some supernatural ability to dissect the world in foreign ways, they were *taught* to use these methodologies. And you know what? I took those same classes after hearing this, and then, just like them, I became "freakishly smart" to people who had not taken said classes. Often, a difference in expertise is disguised as a personality trait of "genius."

The more you meet people who have what feels like "totally outlandish" capabilities, the more you realize that someone, somewhere, taught them how to do that thing. And that you, too, could likely do it if you practiced it as much as they did.

Taylor Swift is no different. In the same way that you may have learned to play soccer as a young kid, Taylor was learning how to play the guitar. As she was learning to play the guitar, someone else was learning biology.

In fact, I recently came across a magazine interview with Dr. Michael Rosbash, an American geneticist who won the Nobel Prize in Medicine in 2017. It included photographs of his school reports over several years. And trust me, the number of "Unsatisfactory" boxes that were ticked through his childhood serves as further anecdotal evidence that for most people, even Nobel Prize winners, Unicorn status is something that is earned, not bestowed.

So how, exactly, does somebody like Taylor Swift go from being an ordinary person learning how to play the guitar to a Unicorn breaking every goddamn music record that was ever set?

Well, Taylor, like every Unicorn, has two things that have gotten her there:

Dedication and intrinsic motivation.

DEDICATION

When I was working on said NASA project, one of the engineers on my team was a pretty cocky guy called Michael, who, one day after work and a few beers, announced: "When I was younger, I used to do track and field. Actually, I beat Usain Bolt at a track meet once. I could have been an Olympian, but I chose to be an engineer instead."

I looked at Michael, who happened to be smaller than me in both height and build, and didn't quite know what to say.

The first thought that crossed my mind may well be the first thought that has come across yours, which is this: If you were to draw a Venn diagram of NASA engineers and international athletes, there would be a very, very tiny and highly unlikely intersection. Most engineers, after all, are closer to Sheldon Cooper than LeBron James.

I remember this exact moment as being the first time I needed to know the answer to the question: Why do some people become Unicorns and others don't? And almost immediately, Michael had answered this question for me.

Maybe Michael *was* in fact a really talented athlete. Although I found it hard to compare the person standing in front of me to Usain Bolt, who was I to argue that Michael wasn't born with some sort of extraordinary ability to run fast? But although a certain amount of talent is necessary to become a Unicorn, by far the biggest and most important determinant of whether a person will do extraordinary things in their field is if they have *dedication* to it.

"It's impossible that you could have been an Olympian," I told him, "because making it to the Olympics isn't something that happens *to you*; it's something you have to *choose*. And you chose something else."

So here's the difference between someone playing the guitar in their bedroom and Taylor Swift: Taylor dedicated her entire life, and the lives of every single family member and friend, to her career from an extremely young age.

For most kids, being very dedicated to a hobby such as learning an instrument means practicing three to five times a week and attending an hour-long lesson at school. The top echelon of extremely dedicated kids may attend several lessons a week, practice every day, and be involved in several after-school and weekend bands and orchestras.

For every few hundred million kids, there's a Taylor Swift, who will somehow convince their entire family to pack up their jobs, their house, and their lives to move to a new city in the pursuit of a career in show business. The more fascinating perspective of a fourteen-year-old moving to Nashville definitely has to be the parents'.

When I was a teenager, I couldn't convince my parents to give me pizza instead of vegetables, never mind getting them to move cities because I wanted to be famous! Clearly, Andrea and Scott Swift are every bit as motivated, in the best way possible, as Taylor. Because that is some *serious* buy-in that I can't imagine anybody I know doing for their own children.

So yes, Taylor is 11/10 dedicated. But what does that even really mean? Sure, she moved to Nashville to pursue music. And sure, her family went with her. But is that the definition of "dedication"? Had my colleague Michael moved to Jamaica to train full time as an athlete, could he have seriously contemplated a place on the Olympic podium?

"What is dedication?" is such a short question, but it's one of the most important questions of our time.

It's not at all uncommon for people in my parents' generation to have had only two or three different jobs throughout their career. Now, people have two or three jobs within the first few years after school. We buy clothes that we wear once before discarding them. My generation increasingly doesn't believe in getting married. It is not unusual to date multiple people at once by swiping through the options on an app, and any outward desire for commitment is increasingly viewed as "obsessive" or "crazy."

Everything about modern life tells us unequivocally *not* to dedicate ourselves to anyone or anything.

And this is why people like my friend the Michelin-star chef, and of course Taylor Swift, are so fascinating and unique: They have defied conventional wisdom, thrown the modern career playbook (which tells you to forgo specialization and instead be an all-rounder) out the window, and dedicated themselves so fully to something that there is no way to see these people as other than some of the most courageous humans who walk among us.

You see, as talented as Taylor Swift is, her talent is not what sep-arates her from non-Unicorns; it's her dedication that does that.

But dedication is not a singular, one-dimensional virtue. It is not purely about allocating an amount of time to a goal or choosing that goal over competing interests, although that is certainly a part of it.

Pete Davis, an exceptionally thoughtful legal scholar, documen-tary maker, and writer, wrote a book in 2021 specifically about this topic, called *Dedicated: The Case for Commitment in an Age of Infinite Browsing*. And yes, you should read it.

He lists what he calls the "dedicatory virtues," or the values that, when found to work in tandem with each other, come together to cre-ate dedication.

Going through this list of dedicatory virtues, I am able to so clearly see the traits of the Unicorns I have come to work with and befriend that I have written them out and posted them on the wall by my desk.

The first dedicatory virtue is *imagination*, something that Taylor has in abundance, and something that a lot of people in the world struggle with. "Oh, I'm just not an imaginative person. I have no creativity." Like Unicornness, imagination is so deeply ingrained in people's minds as being something that you are born with or without that it's hard to convince anybody of the truth:

Imagination is something that everybody is born with, but that not everybody chooses to *keep*.

As I am writing this, I see a child outside my window across the street covered in blankets in the garden, jumping up and down and pretending to be in some sort of a . . . castle? Alternate universe? And every few seconds I hear a scream because her mother has lifted the blankets from her head, and she has forgotten that she can be seen at all.

Everybody is born with imagination. Unfortunately, one of the saddest realities of the human experience is that as we get older, we put self-imposed constraints between our minds and the creative stimuli in the world around us. Eventually, for many people, their worlds turn from omnicolor to black and white, and "using their imagination" is something they think children do before they must grow up.

Connected to imagination, the second dedicatory virtue is *synthesis,* or the ability to connect new and old ideas and thoughts through creativity.

Engaging with creativity and imagination as an adult is something that requires bravery, because reimagining the world, and seeing, hearing, or doing things in ways that others have not, is *not easy.* Taylor's track record for synthesis speaks for itself. My favorite example of this is her song "Vigilante Shit," a revenge fantasy in which two women—both scorned lovers—plot the downfall of the same man. It wasn't until I saw her perform this song on the Eras Tour that I realized it bore many similarities to, and in a way felt like a creative reincarnation of, the hit Broadway musical *Chicago.* Or how her iconic song "Death by a Thousand Cuts" was actually inspired by the female protagonist's relationship failure in the hit Netflix rom-com *Someone Great.* And of course, the most famous Taylor synthesis example of all time is her reincarnation of the romantic Shakespearean tragedy of *Romeo and Juliet* into "Love Story." Connecting old and new is how humans have traditionally made sense of our place in the universe.

The third dedicatory virtue is quickly disappearing in our modern electronically and algorithmically driven world: *focus.* Be honest. While reading this chapter, how many times have you checked your phone, switched tasks, or realized you don't remember what you've just read?

Consider that not even the best writers, movie producers, or even friends can attract and hold our attention for longer than a few minutes. Technology, among other demons, has made it nearly impossible for us to focus on something—*anything*—anymore.

Long gone are the days when star-crossed lovers would write long letters of poetry to each other; today, we no longer expect even a single text back and are delighted if we get even just the dreaded "thumbs-up" reaction. When we do write, we don't use full words but a collection of letters. We consume news through twenty-second TikTok videos. According to the Harvard English Literature faculty, incoming undergrads can't read full sentences.

Our inability to focus is absolutely killing our ability to become a Unicorn at *anything*, because Unicorn-level success requires a singular focus on one thing above all others, and over extended periods. In Power Move Nine I'll go into a lot more detail around the specifics of strategic patience. But for now, suffice it to say that it is impossible to achieve a goal, *any* goal, without one's entire focus on that goal. It is Taylor deciding to keep coming back to writing and performing music, day in and day out and in the moments when you don't see her, instead of vacationing, chilling out, or possibly doing something easier. Focus is about making your goal a part of your very being and not getting distracted by shiny things on your path to achieving your goals. Taylor has not released a makeup line or a fashion brand. She is a performing singer-songwriter and is purely focused on being the best at doing just that.

People like Taylor, who are incredibly focused on their career, tend to exhibit focus in most other parts of their lives too. Unlike you or me, or most people who develop strange twitches when they go more than five minutes without automatically looking at their phones, I have a sneaking suspicion that if you asked Taylor to sit in a room for twenty-four hours straight, she would be able to do it. She'd probably find it deeply uncomfortable, physically and mentally, but something tells me she'd be fine. Because people like Taylor, who have mastered relentless dedication, *have* to have a single line of focus and the ability to be undistracted for extended periods of time.

Like the first two dedicatory virtues of imagination and synthesis, the next two are somewhat connected. *Doggedness* is the ability to keep doing something or to keep fighting for it in the face of difficulty. *Passion* is having continued enthusiasm, even when you've been doing something for a while. These values seem to overlap in that they both require endurance and resilience.

Doggedness is seen in a start-up founder who asks 200 people to invest in her business, and all of them say no. Eventually, the 201st investor says yes, and the company goes on to be a huge success. Passion is when the founder speaks about the start-up to the last investor in the same excited way as she spoke about it to the first.

Think back to those moments on a stage when Taylor was sick, exhausted, and heartbroken. The moments in the Eras Tour when she was visibly crying during a song, when torrential rain made it look like she was swimming, and when she was performing the same set for the millionth time. Yet she still acted as if it were the best, most monumental night of her life.

Even if Unicorns don't feel like they have doggedness or passion all the time, they are usually pretty good at *pretending* they have it until they can get it back again. Some of the saddest lyrics in *The Tortured Poets Department* refer exactly to this difficulty: "*Lights, camera, bitch smile, even when you wanna die.*"

The second-to-last dedicatory virtue is *reverence*, the ability to be awed by and have deep respect for something. It is usually very difficult to remain passionate, unless the object of your passion gives you a sense of internal happiness and wonder, a feeling that there is something bigger in the world than just you and whatever is right in front of you. It's a quasi-religious belief that there is a purpose attached to what you are doing, and that you are doing it for the greater good.

It's a weird value because it's so hard to measure, and so few people talk about needing reverence when they discuss becoming successful. But in order to give your work the dedication required to become Unicorn-level good at it, at least some part of your mind and soul has to be open to being moved by a belief or motivation that is bigger than you. Reverence fuels your purpose, which fuels your passion, and thus allows you to give your full dedication to something.

The final dedicatory virtue is *commitment*, specifically in the context of forgoing all optionality in pursuit of this one thing over all else. For Michael, it would be the decision to become an athlete instead of an engineer. And as we will see throughout this book, it is the commitment to recording music and touring over going to university or pursuing any other career path for Taylor; it is her ability to always and forever put music first—even above the love and relationships she so desperately seeks: "*No, I could never give you peace.*"

I've just outlined to you what dedication looks like by describing what it *is*. Most Unicorns that I've talked to about dedication tend to describe it by what is *not* there, which feels like a poignant reflection on what life as a Unicorn is *really* like.

And the way in which Unicorns experience dedication goes to show that Unicornness has very little to do with natural talent and absolutely everything to do with what you build in your own life.

Dedication is not having any money. It is not controlling your own schedule. It is not being able to know where you'll be in a week, a month, or a year. Dedication is not being able to go to your best friends' weddings, and it is missing the important funerals. It is working so hard that you might die, and secretly hoping that you do die, because then at least the hard work can stop. Failing death, dedication is never knowing when things might get easier. It is having no sense of normalcy. It is having far too many people relying on you to do something that is statistically impossible, while knowing that failure is not an option. It is having far too many people impatiently asking you how soon you are going to achieve the statistically impossible feat. It is realizing that when you "win," you don't get to stop working hard, but actually have to work even harder.

Dedication is *hard*.

INTRINSIC MOTIVATION

I said there were two things that an ordinary person needs in order to do extraordinary things.

The first, as I've just pointed out, is dedication. But as should be obvious by now, achieving *real* and *life-encompassing* dedication is really hard. Really, really hard. And actually quite painful. Not just for the person trying to become, or actually being, a Unicorn, but for absolutely everybody around them.

It requires dedication from friends to be okay with never seeing you. It requires dedication from family to, I dunno, move to Nashville when you're fourteen. It requires your partner to live the crazy highs and lows of your life, but without the benefit of feeling the reward of achieving greatness for themselves. In fact, Taylor alludes to this frequently, with some of her most direct lyrics asking the question: If you have to sacrifice so much to be with me, am I enough?

"But the rain is always gonna come if you're standing with me."

So, you get it. It's tough for everybody, which is why these Unicorns are statistical anomalies—there simply aren't that many people in the world who can bear the burden of Unicornness.

But the next question is, *How* do these people bear this burden? I've already made a long list of the ways in which becoming a Michelin-star chef or a Nobel Prize winner is challenging.

But consider this for one moment: For every Taylor Swift, who has dedicated her life to being a singer-songwriter, there are hundreds more who have similarly dedicated their lives but have not achieved the goal of greatness.

For every restaurant that gets one, two, or three Michelin stars, there are thousands that do not. For every professor who dedicates their entire life to biological research, there are thousands who will never even be nominated for a Nobel Prize.

So while it might make sense for Taylor Swift to forgo "normal" relationships and the college experience as a young adult, the next obvious question is, Why the hell would anybody else do it, especially if success wasn't guaranteed?

Why would you risk turning your life upside down if you didn't know whether or not you'd eventually become a Unicorn?

The answer to this is surprisingly simple. It's because real Unicorns feel compelled to dedicate themselves to their expertise, whether they will be rewarded for it or not.

They are, in other words, total psychopaths about needing to do *their thing.*

One of the weirdest things about spending time with Unicorns is that, despite the fact that they are incredibly high-functioning and intelligent people, they make seemingly insane choices about their lives that don't, on the surface, make any sense.

Why did the Swift family move to Nashville when Taylor was just fourteen? Who knows.

Why does Professor Rosbash still go to work every day, working hard to publish biology research, when he's already won the Nobel Prize? Who knows.

Most ordinary people, at some stage, would say: *Okay, I've proven that I'm extraordinary. Now I can rest!* But Unicorns just don't do this. If you were a behavioral economist studying human incentives, you'd probably come to the same conclusion I have—that there's probably something a little bit wrong with them.

Not too long ago, I was chatting with my friend Paul O'Donovan, an Irish lightweight rower. His recent achievements include winning several Olympic gold medals in lightweight double sculls, in which he set a new world record time. Apart from that, he is a six-time world champion in single and double sculls. No big deal, right? Just another Unicorn.

It was approaching the World Rowing Cup, and when I asked him jokingly (but also kind of not jokingly) what he's going to do with his new trophies and medals when he surely wins, he replied rather seriously, "Who cares? What good is another medal?"

It sent chills down my spine. I was friends with a person who in many ways was just like me (a normal person). But in a brief moment, I realized that I knew nothing about how his mind worked. We couldn't have been more different.

"Okay . . . so why do you do this?" I asked him. "It's so hard, and you've won everything. Why keep going?"

His response was equally eerie: "Why not keep going? I don't have anything better to do."

And there it was. This is what I mean. Paul is the very definition of Unicorn. Most people enter competitions to win. Most people inflict years of pain upon themselves to become the best. But what happens when you've won everything? And broken all the records? What do you do *then*?

There are very few people in the world to whom you can pose such a question. Taylor Swift is definitely one of them. She broke all the records with her albums, like *three albums ago*. Now what? She's just breaking her own records, over and over. So why bother? Why not . . . rest?

There are two main reasons why Unicorns do seemingly weird stuff like never *not* doing their thing.

The first has to do with motivation. You or I might indeed stop after we've broken records and do something else, preferably something a little bit easier. A lot of people might do absolutely nothing at all. But breaking records is not why Taylor Swift gets up in the morning. I mean, sure, it's *nice* to break records, and she sure as hell notices when she doesn't. But is that why she's relentlessly working? Not at all.

People like Paul and Taylor are motivated to keep doing the thing they're good at because they have some internal drive to do that very thing, over and over and over again, perhaps until they die. Winning or losing comes secondary to participating (although, of course, winning is preferred). They must keep doing it, and perfecting it, and improving it, and advancing it. That is their motivation, and it comes from deep within them.

It is *intrinsic* to their very being, and it is central to their core.

Along a similar vein, I asked my Michelin-star friend if the always-on, always-working kitchen lifestyle, decades in a row, ever got to him. You know, like how he can never go out for dinner on Friday or Saturday nights. *"Get to me?* But it's my life. It's just . . . it's what I do," he replied.

Rowing is just what Paul does. Music is just what Taylor does. Cooking is just what my chef friend does. Medals? Sure. Platinum albums? Why not. Michelin stars? Yes, please. But with or without, and in fact long before these accolades ever came along, Paul was in the gym at 6:00 a.m., and Taylor was writing hundreds of songs in her bedroom.

Being motivated by something inside us, instead of something external to us, is one hell of a force field. It is a powerful indicator of how successful a person may eventually be because it makes one thing clear: They do not care about the things that ordinary people care about, the things that often sidetrack ordinary people from finding long-term success.

There is something so small and so powerful inside of Taylor Swift, akin to a fire in her chest, that is so deeply a part of who she is and what she does that not even Taylor can change it or get rid of it. She can just use it as a way to direct her energy.

And Unicorns are like this; they find that intrinsic motivation, and they nurture it until it becomes much stronger than the validation they can get from other people, from money and status, from an easy life.

Consider a typical non-Unicorn. Several years ago at Harvard I met a young American woman who told me her dream was to open a bakery in the French countryside just outside Paris. She loved cooking, baking, and speaking French, and so this was her lifelong ambition and goal.

"But," she told me, "before I do that, I'm going to work on Wall Street for ten years to make a shitload of money so that I can afford to open a little bakery."

To this day, I can still remember the seriousness on her face as she lied to me, and to herself, about what her dreams and ambitions *really* were; they had nothing to do with bakeries, and everything to do with power, prestige, and money.

Unicorns don't think like this. They simply don't care about what others think of them, or how many millions they'll need in their bank account before they can really start doing the thing they love. They just *do* it. Taylor Swift did not follow in her father's footsteps and work in finance so that she could afford to be a musician at the age of thirty-five; she just became a musician.

My point here is that when you meet enough Unicorns, you learn that one of the things that makes them all nearly identical is that they have a feeling in the bottom of their stomach that if they couldn't do the thing they love, they would just *die*.

They have no choice but to commit themselves and dedicate their lives to "their thing." It's just who they are. In recognizing this simple fact, they are able to accept the trade-offs that come with it: the dedication, which is hard, and the uncertainty of their life that results from a commitment to their goals.

Now, I'm not saying that we should all quit our jobs and move to Paris, although that *would* be lovely. But instead, I'm highlighting the fact that it is only possible to be a Unicorn when you are doing something that you feel so compelled to do, you might die if you didn't do it. And everybody—absolutely *everybody*—has something, no matter how niche, that they feel this way about. Even if it takes a while to find it.

For my former colleague Michael, that was decidedly *not* track and field. It was obviously engineering. That is, after all, why I met him at NASA, where he went on to be a highly successful and senior space mission designer at the Jet Propulsion Laboratory. I used to see him spending time in his lab, even after he had "clocked off." He was never going to beat Usain Bolt, because he was intrinsically motivated to be a NASA engineer, not an athlete.

If you want to achieve greatness, it is only possible to live with the dedication to this calling when you are motivated to do it from within—not for the money, trophies, and power. Because it is statistically unlikely that you'll ever actually get any of those external rewards. As wise people will tell you—greatness is about the journey, not the destination.

• ⬤ •

Taylor Swift, despite the painful lengths she goes to in her own life to appear ordinary, is anything but. I mean, I have some pretty high-energy friends, but I get exhausted simply by *reading* about what Taylor gets up to in a single day.

One of the strange things about Unicorns, as I've mentioned, is their unfulfilled desire to lead more "normal" lives, to be more ordinary. In many ways, Taylor and I are actually very similar. I mean, we're the same age and we both have blue eyes. No, I don't travel around the world in a private jet. But I do spend a lot of time wondering if I said or did the right thing in certain situations, or whether the person I like actually likes me back.

And Unicorns are human too. I can't imagine how much it must suck to have stadiums filled with a hundred thousand people who would cut off their left arm just to stand a little bit closer to you, yet finish a sold-out show and wonder why someone still had not texted you back. Because for Unicorns, rather incredibly, constant rejection *does happen*!

For most of the rest of this book we're going to work from the assumption that Taylor is actually a very ordinary person and look in more detail at how she uses her ordinariness to do extraordinary things.

But let's face it. Nobody writes books about ordinary people, and certainly nobody bothers to read books about ordinary people. In the ways that matter most, Taylor Swift is one of the most extraordinary people alive. And she isn't extraordinary because she was born that way; nor is she extraordinary because someone else wanted her to be that way.

The amazing thing about the way that Taylor Swift became extraordinary is that it was in the most ordinary way possible, using mechanisms that any of us could copy and use for ourselves, should we ever choose to accept the brutally painful difficulty of attempting it.

Everything about Taylor being a Unicorn, and what she has achieved, and the ways in which she's done it—whether it's building the business empire that she never needed or having the billions of dollars that never motivated her—comes down to one thing:

She's in the top 0.0000028 percent of her industry. A statistical anomaly. She's a Unicorn.

POWER MOVE TWO

MAKE A STRATEGY
AND FOLLOW IT

"A MAN DOES SOMETHING. IT'S STRATEGIC; A WOMAN DOES THE SAME thing, it's calculated," said Taylor Swift in a 2019 interview.

"Strategy" is a loaded word. It's also an incredibly misunderstood word that is rarely used properly, yet can often make multiple appearances in a single sentence in a writer's effort to sound like a business pro.

"To deliver on our strategy, it's crucial to streamline our strategic operations to enhance our strategic responsiveness in a volatile market landscape. We have the strategic initiatives in place already to execute on this strategic framework."

I kid you not. As somebody whose livelihood relies on engaging with companies, brands, and executives on their strategy, I get to hear word salads like that daily.

There are three main uses of a strategy in business and finance.

The first and most common is that the word "strategy" itself is often used as a filler word in much the same way as "ummm," "errr," or "ahh" are used in speech. If you listened in on a board meeting (or any meeting, in fact) and played the "strategy" bingo game, you'd be drunk in the first five minutes.

The second way that "strategy" is used, like the first, is to place "strategic" in front of any and every other word to make it sound like somebody knows what they're talking about. There are no longer operations, only *strategic* operations. Hiring? What about *strategic* hiring. Insights? *Strategic* insights. I kid you not, I have actually had to sit and listen to somebody discussing a strategic strategy (take a double shot).

The third and most seldom use of "strategy" is when it means the creation of a clear road map, consisting of a set of guiding principles or rules that defines the actions that people or businesses take and the things they should prioritize in order to achieve their goals.

The business world is just *drunk* on strategy. So it may come as a huge shock and surprise that very, very, very few executives—even in the world's largest global corporations—have a strategy. And then, even fewer of them have a *good* strategy.

But why do they care? Well, given that most businesses, corporations, and indeed everyday normal people like you and me don't have a strategy, the implication is that it's not that important, right?

This kind of resonates with my anecdotal data on the topic. In a board meeting, "strategy" often becomes the word that is thrown around so that executives can tick the box and say that the business is a well-planned, well-oiled machine.

In our daily lives, however, there is a complete, total, and utter *dearth* of strategy. The number of times I've asked the chief strategy officer of a multibillion-dollar company what their *personal* strategy is, only to hear "Uhh . . ." back, is totally wild. If someone who creates strategy for a large organization cannot see the value of having a strategy for their personal life, they're probably in the wrong job.

So, why do so many people manage to mess it up, what even is it, and why is it important?

I'll get into the *what* of strategy when I outline Taylor's, which happens to be one of the most phenomenal I've ever seen and the exact reason I think she's a business-finance-strategy *genius* who should be made an adjunct professor at Harvard Business School *right now.*

But first I want to get into the *why.*

When you woke up this morning, what did you have for breakfast?

Cereal? Well, Kellogg's makes breakfast products.

Toast? There are at least twenty types of bread in my local supermarket.

Fruit? There are hundreds of types of readily available fruit in most parts of the world.

What you eat for breakfast usually correlates to what you're trying to *get out* of the meal. If you're fasting, you'll have nothing. If you're a sugar fiend like me, you'll have Frosted Flakes. If you're looking for a concentration of slow-release energy, you'll have oatmeal.

Every day you wake up and likely eat the same thing for breakfast, so it's pretty seldom that you think: Wow, there are so many goddamn choices that I can make for breakfast that it's exhausting.

Every single day, we have hundreds of millions of choices in front of us.

What should we wear? It depends on the occasion and what message we're trying to convey with our clothes. Where should we go? What music should we listen to? Through which device should we communicate? Should I go to college, and if so, what should be my major? Should I live in City A or City B? Should I invest in this stock, and if so, how much? Should I take this job, or look for another one? Should I marry my boyfriend or wait for another?

Today, we have more choices and options available to us than anybody has ever had in any form of civilization. And it is, frankly, *overwhelming*. I get a weird number of people, usually students I'm teaching, asking me questions related to their personal lives, and I *feel* for them. It feels like people increasingly don't know how to manage the choices and options that are in front of them.

The answer, by the way, to all of the questions above is: It depends.

When a student asks me if they should take Job Offer A or B, or whether they should drop a class, I always tell them: It depends. To which they always reply: It depends *on what*?

It depends on what their goal is. Because until there is a goal, it is impossible to determine which of these options will get someone closer to or bring them further from that goal.

A strategy is an imperfect but extraordinarily important blueprint that you can overlay options onto before making a choice, in order to be able to say, Ah! These options align with the goal, and these other options do not!

Doing anything other than this is like playing the lottery with your life and your business. It's being blindfolded, spun around ten times, then throwing a dart in a random direction, anxiously hoping that it'll land on the bull's-eye.

Having a strategy is, however, often confused with having a goal. While a goal is a very necessary component of a strategy, it alone is not a strategy. I meet with people and companies all the time whose strategy is something frankly absurd like:

My strategy is to become a billionaire.

The company's strategy is to become the world's biggest company.

My strategy is to be the next Taylor Swift.

These are not strategies; these are *wish lists*. I, too, would like to become a billionaire. But when deciding between Job A and Job B, which both offer roughly the same (less-than-a-billion-a-year) salary, saying, "I will become a billionaire" is not very useful for helping me figure out what choice I should make.

Instead, a strategy will carefully map the ways in which I can become a billionaire. Part of that will include having a salaried job, but other parts will comprise investments I'll make over certain time frames, the risk that I'm willing to take to generate the high returns of a billion dollars, and what I want my day-to-day lifestyle to look like.

Only when I have a fully baked plan am I likely to know what a good or bad option may be for fulfilling these (extremely lofty) goals.

The important thing to realize, which is directly tied to Unicornness, is that there is no such thing as an *accidental* billionaire. There is no such thing as an accidental record-breaking performing artist. There is no such thing as an accidental Unicorn.

Choosing not to have a strategy, whether professionally or personally, is exactly the same as saying that you accept the random dart throw to determine the outcome of your life. And the number of times I see large corporations invest millions into their innovation, products, and staff, but have no concrete plan for how to develop this into a successful outcome, is quite amazing.

In the same vein, I see people around me all the time who work really, really hard. Like, *exhaustingly* hard. Yet without a strategy, this hard work disperses into thin air every time they throw the dart in a random direction.

They say that you should always work smart, not hard. And "smart" is directly tied to the word "strategy."

But here's the thing: Most people in the world actually don't work hard *or* smart.

Some work hard, not smart, and don't get very far.

Some just work smart and do get somewhere.

And then there are people like Taylor Swift, who work hard *and* smart.

They are the Unicorns, and they all have a strategy.

• ◉ •

There's a way to figure out if a company or a person has a good strategy without having to sit through their board meetings or speak to their chief strategy officer. Or, in fact, without knowing anything about strategy. I can do it, and you can do it too. In fact, we are all born with a *sixth sense* when it comes to this matter.

Most Swifties, by virtue of the fact that they live as an extension of the music and products that she gives them, would think that Taylor has a great strategy. They just don't know exactly what it is (yet).

You can pretty much tell if a brand has a good strategy because it just kind of feels like the whole brand, product, and company make sense. In fact, it's easier to tell when a company doesn't have a strategy because the opposite becomes true: Neither the brand, nor its products, nor the company seem clear in what they're offering.

Consider two brands, one with a great strategy and one with a bad strategy, if any strategy at all: Ryanair and British Airways.

Now, if I asked you which one you thought had a bad strategy, you'd probably say Ryanair because most people who have ever flown this airline *hate* it. But you'd be wrong. So cast aside any biases due to how you feel about its service for one moment.

Ryanair was the first "ultra-low-cost" airline in the world, meaning that it was cheaper than cheap. To this day, I can fly from Dublin to Paris for a weekend trip for thirty dollars. For reference, the last time I flew from Boston to anywhere for the weekend, it cost me at least three hundred dollars.

Ryanair provides ultra-low-cost travel because there are absolutely *no* bells and whistles. You want food? You pay extra for it. You want to bring a bag on board? You pay extra for it. You want to use the bathroom? The Ryanair CEO once joked that they would start charging for that too.

Look, even if you don't love Ryanair, it is consistent. You get the lowest price in exchange for the lowest service and the lowest number of perks. You know what to expect. However, Ryanair delivers on its promise to get you from A to B at the lowest cost. In fact, in 2024, Ryanair was Europe's most reliable airline. It may be uncomfortable, but it gets you places, and *on time*!

On the other hand, flying with British Airways is more expensive and caters to higher-income passengers. While it appears to be a posher, upmarket airline, its offering is . . . confusing. You will pay more for your airfare, but if you want to bring a bag with you? Well, you will have to pay to check a bag for even its more expensive, long-haul flights (and from experience, I can say that you won't know whether it will actually arrive or not!). You want food? You pay extra. You want to get somewhere on time? Probably not. You will likely end up paying more money, and you may actually end up being worse off than a Ryanair passenger.

In many ways, British Airways underdelivers to its passengers, who end up paying more to receive the same as, or less than, Ryanair.

When you look closely, you'll find that there are so many examples of companies not having a coherent, consistent offering. Like the expensive airline whose offering is worse than an ultra-low-cost airline. Or the makeup brands promoting natural beauty that use surgically enhanced models for their ad campaigns. The sustainability-first fashion houses whose manufacturing supply chain undermines local, developing economies. The privacy-centric tech companies whose business model relies on them selling your data. The diversity campaigns that don't pay their minority contributors an equal wage. The environmentally friendly food that uses twice the packaging. The luxury brand that has collaborated with a lower-tier, mass-market franchise.

The list goes on, and on, and on. And when you come across inconsistencies like this, it makes you think: Hang on a second, what is this brand even trying to do? It seems . . . confusing.

That feeling of confusion is the voice inside your head saying, "There is no strategy."

Remember, a strategy is about making a map so that you can figure out which choices are *good* ones and which choices are *bad* ones. More often than not, if a brand or a business makes a bad choice, it's because they had no map to help them figure out it was a bad choice in the first place. There was no *strategy*.

Which brings me to Taylor Swift. When people say things like "Taylor Swift is so smart," and "Taylor is such a good businesswoman," what they actually mean most of the time, even if they don't know it, is "Taylor Swift is one hell of a business strategist."

I'm going to give you an example of a strategy by using one of the best ones in the world (Taylor's, of course), but first I want to take a moment to reflect on why, exactly, so few other executives are able to create a strategy. How is it that Taylor is a better strategist than the executives and consultants who are paid millions every year to create a strategy, yet still don't?

In essence, a strategy is the connection between the everyday actions that are undertaken by organizations and the lofty goals and ambitions that the company may have. The strategy is the part in the middle: the messy, uncertain, hard-to-determine, sometimes even hard-to-measure bit that requires you to look forward and backward in time simultaneously.

And so there are three types of executives: those who spend all day thinking exclusively about the Big Picture; those who spend all day fighting the everyday fires in their path; and the third, elusive set to which Taylor belongs—those who manage to do both, in exactly the right amounts, at the same time.

This third set of executives consists of the best strategists in the world, and their organizations are the most successful in the world. They have the vision, like Apple cofounder Steve Jobs, and the ability to execute operationally, like longtime Disney executive Bob Iger.

Existing in this third group requires an executive to live in many parallel worlds at the same time. They must be Big Blue Sky thinkers and dream incessantly about achieving the impossible while simultaneously thinking about minute details of individual products. They must be incredibly optimistic about the Big Picture future while being neurotically pessimistic about the little details. They must be totally unaware of the trillions of ways that their corporate ambition could fail so that they can get out of bed every day while being fully aware of how close they are coming, each and every single day, to being a total, utter failure. They must sprint, all day, every day, to release product after product, but be unbearably patient about long-term progress and stick with the course despite the temptation to alter the strategy at the sight of danger.

These are the traits of Unicorns, which we will discuss later in great detail. However, right now I want to discuss strategy itself: what it is, and how to make one.

Taylor's strategy has created a global corporation that is infinitely better at multiplying money than even most hedge funds, and that has catapulted her past every record of note in existence, now including her own.

So if you're going to learn about strategy and try to implement one yourself (which I highly recommend), let it be Taylor's.

STRATEGY (TAYLOR'S VERSION)

I need to take a moment to say that I have never discussed Taylor's strategy with her or anybody on her team who may be working on it. So anything I write here about her strategy is purely conjecture. It is worth noting, however, that when you come across a strategy that is very good and very clear, it is also very easy to work out what that strategy is. And this is a *good* thing. The fact that I can look at Taylor Swift, Inc., and deduce from the millions of choices that Taylor has made what her map looks like, means that she's (a) got a map in the first place, and (b) that it's a good one.

So step by step, here's what Taylor has done, and what you should do too.

STEP ONE: TAYLOR HAS A VISION

Something I hear from executives frequently is that "we want to be the best." Great. But what does best actually *mean*? Ryanair is the best at keeping prices low, but the worst at comfort. Does best mean highest company valuation, or easiest returns for customers?

If a strategy is an all-encompassing map, it seems rather obvious that you need to have an idea of where you're trying to go in order to figure out how to get there. Saying that you want to be the best is like telling Google Maps you want to go to America from France. New York, New Hampshire, New Jersey, and New Mexico are all different places that require different routes.

The level of ambition you lay out when setting your vision is an important factor to consider. In fact, one of the reasons I admire and am so drawn to Taylor Swift as a brand and as an individual is that her level of ambition is just absolutely Enormous with a capital *E*. However, it goes without saying that the higher the ambition, the more detailed and the better the accompanying strategy has to be.

It appears that Taylor has a *vision*, a *mission*, and *core values*. A vision is the future-looking lofty and aspirational goal, and the mission encompasses the values and purpose of the organization in the here and now. Her core values demonstrate what she considers to be the most important aspects of the delivery of her product to the world.

Vision (Taylor's Version): To become the most iconic brand in contemporary culture.

Mission (Taylor's Version): To bring people together through culture, using authenticity and friendship.

Core Values (Taylor's Version): Authenticity, empowerment, compassion, resilience, and innovation.

There is no doubt that Taylor's vision for what her brand can achieve is much bigger than any single album, music video, or genre or type of art. Her mission statement alludes to the way in which her business is currently delivering on this strategy and working toward her goal, while her core values are the values with which every decision in her business must align.

Most of the time when a company has a badly thought-out strategy, it is demonstrated in the lack of connection between the mission and core values and the operational execution of growing the company. For example, the word "authenticity" is thrown around a lot, especially with brands that are trying to connect to younger consumers.

While "authenticity" is an easy word to use as a core value, it's a decidedly hard standard to live by, especially as so many brands say one thing but then are financially incentivized to do the opposite. A famous example of this mismatch in the wider corporate world is Nike, which has long espoused being a brand led by innovation, inspiration, and social justice. However, in the early 1990s, abusive conditions of workers in Nike's factories in Indonesia were widely reported on, leading to a crisis for the brand that prides itself on authenticity. A more recent example is Nestlé, which says it promotes values such as nutrition, health, and wellness. However, the company has been criticized for its aggressive marketing of infant formula in developing countries, which some argue has done grave damage to community and environmental health in those countries.

Through Taylor's vision and mission, we can see that the internal growth engine of her business is predicated on her ability to bring people together, and that only when her music is shared and consumed authentically among friends will her brand and her business grow. For example, every time a friendship bracelet is exchanged between strangers, or every time one Swiftie connects with another online, her market share in the global attention economy and thus the music industry is strengthened, as there is a higher incentive to listen to her music and engage in her fandom. Bringing her fans together does exactly the thing that she needs to be successful: It encourages them to communicate with each other through *her* music, not somebody else's, like Olivia Rodrigo or Beyoncé.

As will be demonstrated more clearly later, Taylor lives and dies by this mission. She has made hundreds of thousands of decisions throughout her entire business—across music production, songwriting topics, merchandise collaborators, social media presence, and more—to facilitate exactly this: the sharing of her music and the "togetherness" of Swifties as they digest her work.

Very, very few executives have shown as much commitment to a mission and set of core values as Taylor Swift, and it is incredibly hard to find even single instances of her work, her business, her products, her organization, or her logistics that don't very tightly adhere to her mission and values.

STEP TWO: TAYLOR HAS INTENT

It's not enough to know where you want to go; you need to have a really good plan for how you're going to get there.

If the vision is the destination, and the mission and core values are the mode of transport, the intent is the route you're going to follow. And this is where Taylor has been *incredibly* creative.

There are two major aspects of Taylor's intent that are worth discussing here. The first is her *focus* on the market she approached, and the second is the *mechanism* she used to capture that market.

As far as the broader music is concerned, there are two main categories that Taylor would want to focus on. The first category is demographic: the age, gender, location, income, and personality types of her fans. The second is the genre of music she is creating.

Taylor started her career in country music, which is an established genre with a very high emotional attachment between the music and its fans. Within her demographic focus, she started off by appealing to teenage girls.

As she grew significant support in this genre, she used the strong support she had with her teenage fans to expand into more mainstream pop—a far bigger, more competitive, and more financially rewarding genre in which she could make a much bigger name for herself.

And once again, after she had accrued support in the pop genre, she expanded to other genres, sometimes by writing a whole album in that genre, other times by doing collaborative, one-off songs.

Once she had a very strong core fan base among teenage girls across multiple genres, she started to grow her base by diversifying her appeal to other demographics that were no longer limited to female, teenage, or predominantly white Americans. As her support in every new genre and demographic grew, her appeal to the mainstream deepened, and she became the poster singer-songwriter for nearly every person and type of music that was worth capturing.

Her mechanism for being able to scoop up all these fans in all these demographics across all these genres? The universe she created to home them all—the Swiftverse—which was predicated on her core values and will be explored in detail in the next chapter.

But for now, suffice it to say that she spent many years creating what was essentially the world's biggest and strongest net for scooping up high-value fans of all demographics across the whole world.

STEP THREE: TAYLOR EXECUTES LIKE A BOSS

You have a destination. You know your mode of transport. You have a route. The only thing you have to do now is make sure you actually *follow* it.

Executing on a strategy is equally as hard as creating a strategy, because it is usually in the execution that you realize: Oh okay, this is harder than I thought. Or, Oh okay, this is not actually possible. Or, Oh okay. I hadn't thought about that *at all*.

Some executives, like Disney's Bob Iger or Microsoft's Satya Nadella, are really good at executing—or actually *doing* the stuff that the strategy outlines. Just as some executives are really good at creating the vision and mission, executing is a whole skill set in itself, and one that is incredibly hard to find.

The really hard part about being a good strategist, however, is tying in the execution (the all-day, everyday *activities* of an organization) to the *vision*, in an attempt to answer the question:

Am I any closer to achieving my vision today than I was yesterday? If not, why not?

The execution of a strategy is where people can get lost in the details; you can spend so long trying to change lanes that you don't realize you've missed your damn exit.

The execution is where numbers really start to matter too. Like: How many people streamed Taylor's *Red* album this month compared to last month? What about this year compared to five years ago? What about *Red* versus *TTPD* in their respective opening weeks? What about *TTPD* versus *1989*?

Once, I sat through a three-hour strategy meeting that had over one hundred slides of already summarized data points. At the end of the presentation, I had to ask the person leading the meeting: So are you on track to being the highest-quality provider of household wall paint or not?

The executive didn't know. Because, at the risk of repeating myself, it would be hard for most people to see their monthly Spotify streaming data and say: Ah yes, this 2 percent change this month means I'm well on my way to being the most iconic brand in contemporary culture! But this is exactly what Taylor *has* figured out how to do. Because the success of a strategy comes down to being able to set targets and to achieve these targets, before setting bigger targets.

One of the critical pieces of feedback that reverberated in the music industry echo chamber around the release of Taylor Swift's *The Tortured Poets Department* was in connection with exactly this: targets, numbers, and data.

Specifically, some people said that Taylor had released a second album within a couple of hours of releasing the first, turning *TTPD* into a double album, in order to *play the numbers*. The stated assumption was that Taylor was willing to sacrifice the quality of her music in order to release a large number of songs, to "flood" the market with music, making it impossible for anybody *but her* to be present at the top of the music charts.

Now, leaving aside the central criticism of this argument related to Taylor's core value of authenticity, which I will deal with in more detail in Power Move Ten, I think it's important to say, out loud: Yes, of course Taylor cares about data and streaming numbers and playing the numbers game. She does it, as do all artists. Being the "best" in the music industry is pretty much *defined* by these numbers. And of course, Taylor has more likely than not figured out a way to do it better than all other artists, who are openly and fairly able to compete against her, should they wish to.

I want to keep focusing on the idea of *playing a numbers game* though. This is exactly how we have seen Taylor's career, her music, and her brand evolve, and it is exactly how we know that she actually is in fact bang on track to achieving her totally insane vision of being the most iconic brand in contemporary culture.

For every time she has become the "best" in something, she's moved her own goalposts and expanded the definition of her own market.

She became the chart topper in country music, so she went to pop. She topped those charts, too, so she moved to electropop and R & B. Winning the numbers game in that, too, she moved to indie folk and scored a home run.

Consider that even before she was criticized for playing the numbers game in the midst of *The Tortured Poets Department* release, she released not one, not two, but three album variations of *folklore*: the original, the deluxe version with a bonus track, and then the Long Pond Studio Sessions, which were live recordings. This was an insanely clever way to consistently remarket the same material, giving what is essentially the same album three times the number of streams, and keeping it in the charts for three times as long, for the same investment of time and creativity as a single album.

Likewise, with her close follow-up album *evermore*, she released multiple versions of her song "willow": the original, the coven of witches version, the dancing witch version, the lonely witch version, and the moonlit witch version.

The woman has won so many numbers games at the minute that the game has probably become *boring*, but in trying to beat her own records, she has become even more competitive.

But here's what I think the most interesting thing about Taylor's strategy is. We've seen that she has a natural progression from dominating a small demographic within a small market, before moving to bigger markets and widening her demographics.

Well, she's pretty much won the entire music industry numbers game at this stage. So what is next?

The progression of her strategy is why I suspect her vision is to be the most iconic brand in contemporary *culture*, not just contemporary music.

Her *TTPD* album was a departure, in many ways, from traditional singer-songwriter album development and release, particularly in how it leaned into her specifically stated poetry undertones.

Now that she has developed such a strong mechanism for bringing people—the highly emotionally attached Swifties—with her, it's extremely likely that we're going to see Swift using her core values to bring fans together to form friendships over new forms of cultural media, through an expansion into literature, cinema, and documentary making.

Her executional strength and the ability to use performance indicators, such as chart placements and streaming data, are what have allowed her to flawlessly move between genres and in doing so to capture more of the "fan" market share.

In every industry and across all parts of our personal and professional lives, we can similarly look to Strategy (Taylor's Version) to see a clear example of where a vision, combined with intent and execution, creates success. Whether it's in building a social media following, or finishing college, or even (and maybe especially!) dating, having a personal and professional vision, mission, and set of values is imperative, but still not enough.

A successful strategy marries these elements and allows them to work together to reinforce a goal and create a road map for how to achieve it. In fact, creating these personal strategy statements is one of the first things that MBA students at Harvard Business School are asked to do, and they are constantly revisited throughout the two-year program. It allows you to be able to understand whether or not a job offer aligns with how you want to live your life and the things you want to prioritize, and in a more professional setting it allows you to take nearly all of the "guesswork" out of running a business, whether it's a one-person-strong team or a one-hundred-thousand-person workforce.

Nobody should ever be closing their eyes and throwing darts aimlessly. Taylor Swift sure as hell doesn't, and neither should you.

A *GOOD* STRATEGY

How do you know if your strategy is any good? If a strategy makes or breaks billion-dollar corporations, how do you make sure yours isn't going to kill the business?

Or, more terrifyingly, how do you know that a personal strategy isn't going to force you down the wrong career path, leaving you penniless and broken, after also suggesting that you marry the wrong person?

Well, the nice thing about a strategy is that even a *bad* strategy is better than *no* strategy, so you're always somewhat protected from the elements as long as you've semisensibly thought through your strategy in the first place.

The obviously very easy way that we can figure out Taylor's

strategy is good is because, you know, she's now the world's first singer-songwriter to become a billionaire on the back of her music alone. So, sure. Somewhere along the way, she did at least one thing right.

But in November 2017, when she released *Reputation*, how do you think she knew if her strategy was good or not? As we learn in her Netflix documentary *Miss Americana*, at that time, she felt like public enemy number one. She was having a very public *thing* with Kanye West (no, not *that* type of *thing*), and her new album was not nominated for the big, fancy music awards that seemed to be a given by that stage. Of course, it's so hard to fathom anymore that those moments even existed, given that her success today feels like it was as inevitable as Kanye's downfall. But in those moments, there was absolutely nothing that she or her management team could point to that said: Yup, we're right on track here folks! In fact, it was quite the opposite.

I mean, after her yearlong hiatus from life, both professionally and personally, she finally reemerged with an album—*Reputation*—that featured an entirely new creative direction. Analysts in music and on Wall Street alike reported that her corresponding tour was going to be a flop. Her album wasn't even nominated for Album of the Year at the Grammys. Headlines consistently reported that her friends had fallen out with her, that she was an unlikable and back-stabbing person, and that her star had finished shining. There's no way that any sane or rational person could have felt that this was part of a successful journey to superstardom.

There comes a moment (or two, or three, or ten, every quarter) when an executive thinks, What the hell are we doing? And why is my strategy not *working*?

Judging the strength of a strategy when you make one is actually not possible; it takes a really long time and deep commitment to sticking with it to figure out if it's actually working.

However, there is a difference between a good strategy and a bad strategy as measured by its *design* instead of its outcomes. And here's how we know just by looking at Taylor's strategy, and momentarily forgetting its outcome, that it's a pretty good one.

RULE ONE: TAYLOR KNOWS WHO HER COMPETITORS ARE

There's a phrase that, if your parents are anything like mine, you will have heard a lot growing up: "You are what you eat." Well, I want you to forget about that for a moment and think about the following:

You are who you compete with.

In the same way that you are often judged by the company that you keep, you are also judged by whom you dedicate your time and resources to competing against. The easiest example I can give you that probably feels relatable given the toxicity of online discourse are the dumb fights people have online.

When you see somebody that you really respect, like a famous TV producer or a learned academic, having a fight with a dumb anonymous account online, you think: Wow. The person that I held in such high esteem for so long is actually just the same as an anonymous loser.

Where we dedicate our time and resources says a lot about how we think of ourselves. So if you believe this to be true, you'll realize that the success of a strategy—the very tool for deciding how and where to spend your resources—is closely linked to who you view as your competitor, or not.

I tend not to engage in online fights with weirdos because I, rightly or wrongly, see myself as better than that. I would much rather spend my time publishing a paper that argues my point against an economist with a PhD than some loser sitting in their parents' basement.

But this ultimately begs the question: *Who* are my competitors?

Not having a properly defined set of competitors means that, more likely than not, your strategy is going to tell you to allocate your very scarce time, energy, and money in the wrong places.

For example, if Taylor decided that her competitors were Garth Brooks and Carrie Underwood, she would surely end up recording another country album so that she could beat both of them in the country genre numbers game.

If she had decided her competitors were Usher and Tina Turner, she certainly wouldn't have released *TTPD*.

Your competitor is the entity against whom you are fighting for market share. Consumers have a limited amount of money and time to spend buying albums or listening to music. Your competitor is the person, brand, or organization that will make people stop and think: Should I give my resources to this brand or that brand, because I cannot give them to both?

If I argue with some anonymous account on Twitter instead of a highly esteemed academic, I am de facto making the assumption that people, when reading our exchange, are just as likely to take my side as theirs. Which means my ability to argue is only as good as some person who likely did not misspend their youth in academia trying to become a better communicator of ideas.

I once sat down with the CEO and chief strategy officer of a multibillion-dollar luxury goods corporation. While they did indeed have a strategy that was easily explained over two hundred PowerPoint slides (!), their strategy was just never going to work. Because while this company sold luxury $400 handbags, its strategy made the assumption that it was competing against $15,000 handbags. And a person who is about to buy a $15,000 handbag is never, not for a single second, thinking: "Perhaps I should buy the four-hundred-dollar bag instead."

Taylor's competitors have been easily defined throughout her career, and it's always been kind of easy to tell that she had a very strong idea about who she was competing against. Interestingly, when it became obvious that *folklore*, her indie folk pop album, was able to win the numbers game not only against indie pop competitors but against mainstream competitors, too, it came as no surprise that she would start playing the numbers game with alternative, double-album formats to test just how far she was able to outcompete her competition in the mainstream music industry. And whatever happened to those artists she historically competed against? Katy Perry and Beyoncé and Kanye West and Lady Gaga? Well, while some are doing better than others, it's fair to say that none are directly competing with her anymore. Indeed, the Eras Tour was in some part perhaps a wink and a nod from Taylor to the people she's shared the limelight with and indeed stolen limelight from. There's an implicit recognition in this global tour that Taylor did, indeed, win. Not everybody, after all, has a portfolio of eras over several decades to showcase across 149 shows globally.

Now, however, as I suspect she's eyeing up an expansion out of music and, à la her "All Too Well" music video, into the worlds of literature and movies, her competitors go from being the entire music industry to the entire attention economy.

Her competition will move from having been Beyoncé and other performing artists to anything and everything that takes time, money, and energy away from Swifties that they could have given to her. Disney World. Marvel movies. Netflix. And as her brand and product offerings evolve, she will be forced to contemplate bigger and bigger competitors and execute an appropriate strategy accordingly.

RULE TWO: TAYLOR IS UNIQUE

In 2016, a now famous singer-songwriter called Maggie Rogers was enrolled in a songwriting class at New York University. All semester, she had been trying and failing to write music. Nothing seemed to work, and she fell behind her classmates, who were progressing their portfolios nicely. And then came her semester showcase, created in only fifteen minutes.

Unbeknownst to Maggie, her professor would call upon his old friend Pharrell (because, you know, who isn't friends with Pharrell) to listen to a couple of the demos and give feedback. When Maggie was picked to showcase her song to Pharrell, she sat next to him as he listened live, right in front of her, ready to critique it.

I'm not going to lie. Watching this recorded scene of her class unfold is a very uncomfortable experience. At least at the start. Having one of the best producers in the world listen to your music right in front of you? You can physically feel her pain!

But then something happens. And it's beautiful. After listening to what would eventually become her hit single "Alaska," Pharrell says the following:

Wow. Just wow. I have zero, zero, zero notes for that, and I'll tell you why. It's because you're doing your own thing. It's singular.

It's like when the Wu-Tang Clan came out and nobody could really judge it; you either liked it or you didn't, but you couldn't compare it to anything else. And that is such a quality. And all of us possess that ability, but . . . you have to be willing. You have to be willing to . . . speak. And you have to be willing to be real frank in your music. And real frank in your choices. And most of the time people will say, I'm going to make this type of a song so that it ends up sounding like something that we've heard before or felt before, you know? And I feel like . . . your whole story; I can hear it in the music. I can hear the journey of you having that kind of background. And I love your singer-songwriter verses. That's what I love about Stevie Wonder's music. Because as much as he was in pop, he was a singer-songwriter and he told stories. And I felt that. Just then, what I felt . . . I've never heard anyone like you before and I've never heard anything that sounds like that. So that is the kind of thing that like . . . that's a drug for me. So that was . . . that was cool. And I'd be very curious to know what your visuals would look like, because you seem to know what you want.

In short, what Pharrell described in the most amazing and beautiful and to-the-point way is that Maggie's music has an incredibly distinct and differentiated value proposition. Her music is so different from anything else out there that she doesn't have to *compete* against other musicians. Her music isn't going to try to steal market share and fans from other pop singers; she is her own genre. And she gets to own 100 percent of that genre.

Being different from everyone else is a *phenomenally* good strategy.

Why? Because nobody else can copy what is unique. In a similar vein, as you read this, millions and millions of young women are desperately trying to make themselves look like Instagram or TikTok stars. How many people are trying to make themselves look like Sinéad O'Sullivan? Zero. There are many reasons why that may seem like a bad thing (why does nobody want to look like me?). But why is this *good*? Because I don't have to compete against people who could be better Sinéads than me. I get to own 100 percent of the Sinéad market. Admittedly, it's a tiny market that nobody is interested in, but you get the idea.

Put another way: The best way to be number one at doing something is by being the only person doing that thing.

It is incredibly difficult for someone to try to mimic Maggie Rogers. It is incredibly easy for someone to try to mimic one of the thousands of mainstream pop stars who have come and gone in the last decade. In business, this is what is called a "competitive advantage"—nobody can make music in the genre of Maggie Rogers as well as Maggie. Her unique sound and the creative duvet that her music pulls you into as you listen to it.

With that in mind, what is Taylor Swift's competitive advantage? What makes Taylor unique?

Well, Taylor is your best friend on demand, 24-7, available to hold your hand at the push of a button. Never dressed too well, never dressed too badly, never about to upstage you, never going to put you down, just aspirational enough to make you want to be her, but not too aspirational that she feels out of touch or that being her is out of the realm of possibility. Taylor's competitive advantage is being Goldilocks: not too big, not too small, but *just right*. She knows this, of course, and she has fucking *nailed* it.

How does this contribute to her vision of becoming the most iconic brand in contemporary culture? Because listening to Taylor makes you feel like you are spending time with your best friend.

It's an incredibly smart way to differentiate herself, for the following reason.

Most female artists are told that they need to use their sex appeal to sell music. However, "sexy" is not a long-term strategy and is very specifically only useful when you are seeking an audience to listen to your music when they themselves want to feel sexy. Which, let's be honest, *works*. Want to feel sexy in a club? Listen to Cardi B. Want to feel sexy getting ready to go out? Listen to Ice Spice.

But you know what people want much more than the ability to feel sexy? Not to feel lonely. Making people feel less lonely is a multibillion-dollar market, and Taylor looks likely to impact a large part of that.

So while it is very likely that when breaking out into the music industry as a blue-eyed, blond-haired teenage girl, she was told to "be sexy." And while that may have made her more immediately recognizable and had a bigger short-term impact on her career, she would have been sacrificing her streaming records in the long term. Her initial and unique positioning as "the girl next door" may have gone against what was conventionally normal, but sticking with it was the only way she would have been able to achieve her mission of connecting people through *friendship* and authenticity, not sexiness.

"What makes you different?" is, sadly, the question that we're taught instinctively to answer: *Nothing. I am just like everybody else.* We have been trained our whole lives to pretend that we're average in any crowd, and to follow the mainstream, not to stand out.

But that's just plain wrong. It's time to throw that playbook born out of high school fear away right now! Because a good strategy, whether personal or professional, relies on you being different and embracing that difference.

Define your own category. Be the only version of you that could possibly exist in the world.

• ● •

I have a confession to make: There are very few strategies I come across that make me fangirl the way I do about Taylor Swift's, and oh my gosh she has me weak in the knees. If creating strategy is an art, I'm not sure which she is more talented at: being a singer-songwriter or being a strategist.

Unfortunately, because so few people really understand or know what constitutes a good versus bad strategy, what I think actually makes her one of the strongest businesspeople in the world tends to go largely unnoticed.

So just like clockwork, Taylor's dominoes have cascaded in a line. What if I told you she's a mastermind?

Because in a world where simply choosing what to eat for breakfast leads to a combinatorial explosion of options, it is becoming harder and harder to pass off *not* having a strategy.

Whether you're the chief strategy officer of a multibillion-dollar corporation like Taylor Swift, or you're the chief strategy officer of Sinéad, Inc., it doesn't matter. The world has become fiercely competitive, and even if you work hard, working "dumb" is no longer an option for anybody who wants to succeed in what might seem like the smallest of ways.

Having a strategy is like taking the blindfold off before the world starts spinning you around so that you can at least see the dartboard before you make your shot. It doesn't, rather obviously, guarantee that you'll hit a bull's-eye, because that in itself is a yearslong game of practice (or so I presume, for someone with my bad coordination).

However, creating and executing on a strategy, just like having a devotion to practicing the dedicatory virtues, is about focusing on a desire to achieve *excellence* across personal and professional domains, and people who have the ability to think strategically in one domain usually bring that skill with them to other domains, making the process of learning how to create a strategy such a valuable investment.

It's yet another mechanism used by Unicorns that we can beg, borrow, or steal to get ahead in our own game.

Because, you know:

If you fail to plan you plan to fail. Strategy sets the scene for the tale.

POWER MOVE THREE

BUILD WORLDS, NOT PRODUCTS

WHAT IF I TOLD YOU THAT MATTEL, THE CREATOR OF BARBIE, sells toys, but is not a toy company? That Louis Vuitton sells handbags, but is not a handbag company? Or that Taylor Swift makes music, but is not selling albums?

You see, each of these brands is actually in the business of selling something much, much more valuable than toys, handbags, or albums. And this value has translated into the Barbie movie being the biggest box-office hit in Warner Bros. history, Louis Vuitton's owner being one of the richest people in the world, and Taylor Swift being the first singer-songwriter to generate billion-dollar wealth from music alone.

So what are they in the business of if it's not selling us their products?

They are creating and selling meaning, nostalgia, belonging, and, dare I say it, even a sense of immortality.

· ● ·

A few years ago, I was in Manhattan at a birthday brunch for a friend. She brought us to an eye-wateringly expensive hotel restaurant because "Victoria Beckham eats here all the time," and I had to make the trade-off between having a single cocktail or paying for the subway that month. You know when you're sitting in a restaurant, too scared to order, and you can just tell that the person who invited you and over-ordered will ask the waiter to split the check at the end, meaning that the anxiety is eating you inside out? Yeah. That was me.

So naturally I ordered the cheapest thing on the menu—an omelet.

And to my horror, the omelet arrived thirty minutes later *deconstructed*.

I was furious. The entire raison d'être of an omelet is for the heat from the egg to cook the ingredients together, transporting and spreading the flavor and, most importantly, melting the goddamn cheese.

It was at this moment when I learned and internalized one of the most important concepts in business and finance: In a good business, the *whole is always greater than the sum of the parts.*

Eating what essentially were separate ingredients was far less satisfying than eating an omelet in which all these ingredients were combined in flavor and texture. Separately, each ingredient was just fine (apart from raw onion—oh my god). But together they would have been superb.

A properly cooked omelet is inherently more valuable than a deconstructed one.

And in business and finance, it's exactly the same. The goal of most corporations is to have investors value the business as an omelet, cooked together (which is worth more), instead of one egg, half an onion, a tomato, and a sprinkle of salt (which is worth less).

At some stage, the omelet becomes more valuable, because the ingredients, when mixed together, become more *meaningful*. This is one of the most important concepts in the corporate world, yet it's also one of the hardest things to achieve, and in fact very, verrrrry few CEOs have ever been able to do this: bring separate parts of the business together to make it more meaningful. Another term for this is "creating *synergies*."

Why is creating synergies so hard?

Well, it has to do with a term in business and finance called *intangibles*, which are assets that a company has that are often not physical but are highly valuable.

In the case of the omelet, the *intangible* value of all the ingredients being cooked with the egg, thus making the whole greater than the sum of the parts, is additional taste and flavor. What is the financial value of that? That's tricky to answer, but in short, it's whatever a customer in a restaurant is willing to pay for it!

Another simple example of a business in which the whole is greater than the sum of its parts is a supermarket. Instead of going to a butcher who sells just meat, followed by a greengrocer who sells just vegetables, and so on, you can go to a supermarket where everything is sold in one place. Historically, supermarkets have been able to sell produce at a premium because of the *intangible* that is being offered: convenience.

*　　※　　*

Okay, so what do omelets, supermarkets, and intangibles have to do with Taylor Swift?

Well, before Taylor Swift, musicians very much operated off a business model whereby the value or net worth of the musician was the total value of each of the albums they had released, plus the additional revenue they made from touring, merchandise, and brand partnerships.

This way to value looks like this:

Value of Musician's Business = Value of Records + Tour + Merchandise + Partnerships

This has made it pretty damn hard for musicians to become ultrawealthy from their music alone. This model constrains the artist, because it takes so much time to create an album and go on tour. In short, it's not very scalable. There's only one Beyoncé, and there are only so many albums and tours a single artist can create in her career.

In fact, most ultrarich musicians have found themselves in positions of wealth because they have done well outside their career as an artist, usually by investing or founding other businesses. I mean, look at Jay-Z, an ultrasuccessful, twenty-four-time Grammy Award–winning musician with no less than fourteen chart-topping albums. But his $2.5 billion net worth? Well, a lot of this came *not* from releasing music but from his side ventures, including his record label, Roc Nation; his music streaming platform, Tidal; his luxury alcohol brands; and his investments in tech start-ups.

In short: I hate to break it to you, but if you want to be a billionaire musician, you will have to make most of that money by doing stuff other than recording music and touring. Or put another way, the whole is arguably *not* greater than the sum of the parts. Your net worth as an artist has no intangibles. Singer-songwriters are basically deconstructed omelets.

That is, until Taylor Swift came along.

In the now infamous interview with Barbara Walters, Taylor is introduced by Barbara saying: "One magazine headline said it best: Taylor Swift *IS* the music industry."

Taylor has used the concept of the "whole being greater than the sum of the parts" to turn the music industry on its head, as she significantly changed the "job" of artists from simply releasing and touring *albums* to world-building entire *fan universes*.

Oh, and in the process she has become the world's first billionaire pop star. No biggie.

BUILDING WORLDS, NOT ALBUMS

Let's rewind. Within the last ten years, world-building has quietly become the most powerful form of building community-based products, businesses, or corporations. In its most simple form, world-building refers to the creation of immersive fictional worlds that are highly detailed and consistent and contain different characters, cultures, and landscapes.

These worlds then serve as the backdrop for stories and experiences that allow fans to move out of their real environment into the newly created one.

It all sounds a bit weird, right?

World-building really took off in the cinematic world, and the concept as a whole is much easier to understand if you look at Disney's Marvel Universe, which is one of the best examples of a cinematic fan universe in the . . . well, universe. The Marvel Universe is a fictional shared world where the deeply connected stories in Marvel comic books take place; it features a whole load of superheroes, villains, and side characters that directly and indirectly mix with one another in separate movies.

It's basically a fictional subuniverse where fans are transported to engage with the themes and characters in that universe and with one another.

Although the age demographic reading this book may be too far removed from arguably the first-ever example of a successful fan universe, think momentarily about Star Trek and its "Trekkies," the fans, many of whom chose to live their lives with one foot squarely in the Star Trek universe.

So you might be wondering what the big deal is. Star Trek is only a TV show. Marvel is only a bunch of comics and movies, now owned by Disney. "It's nothing more than a series of films!" people have remarked. A lot.

Well, it is actually a huge deal, because before Marvel came along, Disney used to make movie after movie, with separate characters living in separate worlds with separate storylines. And like most musicians, the value of Disney's movie business was equal to the value of each of its separate movies added together.

Disney, in this way, used to be a *deconstructed omelet*, serving people a bit of onion and a bit of cheese, one ingredient at a time.

But by starting to build the Marvel Universe, in which each subsequent movie or plot or character was deeply connected to the other movies, the rest of the universe was made more valuable, in large part because fans became more involved in the story over longer periods of time and even began to participate in the shaping of its narrative landscape.

The idea is that you watch one Marvel movie to see a story from one perspective, and can then watch another Marvel movie to see that same plot play out through a different lens. Each additional movie adds new context and layers of meaning that, over time, change how the viewer understands the world in its entirety.

Marvel took the idea of creating a collection of separate movies to being a universe in which fans "lived."

This large, complex, and ever-changing universe consists mostly of numerous interwoven elements. Consider the characters themselves: heroes (Spider-Man), villains (Green Goblin), sidekicks (Happy Hogan), and antiheroes (Deadpool). The teams: X-Men and the Fantastic Four.

The locations and physical places involved: Wakanda, Avengers Tower, and Titan. The artifacts and objects: Infinity Stones, Captain America's shield, or the Cosmic Cube.

And then there's a whole other layer of universe that sits on top of this: alternative storytelling formats, such as comics, movies, TV shows, and video games; novels and spin-off series; and merchandise, like action figures, apparel, and collectibles. And yes, fan engagement. Conventions like Comic-Con, fan sites, famous social media hashtags, and cosplay events.

What does most of this universe focus on? The crux of it is, of course, the mythology and lore: the backstories, origin stories (Spider-Man's bite), and infamous character arcs (Tony Stark's redemption); and the legends and myths of superheroes. A lot of this is brought together and continued, without the input of Marvel, through fan contributions to the stories in written fan fiction with alternative plotlines and crossovers, fan comics, videos, and art.

Each of these interactions between Marvel and its fans, and the fans with one another, creates a distinct and important piece of the fan universe.

The business model of the universe, therefore, is extremely different from that of regularly sequenced and separate movies—specifically in this extremely positive way:

- The value of *previous* Marvel movies actually increases with each *new* movie being released, because it adds additional perspective and greater depth to the universe, making it an inherently more interesting place.

- Each new release is worth more upon release than the last, as there is an even bigger fan base anticipating its arrival.

This means that each new movie becomes exponentially more valuable in itself, while making the rest of the portfolio exponentially more valuable as well.

So whereas before Disney was making deconstructed omelets with single-release movies, world-building Disney is now in the business of making all-in-one, fully baked, amazing ultratasty and super-melted-cheesy breakfasts.

And the *intangibles* of this fan universe that it's expanding? Why can the value of the whole be greater than the sum of the parts? It all comes down to the most highly sought-after intangible that exists for brands selling products and entertainment: the feeling of "belonging." Through a shared story, or world, people can connect over their interest in and passion for the specifics of some part of that world.

So this new model may have been proven by Disney's move into Marvel world-building, but we can see that it works for other movies too. Consider the fact that the ultrasuccessful movie *Barbie*, which followed this model, is the beginning of the *Mattel* Cinematic Universe, as an additional forty-five movies featuring different Mattel characters are in development and will be based in the Mattel toy landscape.

Indeed, although world-building started with media, it has since expanded into other more surprising places, such as the luxury goods industry. Who knew that handbags and glad rags could become immersive worlds! Similar to the cinematic fan universe, LVMH, the largest luxury goods company in the world, creates community and engagement among its die-hard fans who share a passion for luxury fashion and lifestyle.

Through incredibly and meticulously curated marketing campaigns and customer interactions with luxury goods, LVMH is trying to bring the world of immersive branding to fans within luxury markets.

Yes, sure, this sounds like marketing jargon. But consider that LVMH owns more than just Louis Vuitton and other makers of extremely expensive handbags. It now owns the brands that people who buy expensive handbags engage with on a day-to-day basis. What champagne do luxury connoisseurs drink? The same champagne that LVMH owns. What watches do they wear? The ones that LVMH owns. What hotels do they stay in? Or what restaurants do they eat in? Yup, the ones that LVMH owns.

LVMH is trying, in other words, to build a luxury world in which you can live. For example, in late 2022, the company collaborated with famous (and somewhat absurd) Japanese artist Yayoi Kusama, whose art is known for its multicolored "dots." This collaboration was one of the first, and the largest, LVMH universe campaigns. Everything (and I mean *everything*) from bags to shoes and champagnes, from buildings to museums and even cities, was covered with Kusama's legendary dots. The Eiffel Tower was covered in them. Art museums were exhibiting her work. Louis Vuitton handbags were suddenly covered in her dots, leading their prices to increase. For a few brief weeks, whether you were a Louis Vuitton die-hard or not, the luxury-driven LVMH universe was inescapable. You may not have recognized it at the time, but it's likely you saw Yayoi Kusama's infamous dots somewhere!

Most important, the very rewarding *intangible* for LVMH is just as rewarding for customers as its luxury goods: They are in the exclusive club of cult fandom.

So whether by coincidence or on purpose, and I suspect it's a mix of both, Taylor Swift has managed to do what has never been done before: move away from the *deconstructed omelet* model of the music industry, which releases one unrelated album after another, and instead build the biggest goddamn universe that has ever existed in music, and likely will continue to exist as the largest for many years to come.

● ● ●

While many of her peers in the industry focus solely on producing hit singles and touring relentlessly, Taylor has her sights set on an insanely loftier goal, as we discussed in the last chapter: being the most iconic brand in contemporary culture. To do this, it's likely that at some stage she came to realize that she needed to create a cohesive brand universe that would resonate with her audiences on a much, much deeper level than ever before.

She needed to build the Swiftverse. And much like the Marvel Universe, you can map it into very specific elements.

You've got the characters: the heroes (Taylor Swift, Joe Alwyn, Travis Kelce); the villains (Kanye West, Scooter Braun, Kim Kardashian, John Mayer); the sidekicks (Jack Antonoff, Selena Gomez); the antiheroes (Karlie Kloss); the teams, like HAIM; locations of importance upon which narratives are interwoven, like Nashville, New York, London, and (question mark) Kansas City; the artifacts and objects of importance, like cardigans, car keys, snakes, champagne, cowboy boots, and red sunglasses.

The Swiftverse storytelling formats include, obviously, songs and albums, but also music videos and extended movies like *All Too Well: The Short Film*. Indeed, poetry and writing have become larger parts of Taylor's musical releases, and her expanded universe now includes discographies of closely related artists like HAIM, Ed Sheeran, and notably The 1975, after her failed relationship with front man Matty Healy.

Her merchandise and collectibles are such an important part of the Swiftverse that the Victoria and Albert Museum in London curated a Taylor Swift exhibition, *Songbook Trail*, which included items from her personal archive as well as her fans' collections.

It's in fan engagement that the Swiftverse really comes into its own: Her influential fan groups, which collaborate online, have even forced journalists who have reviewed Swift's music to remain anonymous for fear of a coordinated backlash against them. The cosplay, of course, has been most noticeable at her Eras Tour concerts, where hundreds of thousands of people—men, women, and children alike—spent millions of cumulative hours preparing their favorite Taylor "look" to wear to the show. And if you venture online, you will see really standout profiles of artists who have risen to fame by rewriting Taylor's songs from other characters' perspectives or writing music in response to Taylor's.

But of course, none of this would be worth mentioning if it weren't for the two decades and more of mythology and lore that has created the Swiftverse in the first place. Consider her backstory: the quiet girl next door who makes good in Nashville against the odds. Just like Peter Parker, who eventually became Spider-Man, she was the unlikely hero. There are the character arcs of her friendships and subsequent fallouts with Katy Perry and Karlie Kloss and the entrance of the supervillain trio Kanye West, Justin Bieber, and Scooter Braun. Like Peter Parker, she is forced to take a stand: Pair with the bad guys, or unleash hell when she goes against them on a path to righteousness? We then see her subsequent redemption from that decision and the formation of a new path of enlightenment with Joe

Alwyn but are constantly reminded of the challenges and burdens that the Peter Parkers of this world carry in trying to make it a more just one. Finally, the plot twist that maybe her One Great Love had been Matty Healy the entire time.

Understanding how she's so successfully gone on to achieve this insanely successful fan universe gives us a clear understanding of how fandoms work, and like everything else that we gain from her, we learn on a personal level about the kind of worlds we're being pulled into by corporations, and even the worlds that we're building and living in ourselves.

According to Ana Andjelic, who, as the former chief brand officer of Banana Republic and Esprit, works in fashion-driven world-building, there are four strategic C pillars to building the Swiftverse or any fan universe. They are: curation, content, community, and collaboration.

So baby, let the games begin . . .

STRATEGIC PILLAR ONE: CURATION

We live in a world where we look to our self-appointed and usually very *celebrity* cultural leaders, whether they are chefs, authors, designers, models, or social media stars, to answer these questions: What should we listen to? What should we eat? How should we look? Where should we go?

The power that we, collectively, hand our many-millions-of-followers curators is huge. And yet very few of them outside of Marvel, Mattel, and Swift have ever turned this opportunity into a world-building endeavor.

But Taylor, whether fifteen or thirty-five years old, has never skipped an opportunity to hold our hands and bring us along with her on a journey of self-curation. Even those who know her as a singer instead of a world-builder will agree that she's one of the best storytellers of our time. Indeed, her fame has come down to her being a phenomenal lyricist, with her "music" now being referred to as her "oeuvre" in the hallways of institutions like Harvard. I mean, even Oxford students have written dissertations about her, claiming she is as culturally important as Shakespeare, Chaucer, and Wordsworth.

But lyrics alone are not going to suffice when creating universe-deep narratives. To curate a universe, deeply interconnected stories and plots are woven together into a single, but often complex, narrative. The story is not told linearly, from the beginning to the end, as we see in most books, movies, and albums. Instead, it is told through numerous pieces of content containing "what-ifs," cliff-hangers, and non-resolutions.

The best universes are curated through collections featuring flashbacks, fast-forwards, and present-day recollections of the complexity of the whole world being built.

And this is exactly how, accidentally or not, we have all come to know Taylor Swift and her life, which in many ways mirrors the complexity and interconnectedness of our own lives.

Not only is the story arc important for highly curated universes, but so too are the specific ways in which it is told through the cadence, rhythm, and rhyme of the collections of pieces being released. Like any good story, this comes down to frequent and repeatable motifs that make us feel like "Oh hey, this is a universe I know, recognize, and trust."

And, honestly, this is where Taylor *shines*. I mean, a short list of her emblematic Swiftic anchors includes red scarves, snakes, the number 13, anything to do with sipping wine, and friendship brace-lets. At Eras Tour shows, nearly everybody had painted the number

13 on their hands, as Taylor Swift had done early in her career. Likewise, many wore cowboy boots and large cardigans, branded and nonbranded merchandise that tell other Swiftverse inhabitants: I am one of you, and we share this thing, this *obsession*, together. Of course, non-Swiftverse inhabitants will see these anchors and think nothing of them. They serve, at least in the real world, as very strong in-group signals of the Swiftie elite.

Thematic anchors are more complex, but reappear often enough in the Swiftverse and in our own lives for us to feel like we understand them despite the complexity: heartbreak, loneliness, a constant feeling of not being good enough, and, of course, revenge. After all, hell hath no fury like a scorned Taylor Swift.

In many ways it is very convenient that her competitive advantage and industry uniqueness come from being the girl next door, our best friend, and even someone we have the tendency to feel sorry for. The authenticity we feel in her sharing her life with us makes it so much easier for us to jump with both feet into her world. Because *her* world, fictional or not, is largely the same as *our* world. Right?

It would have been a hell of a lot harder for her to have created the Swiftverse, which homes more than fifty million Swifties, had she not made a very early decision to wear her heart on her sleeve and sing about what (or more specifically *who*) has pissed her off that day, week, or month. These lovers, friends, and even frenemies have become characters in our own lives too. I mean, there isn't a single living person on this planet who couldn't conjure up someone they think about when listening to "I Forgot That You Existed" while deeply trying to pretend that this person no longer lives rent-free in their mind.

Apart from connected stories and narrative motifs, Taylor is slaying one of the most important curation techniques of universe creation: remakes and sequels. Sure, the rerecordings of Taylor's Versions were born out of a desire to protect and control her own music catalog, but one of the most genius Swiftverse moves she has made yet was to rerelease her albums because, if for no other reason, *nostalgia* is extraordinarily valuable. It *sells*. Everybody wants to feel like they're reliving the *1989* Era.

Which brings me back to the tool of "time" within the realm of strategy. Anytime a competitor tries to release a new album and attempts to shift her fan base to theirs, Taylor says, "Not today, and not on my watch," and drops an album that deeply connects us to the reasons we loved her during *Red*, *1989*, *Reputation*, and beyond.

And not only does she remake her previous albums, doubling down and bringing her past success forward to compound with today's success, but she changes some lyrics, adds additional meaning to the music through music videos (uh hello, "All Too Well"!), and releases previously unheard tracks, allowing Swifties to further understand and engage with the landscape in which the Swiftverse was created and curated.

So, understanding this, you can see that the role of her infamous secret and hidden messages in her music and communications, her Easter eggs, is incredibly important. It's the way that she communicates directly to the people living in her universe, and it's the way that she allows those people to shape their own narrative of the world they find themselves in; she listens to what Swifties say they want in their universe, and she reciprocates the affection by giving it to them in the same way that someone might give a puppy a treat.

Even in her earliest years of music making, and long before Marvel or Mattel or other worlds were created, much to the delight of Disney shareholders, Taylor started building hers. And very much unlike Disney's creation of a cinematic universe around the Marvel comics and Mattel's around their toys and games, hers is completely organic.

Making it *even more* valuable. Because there is nothing more alluring in an age of hypercapitalism than saying, "I'm not trying to trick you into being friends with me; you can take or leave this friendship; I'm not doing it for the money."

STRATEGIC PILLAR TWO: CONTENT

Simply put, musicians release *albums*, and world-builders like Taylor Swift release *content*.

Consider that it's been a long time since Taylor adhered to the concept of traditional music industry norms. I mean, she has taken "conventional" and thrown it out the top-floor window. Her albums have insanely long track lists; she has shocked the world by releasing successive albums within a couple of months (*folklore* and *evermore*) and then within hours (*The Tortured Poets Department: The Anthology*); there were rumors that she would only tour *Lover* at music festivals instead of stand-alone stadiums (although because of COVID-19, we'll never know); and on occasion she has not even bothered to announce the album until its imminent release!

By throwing away the Very Important Music Industry Playbook, she has created a much more expansive and multifaceted approach to world-building, whereby music is just one (although arguably large) piece of the Swiftverse narrative tapestry; her complex stories and lore are increasingly being told by the colors of the clothes she wears, the poems she writes, the music she listens to, and even other musicians' music she co-opts, like that of HAIM or The 1975. While the Swiftverse is largely predicated on her songs, there is a strong and permanent sense among her fans that "she is trying to tell us something" in nonmusic ways, mostly through the use of her famed Easter eggs.

Indeed, as Taylor's repertoire grew, she began to embrace a more *holistic* and connected approach to content creation, which allowed her to reach a higher potential for richer, more immersive stories across multiple mediums. Rather uncoincidentally, this progression just happened to occur in tandem with bigger picture changes in the music industry, including the growth of digital streaming platforms and social media.

And yeah, you could probably say: So what? Everybody has an Instagram and a TikTok page. What's the difference between that and world-building?

Which is a fascinating aspect to consider because for a long time Taylor Swift was one of the only Big Artists who did *not* have a TikTok, and who rarely or never used Instagram. She showed the world that there's a big difference between "having a huge online following" and "building a fan universe." A huge online following no longer means the existence of deep fan connections.

But more to the point, the difference between Taylor and other artists when it comes to social media is that other artists tend to use these platforms as an end in and of itself. As in, this social platform is where they "engage" in a rather one-dimensional way with fans. They'll post a photo, maybe "like" or comment on a couple of responses.

On the other hand, Taylor uses social media platforms not as the goal but as only a way to create something much bigger with her fans: the Swiftverse, which does not "live" on a digital platform owned by some other corporation. Instead, like Kim Kardashian and Kanye West, the Swiftverse lives rent-free in our hearts and our minds. For Taylor, TikTok is a way, not a product.

Something else that really differentiated Taylor throughout this *industry-meets-disruptive-technology* transition was her embrace of visual storytelling through music videos and short films. As she did with social media, Taylor rejected the idea of simply releasing music videos as a way of promoting her singles and began to treat them as stand-alone works of art, each with its own narrative arc and visual aesthetic.

Not to sound like my mother, but the music video scene got to a stage where I started to think: *They just don't make them like they used to.* And they didn't, because Facebook, Instagram, and TikTok replaced the need for videos at all. That is, until Taylor started using them for something else entirely—as a medium for dropping Easter eggs. Videos like "Blank Space" and "Bad Blood" gave Swift's fandom a visual representation of the Swiftverse—a home of sorts—and a more tangible spectacle that outlined the landscapes, characters, themes, and plot progressions that defined her kingdom.

Take "Bad Blood," which introduces her sidekick Selena Gomez as the character "Arsyn," and the Swift alter-ego characters, such as "Catastrophe," who are displayed across the bounty hunter's office. The color theme of the video is, unsurprisingly, red, connecting her bad blood to another album era entirely, based in the past. At one stage we see graffiti that says, "This is why we can't have nice things," a reference to a future (yes, a future!) song on her *Reputation* album.

And if linking to her next album doesn't seem crazy enough, in a later scene featuring a large target there is the prominent use of an arrow, perhaps alluding to "The Archer," a song from *two* albums into the future. Of course, at the time, the arrow would have meant nothing to Swifties, and maybe it's purely coincidental, but looking back and seeing it there suggests to fans that the Swiftverse is a multi-decade curation of Taylor's. And indeed, such coincidences force Swifties to purposefully go back and reinvestigate all previous content that Taylor has released, looking for more clues as to what the universe is *really* like. This leads to—you guessed it—continually high music streaming across all her albums.

And Swifties really obsess over these glimpses of the Swiftverse in their hunt for behind-the-scenes views of Taylor's life. What is scribbled on the piece of paper on the desk in the background? What does that number *mean*? Why was she wearing red in one scene, and then blue in another? Why was the picture hanging on the wall not entirely straight?

Consider that multiple people made multiple videos on social media about the color combinations of her *1989* Era outfit on the Eras Tour in her Dublin and Cardiff shows (green and orange), while doing some pretty weird math relating to the number of shows ago that she wore the same outfit with inverted colors (orange and green). Insert something about the color of the microphone she used, divide by ten, and multiply by thirteen (because, you know, thirteen), and suddenly Swifties were convinced that she was going to announce the release date of her *Reputation* album rerecord on the third and final night of her shows in Dublin. Did she? No. But regardless, the Swiftverse for a short moment all had PhDs in Taylor Math.

And for those who were struggling to do the math themselves, there was even the creation of an app called Swift Alert to help Swifties figure out the statistical likelihood of Eras Tour–related shenanigans, such as the color of her outfits or the surprise songs she might play.

These glimpses, peppered with Easter eggs—some real, some imagined—create absolute hysteria in the fandom.

Which begs the real question: What is her content actually delivering us? What sort of universe does it create? Because this is the defining question that surrounds the strategy of social media in the first place. What does she want us to take away from this engagement?

In thinking about the role of content from an artist, a business, or an organization, I refer back to what my Michelin-star chef told me when I posed him this question: If you had to give up one of these ingredients in your cooking, what would it be—butter or salt?

He cheated on the question and told me, with a serious face, "Neither." For the simple reason that butter, or any fat, is used in cooking to release, transport, and deliver flavor from the ingredients to your mouth. Salt is used to amplify existing flavors. They work in tandem.

Content creation is like butter: It is used to deliver messages and meaning from the artist to our minds. The platform, social media or otherwise, is the salt that can amplify it.

And the tastes, feelings, or meanings that Taylor wants to deliver to us? Well, this, as always, goes back to her unique selling point and her industry differentiation.

Taylor is your best friend, your sister, your agony aunt, your mother. As she has said in countless interviews, "I want to write a song for the person going through a breakup, for the person who feels left out, for the person who is really angry."

She is giving you a sense of *belonging*, through a deep emotional connection and empathy for the biggest issues in our lives as we grow older and transition through life stages. She is giving us a space to share our wins, à la her *Lover* album, and commiserate our losses, à la *Red*. Her content says, "Feel free to stop by when you're feeling betrayed" (*Reputation*), and "Come here to frolic in imaginary lands" (*folklore*), and even "This is how sad I felt when I was on stage with all of you" (*The Tortured Poets Department*).

Through the creation of the Swiftverse, Taylor's content has moved far beyond the idea of a single album release, and instead is used as her most impactful tool for doubling down on her strategy to be the most iconic brand in contemporary culture, possibly *ever.*

STRATEGIC PILLAR THREE: COMMUNITY

Of course, behind every song stream, album purchase, and filled concert seat is a human being. A complicated, contradictory, full-of-hopes/dreams/fears human being.

But the existence of "Swifties" in the first place requires some inspection, as people often misunderstand the relationship between Taylor Swift and her fans. There is an assumption that Taylor is their deity, and they worship at the altar of her righteous music. That she controls their minds, their opinions, and, importantly, their wallets. While this sounds like a convenient mechanism for understanding the ways in which she has grown in popularity and enriched herself both in the currency of money and music awards, I'm sorry to say that it's a complete mischaracterization of reality.

It's a compelling narrative simply for the reason that most of the time this is actually how power *is* created and sustained: in a top-down, heavy-handed manner. And not only in cults and religions, but in corporations and capitalist markets too. Think about the number of times you have inadvertently become beholden to a company that has slyly convinced you to click the "subscribe" button and hand over your credit card details in a matter of seconds, before you realize that you can never unsubscribe and that you'll be paying for a shitty and useless subscription for years. Well, this is exactly what "top-down" power looks like, and it leaves such a stale taste in our mouths that people actively try to overthrow it.

Power and hierarchy go hand in hand. *Most of the time.*

But upon closer inspection, and with a little more intellectual integrity, it becomes clear that this is not what Taylor has done at all. This is not even remotely how the Swiftverse and the community of Swifties is organized.

Unlike nearly every powerful person, organization, and institution, Taylor's power base comes not from being at the *top* of a hierarchy but by being on the *same level* as her fans. She has grown so insanely powerful because of the very thing that she is willing to give away in the first place: power.

To quote Taylor herself, "When I meet my fans, it's not like meeting a stranger. It's like saying hello to someone that I already know."

Swifties do not see Taylor as a god that they look up to; instead, she is an equal. And this is one of the most important aspects of Taylor's business, which has been repeated throughout her entire career.

Her value to her fans is that she is with them—as a sister, an aunt, a mother, and a best friend—in the trenches. She is not the general screaming orders at her army of relentless followers; instead, she is the teammate who goes through basic training with you. She is the person who carries your hundred-pound backpack when you are struggling to finish the obstacle course, not the person who punishes you when you underperform.

This, by the way, is an incredibly rare form of power known as *distributed power*, and it scales incredibly quickly. In contrast to top-down hierarchical power, distributed power is how populist politicians connect with their citizens to become overnight electoral sensations; it's how social media platforms like TikTok grow from nothing to having billions of users; and it is how Taylor Swift became the world's first musician to become a billionaire.

Decentralization is the cornerstone of huge communities; just look at Reddit, Twitter, or Facebook. People can pop in and out of conversations, make new and different friends on their own terms, and make the place their own home without being told how to act, what to say, or what they should feel.

Like many gods and their temples, Taylor has built a universe in her name and in her likeness, where those who worship her can congregate. However, being decentralized changes the dynamic from "you are here to worship Taylor" to "you came for Taylor, but stayed for the friends you made along the way."

Because one of the most fascinating and unique things about how Taylor interacts with her fans is that even in an age of technology and unprecedentedly fast communication, Taylor doesn't actually communicate with her fans that often at all. An Easter egg here and there. A few words in the middle of her concerts. Unlike a lot of artists, she refrains from doing lots of interviews and does not chronically catalog her life online.

So why does it feel like she's ever-present?

Because fans are not communicating with *Taylor*; they're communicating with *one another.* They just happen to be doing it in the Swiftverse, which brings a heightened sense of closeness to Taylor.

In the same way that writing letters is not scalable but Twitter is, communicating with your fans is not scalable in the way that allowing them to communicate with each other is.

Consider the Swiftie Jessica Buchanan, who went viral on Tik-Tok after her fiancé ended their relationship right before the wedding. So on what would have been her wedding day, this (extremely tearful) *bride-no-more* booked a flight to the Eras Tour and, while crying her way there by herself, became friends with the Swiftie sitting next to her on the plane, with whom she proceeded to make friendship bracelets.

Or consider the evening of the first show of the Eras Tour in Vienna, canceled due to security concerns after a terrorist plot was uncovered, when thousands of Swifties self-organized to gather en masse along Corneliusgasse, after her famed song "Cornelia Street," and sang her entire set list themselves, creating their own Eras Tour.

There are just no words for the hundreds of stories like this that have become commonplace as a result of the Swiftverse being a very online place, where fans connect over Instagram, TikTok, and through pretty much any communication means possible. It is this type of agency that Swifties feel, this sense of empowerment to substantiate change in their own Swiftverse, that has made Taylor such a powerful leader in a very novel and refreshingly bottom-up capacity. The Swiftverse, if you need it, is there *for* you, but it is also *by* you.

Perhaps one of the more unique, but telling, stories of such heartwarming intra-Swiftverse communities became known to me after I had publicly written about Taylor Swift. One day, I got an email from a woman who was organizing a Swiftie-led alcohol and substance rehabilitation program, whereby Swifties would come together through rehab activities like singing, dancing, making friendship bracelets, and more. Would I, this woman reaching out to me wanted to know, be willing to give a talk about Taylor Swift to the program participants? People were literally coming together through the Swiftverse to radically enrich their own lives.

If Twitter is the platform for scaling news and opinions, the Swiftverse is the platform (albeit without a circumscribed home) for scaling friendship and belonging. All Taylor has to do is drop some content, hide some Easter eggs, or occasionally drop in to say hi, and her fandom will do the rest, which includes obsessively investigating, theorizing, and archiving the universe that she is building.

STRATEGIC PILLAR FOUR: COLLABORATION

If there's anything we can learn from the Mattel Universe created around the Barbie movie, it's that the fastest way to expand and deepen a fandom universe is by collaborating with those outside the universe. Barbie's unprecedented marketing drive through collaborative merchandise, dubbed "merchtainment," changed the paradigm on how to bring people from the outside into the universe. And it did this, rather simply, by bringing the Barbie Universe to the real world.

For several months, you could not go anywhere, read anything, or speak to anybody without Barbie being involved in merchandise, conversations, or the economy. I mean, "the Kens" even get a mention on Swift's *TTPD*. There was a full-scale Barbie house created in partnership with Airbnb. Barbie and Ken were on the dating app Bumble. The hot-pink Barbie color became a nail varnish, a Chanel handbag, a Porsche vehicle. Clothes, food, haircare, makeup, even *airlines* went Barbiecore—the name given for what essentially turned into a society-wide trend of living in the Mattel Universe.

Taylor Swift, on the other hand, has never needed the Swiftverse to infiltrate the "real world" in the same explicit manner because she is already there, living in the Swifties' minds by essentially branding, in a much more subtle way, not their Porsche cars or their Rolex watches, but their emotions. Taylor Swift does to our minds what Barbie has done to consumer goods.

Nonetheless, she does indeed engage extensively with artistic collaborations, which serve an entirely different purpose: not to bring people into the Swiftverse, but to give it additional dimensions and new layers of complexity and depth, essentially in an attempt to keep people there for longer.

Her collaborations, which are nearly always through music and rarely through brand partnerships, help her do two things. The first is to use external voices to double down on her message and bring external validation to what she has built. It sends the message that Ed Sheeran likes the Swiftverse so much, and so should you.

The second use of collaborations, as mentioned, is to add layers of complexity to the fan universe she is building through diversification. Is this universe a pop universe? A country universe? An R & B universe? Yes. Regardless of the genre you are into, this is a home *for you*. For *all*.

Think about the diversity of people she has worked with: Brendon Urie, Zayn, Aaron Dessner, Gary Lightbody, Kendrick Lamar, Ice Spice, HAIM, Shawn Mendes, Future, Florence Welch, Fall Out Boy . . . the list goes on.

Now think about the depth of one collaborator, and how much this one person impacted the dimensionality and directionality of the Swiftverse: Matty Healy and his band The 1975. Taylor's *The Tortured Poets Department*.

The superpositioning of Taylor's *TTPD* over what has been years of back-and-forth dialogue, engagement, and dare I write . . . *feelings?* between these two recording artists is the most *exquisite* example of "the whole is greater than the sum of the parts." Her song "imgonnagetyouback" was a natural response to his "Fallingforyou" (both songs even mention bikes), the titles of which have brought fans to consider that her song "Blank Space" was about Matty Healy. The intro to "Fortnight," it has been discovered by fans, is the same as The

1975's "Heart Out," but slowed down. Both Taylor's "imgonnaget-youback" and The 1975's "Looking for Somebody" have the same synth underlay. Both artists said, "This is about you. You know who you are. I love you," before singing a song on their respective tours, after which Taylor sang "cardigan" from her 2020 *folklore* album.

Immediately upon release of *The Tortured Poets Department*, a new dimension of the Swiftverse had been revealed after years of secrecy: that the previous several albums were, perhaps, somewhat related to Matty Healy and The 1975 the whole time. This new narrative, carefully exploited through shared imagery, lyrics, and music overlays of *TTPD* with The 1975 works, sent the Swiftverse into a maniacal frenzy and had every song from prior albums being excavated, reexamined, and ultimately redefined through a new lens. Thus, long-forgotten songs from five albums ago were suddenly important evidence for a new theory underlying the principal lores of the Swiftverse.

Clever? Yes, insanely. I cannot think of a single recording artist whose new music releases make fans listen to the rest of their works on repeat, as if they had never heard any of it before.

The power of collaborative world-building knows no bounds.

And as well as being a way to welcome in a higher volume of more diversified Swifties, collaborations align perfectly with her goal of becoming the most listened-to artist in the world. Can she own the rap *and* the R & B *and* the country *and* the pop market share of the music industry? Who knows, but you can sure as hell bet she is trying. Broadening her audience appeal and reaching new demographics through shared exposure and cross-promotion is how she has become the only artist not only to retain her existing fan base from her work but to increase her fan base from her *older* album releases.

Ever wonder how ten-year-olds and thirty-five-year-olds love her equally? It's absolutely bizarre, if not unheard of, for a brand to have such a wide variety of fans in an intense base. The first question that you'll hear someone asking is: How did my daughter come to love the same music I did when I was a teenager?

And the answer is: collaborations.

. ● .

Being able to curate the world you want to live in, create content that mirrors those ambitions, and build communities through collaborations is the engine behind every brand, organization, technology, and individual that is finding and achieving higher and higher levels of success that were previously deemed unreachable.

Understanding that it's better to offer a customer a fully cooked omelet instead of a deconstructed one at a restaurant is not rocket science, but it's a really hard thing for executives to get right. Along the same lines, it should be rather obvious now that building a universe is a much more worthwhile endeavor for a brand or corporation to commit to than just releasing one-off products, which have low future value once the initial usefulness has worn off.

As we can see from the Swiftverse, most of this additional value relative to many other musicians' business models comes down to being able to scale a universe faster than scaling the number of albums being released. And this inevitably leads to the whole being greater than the sum of its parts, which is the holy grail of business and finance.

So why isn't everybody doing this? If I can figure out Taylor Swift's grand plans for the Swiftverse and can see the absolutely enormous impact they're having, why can't other CEOs just be another Marvel, Mattel, or Taylor?

A lot of this comes down to the difficulty in understanding and measuring *intangibles*, those very valuable nonphysical assets that companies have but don't quite know what to do with. Sometimes the intangible is the company's brand, and so the CEO can spend a lot of money on marketing. Sometimes the intangible is quality, so the CEO spends a lot of money on manufacturing.

But in the world-building game that Taylor, Marvel, and LVMH are playing, a lot of the intangibles are just *feelings*. So most of the time, if a CEO can't get an army of MBA-anointed analysts to objectify, quantify, and calculate very high returns on investment for creating . . . *feelings* . . . then it will feel too risky for the CEO to pursue it.

While it feels like there are obvious lessons for corporations and executives from unpacking the unique strategy that Taylor is pursuing in her world-building effort, I think the most meaningful ones are directly pointed at us personally.

We live in a world where most people are sick of being labeled "consumers." I am a human being, and I have a name. I, like every other human, have admittedly very complex emotions and behaviors. I don't want to be targeted by marketing and lumped into what are called *demographics*. But unfortunately, according to most brands and most corporations, I am nothing but a number, signified in a dollar denomination.

World-building, on the other hand, allows Taylor to lean into her differentiation and take an authentic approach to interacting with and growing her fan base. Her fans are not numbers, but people. She is not their god, but their friend. And she is doing this despite the fact that decade after decade, male business executives claimed that it would be impossible to build a company or brand so powerful based on belonging instead of exclusivity, and friendship instead of FOMO.

What Taylor teaches us is that we, too, should be mindful of what worlds we are building for our own personal and professional lives, from what we curate to how we deliver the content of our lives, and to the diversity of who we bring into our world. Our networks matter. Collaborations matter. What we say and do matters.

And the easiest examples of where we see world-building happening every day in our own lives are, well, in our own worlds. Whether it's a fulfilling personal life that is highly engaging and full of meaning, or whether it's a brand, community, or organization that attracts highly emotionally connected people into it, we should take the time not just to deliver one-off interactions with people or one-time products or services but to create something that will allow people to invest their energy and trust.

Recently, a student of mine spoke to me about the lengths he goes to in order to curate the things in his life: He reads classic books, watches movies from before the 1980s, buys long-lasting second-hand attire, and only discusses topics at dinner parties that he thinks he can adequately contribute to. Having curated his own life to such an extent, he finds that he is better able to attract the type of people who are like-minded and share the same level of consideration for what content they consume and put into the world. This, in turn, makes it easier for him to collaborate in a more meaningful way. Before he changed to being more mindful of building a worldview around him, he struggled to find meaning or purpose in many of the interactions he had with people or content.

In a more commercial setting, you can see the same strategic world-building taking place on social media, as influencers are often seen to be "combining friendship groups," appearing as heavily curated characters in one another's content, and collaborating on projects in locations that are usually somewhat defined, such as one person's apartment à la *Friends* or a favorite bar or restaurant. This has changed the nature of digital influencers, who are now starting to turn one-off posts into live-streamed TV shows based on friendships, hardships, and romances.

How we engage with our networks, personally and professionally, has a huge impact on how fast and in what direction we grow, especially if we want the whole of our life to be worth more than the sum of the individual pieces of our lives. Working *with* and not *against* people matters. And finding the people in your universe that you will be able to collaborate most successfully with matters too.

The four *C*'s of world-building—curation, content, community, and collaboration—have to be interconnected and reflect an authentic desire to build a world or universe that is additive, instead of extractive, for those who enter it. It rejects the age-old idea that power is a top-down mechanism, reserved only for the "male, pale, and stale" elite. Organizations, products, and people who use those mechanisms to get to "the top" are consistently underperforming the atypical, community-backed leaders of our generation, like Taylor.

Instead, the premise of world-building your way to success is centered on the idea that anybody can impact and influence change from the bottom up, and that we are all active agents of our own trajectory.

That is, if we choose to be.

POWER MOVE FOUR

NEGOTIATE WITH AUTHENTICITY

ONE OF TAYLOR'S BIGGEST EVER COUPS WAS FIGHTING, AND WINning, against private equity, an investment-asset class worth many trillions of dollars. It's hard to overemphasize what an epic and historic power play this was, and to say that it's one of the biggest achievements by any CEO is probably an understatement.

Although the Great War between Taylor and her nemesis Scooter Braun over her master recordings, as well as the betrayal of her ex-manager Scott Borchetta, is much documented, the fight itself is surprisingly undocumented in terms of how Taylor Swift, a CEO in her mid-thirties, has so successfully defied the dynamics of the $115 trillion financial capital markets that govern our world.

In this proxy battle between Good and Evil in our capitalist system, as Taylor took on Wall Street we saw that one of the only times a CEO has been able to persist and resist the pressure of private equity, they have done so while wearing high heels and friendship bracelets.

What is completely fascinating about this fight to rerecord her catalog and rebuild the Swiftverse around herself is the fact that she has defied traditional wisdom, which tells corporate superstar executives that they need to be tough, and inhuman, and transactional, and instill top-down influence on those around them so that they terrify anybody away from even attempting to screw them over.

Taylor, on the other hand, has provided us with what may be the first example of a transformative and authentic style of management that says: Okay, Wall Street, I recognize that you don't take me seriously because I'm nice and wear pink and sing songs about my diary, but I'm not scared of you. And I might only be one person, but there are 180 million people in the United States alone who are on my side.

I mean, you don't have to dig deep to find the ghosts of women who have lost in tough negotiations by taking this approach; authenticity is rarely valued or taken seriously as a means for securing hard-fought wins against tough competitors.

That is, until Taylor Swift won a $400 million battle through a stunning display of her human-focused strategy and unwavering determination that good wins over bad. By leveraging this style, she not only challenged the norms of the increasingly financialized music industry but also redefined what it means to be a leader in a competitive, male-dominated field.

And hence, we can now see the emergence of a new corporate road map predicated on Taylor's success, which is a testament to the rarely seen power of combining empathy, resilience, and strategic acumen.

Her victory against her former record overlords serves as a powerful example that kindness, authenticity, and emotional intelligence are not weaknesses but *strengths* that can drive success, even in the most unlikely of scenarios.

For the first time in a very long time, Taylor showed us that the good folks can triumph too.

As the famous quote goes: "First they ignore you, then they laugh at you, then they fight you, then you win."

•   ❀   •

I was twenty-five years old when I first learned about the investment class of private equity, from a private equity investor named Ryan, who went on to be one of the worst people I've ever dated. This was approximately two years before Taylor herself would have her heart broken by the sharks in private equity.

My own battle with PE, as it's known, mirrored that of Taylor's; it was a battle royale between an inherently good person (me, of course) and a cunning shark who would feel no remorse for buying and selling his own grandmother in the morning if he thought it might be financially advantageous (Ryan).

So what is PE and why is interacting with it so heartbreaking? Well, before I get into the grim details about how this asset class operates, it's worth noting that there are two useful ways to inspect an industry from the outside to understand it.

The first and most common is to look at the industry from a Big Picture perspective. What does this industry do? How does it make money? Who are its competitors? How does it achieve its profit margin? What are the industry dynamics?

And sure, the answer to all these questions will tell you *most* of the things you need to know about interacting with an industry. However, every industry, organization, or business unit is filled with people, humans just like you and me. Arguably, you could say that Google is not a mega huge corporation but instead a community of people with its own culture, rituals, and gods they worship. And this community is full of people who are incentivized to sell more products and increase the revenue of their business at nearly any cost. We know that people in large corporations are mostly incentivized to do this at the individual level because most people are remunerated by a mix of short-term incentives (a monthly salary), medium-term incentives (an annual bonus), and long-term incentives (shares in the business) that essentially pull everybody's day-to-day behavior in the same direction: to optimize for an increase in revenue and profitability.

These are people, like you and I, that have hopes, dreams, and ambitions. And so, whether you're trying to sell a product or idea to a Mega Huge Corporation or just simply understand it, another way to figure out an industry is to look at the individual people who work in it, and instead try to understand *those people*.

Understanding the *people* in an industry or organization is the most critical aspect of any successful negotiation. Because, as we'll see with the fight over Taylor's album ownership, you don't negotiate with a firm; you negotiate with a person or a small number of people within it.

So before we jump into "what is private equity, and why did it nearly ruin Taylor's life?," I want to tell you a story about one of the people that makes up this financial asset class that caused Taylor to rerecord her entire music catalog.

That person is Ryan, my private equity ex-boyfriend.

Tall, dark, and handsome, he grew up in the Midwest before moving to Manhattan and spending his days at his desk in front of spreadsheets, his lunch in the gym trying to make himself look more ripped, and his evenings drinking away his loneliness at expensive hotel bars surrounded by his loafer-wearing friends with names like Brad and Chad and Hunter.

Of course, he wasn't always awful. When I met him, I didn't know enough about private equity to know that he was a parody of himself. He was funny, sarcastic, and . . . dare I say, even nice? Border-line *boring*?

When we would go for dinner, he'd take me to the usual New York City hot spots filled with other PE guys with their hot model girlfriends, who were there mostly to be seen. When he ordered a bottle of wine, it would undoubtedly be the celebrity wine of the month that he had been told was good, but couldn't taste why. When we went on vacation, we'd go to the resorts that were trending on social media, and he'd want to spend four days drinking by the pool, topping up his tan, and showing off those lunchtime abs.

Ryan's life was predictable, dull, and expensive. We did what his private equity boss told him to do, in an attempt to look just as rich and successful as his investor peers, so that when promotion season rolled around, he would look like partner material. Conversations were beige at best, and "bro" at worst. And when I learned that he barely had a relationship with his Kansas-based family, who seemed delightful from the outside, red flags started flying. Did he discon-nect from his family so that he could live this new life as a finance bro in Manhattan and feel less bad about abandoning his country-living morals? The life he was living in New York seemed worlds away from how he had grown up.

Over dinner, I would hear him say things like this to his friends: "It's a great company, for sure, but it's overvalued. I don't think it fits with the worldview of the partners. If I want a bonus this year, I should get rid of it from the portfolio quickly." Soon enough he'd replaced the word "company" with "girlfriend" and dumped me.

But in those few months, I learned more about the world of Wall Street and how the people of private equity work—the very same ones that buy and sell record labels and artists' catalogs.

Everyone I've met in PE, lovely or not, has one thing in common: They work in private equity because they couldn't figure out what else they were passionate about, and thought, "If I'm going to do something I don't love, I may as well do something that makes me a hell of a lot of money." The people of PE are deeply juxtaposed with everybody else I've mentioned thus far—the two-Michelin-star chef, the Olympic athlete, and most of all, Taylor Swift.

To understand the PE industry, you have to understand that it is composed of many people just like Ryan, who are at best indifferent to the types of passion and dreams that consume Unicorns and at worst seek to feed off other people's passions and dreams to fulfill themselves, emotionally or financially.

●　●　●

Now, think of the most obscure or abstract single object or industry that you can, and I can nearly guarantee you that most of it is owned by private equity. A pen? A streetlamp? The water running through your taps? The sink? The clothes on your back? The chair you're sitting on? The music you're listening to?

In the simplest explanation, PE investors buy companies or assets that are not listed on public stock exchanges like the New York Stock Exchange. Then, to multiply their money, they sell the business they've bought for more than they bought it for. Sounds pretty simple, right?

Well, there are two things you need to know about PE in order to be able to understand why Taylor Swift is such a goddamn genius: The first is that PE typically makes the businesses it owns worse, not better; the second is that it's nearly impossible not to get sucked up into its vacuum.

So let's start with the first thing—that PE destroys nearly everything in its path, nearly always by "cost cutting." If you want to increase the profit of a company, you can either increase the revenue by growing the company (hard!) or decrease the costs (easy!). And how do you decrease the costs? Well, usually by firing a bunch of people, and then by putting a hard stop on any nonessential activities in the company like . . . oh, I dunno . . . innovating.

It doesn't matter that eliminating R & D means that vital technologies aren't created, that businesses don't produce better or more sustainable products, or that society eventually begins to culturally, financially, and physically crumble. We consistently see that the costs of cutting R & D fall on our collective society; however, the rewards are going to benefit an individual like Ryan, who has increased the investment portfolio value and is now closer to making partner.

Yeah, there's a reason that private equity is despised by so many people.

Because it has made every aspect of our lives that it exists in . . . shitty.

In fact, in 2022, the journalist and sci-fi writer Cory Doctorow coined the term "enshittification," which refers to the drastic decrease in quality and simultaneous increase in price (or enshittifying) of nearly everything around us.

I, like many others, believe this is largely due to the impact that PE has on our world. So-called cost cutting and the ensuing degradation of products and services is the reason that trains don't run on time, stores have too few clerks, skiing has become so expensive, the

Google search engine returns fewer queries and more ads every year, the Thames River in London is mostly just sewage, movies and music have become incredibly boring, and the amount of cereal you buy decreases even though the box stays the same size and the price increases.

So, if PE is so bad for our society, why do we keep allowing it to buy all these businesses just to tear them apart?

The answer is very simple and comes down to two words: money and power.

The global PE market is valued at over $5 trillion. That's 120 million Eras Tour tickets. That's 17,000 times the size of the entire Super Bowl economy. That's 33 International Space Stations—one of the most expensive things to have ever been built on Earth.

When private equity comes for your industry or your business, it comes with a team of Harvard- and Stanford- and Wharton-trained lawyers who each have more than thirty years' experience in multibillion-dollar merger and acquisition deals. It comes with pockets so deep and checkbooks so big that the investors think not in *thousands* of dollars but in *hundreds of millions* of dollars, at the least. And it comes with spreadsheets made by people like Ryan, who will tell you: "You're too dumb to understand this, but trust me. It's for the best that we take over your company."

And this is what happened to the music industry just as Taylor Swift was becoming a significant name in it.

This is what Taylor Swift had to defy.

*   *   *

Record labels, as it happens, are just like any other business that PE loves to swallow whole. The simplified version of how it works is pretty straightforward, even if the spreadsheets are not: Recording artists like Taylor Swift sign with a label, which will own the rights to the music being created, and that music will generate revenue over its lifetime through royalties.

But if you are an artist, like Bruno Mars, and the company that owns your repertoire is being sold, you don't get a *big* say in who buys it, for how much, or what they'll do with your music. Most of the time, you don't get a say *at all*, while your music gets sliced and diced and sold and rebought and gradually more boring and *beige* over time.

I mean, you can ask Taylor: In 2005, she signed with a record label called Big Machine Records, which was majority owned by an American music executive called Scott Borchetta. Under this contract, Taylor wrote her first six studio albums and found unprecedented global fame.

During this time, Taylor had apparently been trying to buy her music back from the record label. Although we do not know why she was unable to do this, it's easy to speculate that Scott Borchetta realized that this was another version of the whole is bigger than the sum of its parts. As in, his record label, Big Machine Records, is much more valuable with Taylor's music than without it.

And sure enough, in 2019, Carlyle, one of the largest PE firms in the world, with nearly half a trillion dollars in its war chest, announced that a company it owns, Ithaca Holdings, was going to buy Big Machine Label Group from Scott Borchetta for around $300 million.

This included, as most people are now aware, Taylor Swift's music catalog.

After the sale was finalized, Taylor's music was owned by a person she outwardly despised, Scooter Braun, who managed, among many other famous people, Kanye West.

In Taylor's view, the one person who had overseen her downfall at the hands of Kanye West now effectively owned her business.

After global backlash, Scooter Braun realized he was sitting on a ticking time bomb with Taylor Swift's music catalog and sold it quickly to another PE firm called Shamrock Holdings, owned by the Disney family, for over $400 million.

Think about that for a minute: In 2019, Scooter Braun bought an entire record label for $300 million, and a few months later resold just one artist's portfolio within that label for more than $400 million. This is exactly how PE works in action: Buy a company, strip it down, cut away the pieces, and resell it all for more than you bought it for.

If this all seems very predatory, then yes. You seem to be understanding the private equity model!

The deal to Shamrock Holdings was painfully large, with a lot of financial analysts wondering whether or not they would be able to increase the value of Taylor's first six albums before they inevitably resold the hot potato to another PE firm a few years later.

Shamrock was convinced they would make a killer return on Swift's catalog. Taylor, on the other hand, thought differently.

Taylor used four main tactics to outmaneuver her multitrillion-dollar-size opponents.

TAYLOR'S FIRST TACTIC: CONSIDER YOUR UNIQUE ASSETS

Nearly everybody knows what happened next in this story: Taylor announced that she would rerecord her albums, and that moving forward she would own 100 percent of her rerecorded work. And since then, she has been doing just that.

So what's the big deal? If Taylor can say, "Screw private equity, you're not going to buy and sell me," why doesn't everybody?

Well, in short, Taylor Swift is not just "everybody," and we can learn just as much as the private equity industry did from this incredible act of defiance. Because not even the most senior PE investors in the world thought Taylor would be able to hit them back hard, let alone hurt them.

As Taylor says herself: They *"should keep in mind / There is nothing I do better than revenge."*

In a message Taylor released publicly in 2019, she stated that her ex-manager Scott Borchetta told her team that she could use her music for her Netflix documentary if she promised not to rerecord her albums—that he was essentially holding her music hostage.

If what Taylor says is true, that Scott asked her not to rerecord her music, we can learn something very interesting about the Carlyle-backed investment deal: that the investors knew Taylor Swift was powerful enough to harm their investment.

In purchasing her music catalog, Ithaca Holdings was making a bet that the catalog would become more and more profitable over time, most likely through Taylor becoming more famous, and her music getting more and more streams. In the minds of the investors, the only reason she *wouldn't* make them more money is if people suddenly fell out of love with Taylor Swift, a scenario that financial analysts would have placed somewhere between extremely unlikely and downright impossible.

There is, however, another scenario that could hurt the investment, although it had never in the history of music actually happened: If

Taylor rerecorded her music, and people listened to Taylor's Version instead of the original, they would generate *no money* from streaming.

But how likely was that, really?

The crux of the entire rerecord-versus-don't-rerecord her albums came down to the first, most dangerous assumption that investors made about Taylor Swift: that she was a regular CEO who thought about her catalog the way most CEOs think about their businesses—pragmatically.

However, we already know that Unicorns very much do not think like this; as we've seen, the very focus of their talent is intrinsically, not externally, optimized.

Taylor had one unique asset that differentiated her from every other CEO that private equity fought against: her Unicornness and her blind obsession with and love for her music, which forced her to act in a seemingly irrational way to investors.

There was no way, surely, that a normal recording artist would go to the effort of rerecording her music. Right?

Well, kind of.

Ithaca Holdings suspected that there was a nonzero chance of it happening, hence they allegedly tried to persuade her *not* to rerecord her music. But the fact that they bought her music in the first place meant they didn't take the threat seriously.

Shamrock, on the other hand, seemed to go into the acquisition deal to buy Swift's music from Ithaca armed with a militia of MBAs who were clearly not Swifties, as they didn't really see any threat to the value of her original masters even if there was a rerecord.

This is explained in more detail in a *Rolling Stone* article in which Tim Ingham, the music business writer, describes just how hard it would be for Taylor to impact the value of the original masters over a longer period, let's say ten years. Sure, he explains, the industry might get behind Taylor and throw inordinate amounts of marketing money at her new rereleases. Sure, music streaming networks like Spotify might get behind Taylor and algorithmically help her re-records replace the originals. And sure, there would be some fans who go to the effort of replacing her old with her new. But eventually, Ingham argues, people—especially her fans—would get bored and forget about this whole thing.

And so there really wasn't a single stakeholder in these multimillion-dollar deals who thought it would be anything other than career suicide for Taylor to go through the hassle of rerecording her catalog for what may or may not be a few streams of Taylor's Version.

I mean, think about the *effort* involved. You're Taylor and you're trying to release new music, new videos, new tours. And yet you're constantly being pulled back into the recording studio to redo something from a decade ago. Consider the difficulty of the physical act of traveling into a studio while trying to convince the same A-list performers you collaborated with all those years ago to join you. Once in the studio, you have to record and rerecord until your voice, at age thirty-five, sounds like it did at eighteen, with exactly the same intonation.

And now think of the opportunity cost—the new music that you could have released that would have been a nearly certain bet for success has just been replaced by music that people already know, love, and have access to.

It's a wildly risky move for a payout that seems . . . minimal, at best.

And then, of course, we know that private equity is much bigger, stronger, and more manipulative than a single singer-songwriter who makes friendship bracelets with fans. If there's $300 million at stake, and it looks like a rerecord could make any impact on the catalog owners, investors will happily use blunt force in an attempt to inch toward winning. Nobody else has the time, money, or energy to keep up with the scale and power of private equity, which can only be described as *"Building up like waves / Crashing over my grave"* by anybody who has encountered it.

And I'm not just talking about Shamrock here, although they certainly had a vested interest in Swift's music. I mean the entirety of private equity combined, which invested more than $12 billion in music rights in 2021 *alone*. If Taylor Swift got away with rerecording her music and successfully reducing the value of Shamrock's acquisition to next to nothing, then the entire industry should be very, very worried about what could happen next.

But you know, they *weren't* worried. They bet against her, which, as we now know, was a dangerous mistake for these investors to make.

They say that hindsight is twenty-twenty, however, because at the time the successful outcome of Taylor's revenge on the $5 trillion dollar PE industry was not at all predictable. In fact, the reason I've painfully outlined the industry, what it does, and what these investors are like is because it's important to understand just how strong the current going against Taylor was at this time. There have been many CEOs, in many industries, who have said the same thing Taylor has said: Over my dead body will you buy my business, take my music, or sell my art.

And every single time, somebody like Ryan will make a spreadsheet, take it to the partners, install an award-winning legal team, and find a way to do it anyway.

What made this situation different from nearly every other situation is the fact that Taylor Swift found the assets that made her unique in this deal: her tenacity and blind love for her catalog, and used them against the investors.

In a tough negotiation or conflict, finding and using your unique assets—whether it's specialized or niche knowledge, resources you have access to that others don't, or strategic partnerships—creates leverage. It makes your position stronger and gives you more control over the terms of the negotiation. By focusing on what's unique, you shift the balance in your favor, moving the negotiation away from competition to dialogue.

And in this dialogue, Taylor made one thing clear: You won't be owning my music for much longer.

TAYLOR'S SECOND TACTIC: NEGOTIATE WITH HUMANS, NOT WITH SPREADSHEETS

At some stage, as the "PE-must-own-everything" playbook was rolled out, investors forgot that behind every organization and behind every product are *people*. People who were born with ambitions to do something with their lives and to contribute to society.

In particular, Taylor Swift's catalog of music was made by a teenage girl who created an unfathomably close connection with millions of people by sharing her most intimate experiences, her own fears, disappointments, and tragedies. This, essentially, is what a financial analyst—one who was probably male and who probably acted like my ex Ryan—tried to price by projecting forward-looking numbers on streaming revenue.

Companies and investment funds like Carlyle, KKR, Ithaca, BGM, and Shamrock Holdings, out of necessity, treat their portfolios of other people's hopes, dreams, and fears as numbers on a spreadsheet that either go up or down over time. And while all artists are selling creations that are unique to them, Taylor Swift's music, her *products*, have been created using her unique strategy of wearing her heart on her sleeve.

Unlike buying a business that manufactures inanimate carpets, Scooter Braun buying Taylor Swift's music catalog is like a sixteen-year-old girl's worst enemy stealing her diary; and having been a sixteen-year-old teenage girl myself once, I can guarantee you that this would be a more complex acquisition.

Over time, I suspect that investors got so used to treating people like items of clothing they could just get rid of when they didn't need them anymore (cough, Ryan) that they didn't stop to think that maybe they actually *did* need these people to be on their side after all. Maybe it never occurred to them that they should have treated this one transaction differently.

The irony is that by announcing the value of her master catalog as a function of the revenue generated by streaming and her merchandise sales, it's very possible that financial analysts did not consider the infinitely more valuable thing that she brought to the table: her ability to influence her hundreds of millions of fans. One of the *intangibles* she creates through the Swiftverse.

In other words, analysts saw the terms of the deal for her work as they do for those of most musicians—a deconstructed omelet. And they did not value or take into consideration the risk of buying—or stealing, as many Swifties considered it—the bedrock of the Swiftverse that Taylor has been building quietly but confidently for over a decade.

Buying an artist's catalog is one thing, and sure, for a while the fans of that artist may create some backlash. But Ingham at *Rolling*

Stone is right; eventually even these fans will get tired of the performative outrage on someone else's behalf.

Most fans do not have any skin in the game of who owns the music they listen to. Why should they care if it's owned by one three-lettered financial institution over another, so long as they can keep streaming it?

Stealing the shrine at the altar of your worship, however, is an entirely different proposition. And this is what the millions of Swifties, of *humans*, who live in the Swiftverse felt had happened. They did not switch their streaming to Taylor's Version to help an artist make more money than a private equity firm. Instead, they uprooted their universe and built a new one around their ability not only to protect Taylor Swift, whom they viewed as a friend, a sister, and a mother. They uprooted their universe and built a new one around *themselves*.

And the impact is clear. According to Cecilia Giles, who wrote about the legal impact of her rerecord decision in the *University of Cincinnati Law Review* in a piece very cleverly titled "Look What You Made Them Do," *the rerecords are outperforming the originals by a landslide.*

However, the disconnect between the investor perspective on Taylor's catalogs and the reality remains fully disjointed. Private equity investors just could not, and possibly still may not, comprehend the fact that Taylor's human-centric and trust-first business model would not align with the "growth at any cost, even if we ruin the world" model that private equity created.

These investors, several times over, walked into several hundred-million-dollar deals without any comprehension of what Taylor was actually selling (friendship, not music), to whom (mothers, sisters, and daughters, not "users"), and through which platform (the Swiftverse, not Spotify). They had no understanding of the actual asset they were buying, nor of how Taylor Swift, Swifties, and the Swiftverse would impact its economics.

Not Scott Borchetta, despite being Taylor's manager for so long. Not Scooter Braun. Not Carlyle. Not Shamrock Holdings. And not a single one of the business and finance elite who would have been paid handsomely to consult on the deal.

Who won the battle of business models? Well, for the first time in a very, very long time, we can breathe a deep sigh of relief that Taylor's model may have finally beaten private equity. At least, for now.

Taylor Swift has shown us that the world is full of people who are humans, not numbers on a spreadsheet. Success driven by authenticity acknowledges this and will always be hard for even the most powerful dynamics to counter.

TAYLOR'S THIRD TACTIC: NEGOTIATE SO THAT EVERYBODY WINS

Most people, especially those who have lived in New York City, are scared of rats. Maybe it's because in New York you're technically always less than ten feet away from one at any given moment. Or perhaps it's because the rats in New York are the size of small dogs, not to mention utterly fearless!

But something we tend to forget is that rats are scared of humans too. And if you corner them, or if they *feel* like you're cornering them, they will attack you. Interestingly, rats have a hinged lower jaw that gives them plenty of space to open their mouths, allowing them to sink their top teeth into whatever they're attacking. And once they do this, their jaw locks, making it really difficult to stop the assault once it's in motion.

This is where the expression "never corner a rat" comes from when discussing negotiation tactics. Or, in less rodent-like terms, be careful when pushing people too far, and *never* put someone in a position where they feel completely trapped, with no way out. Why? Because there is a high likelihood that they will respond unpredictably and aggressively, and often in ways that can cause significant harm to all parties involved.

The best negotiations happen when there is an open dialogue between both parties, built on trust and respect (duh!), and where both parties feel like they have some skin in the game.

The worst negotiations, which happen more frequently than is good for the world, are the opposite: They take place with one party feeling like they have nothing to lose while motivated by spite.

If I had to award a Nobel Prize for the worst-negotiated deal in business history, it would go to Ithaca Holdings for their aggressive acquisition and handling of Taylor's master records. In fact, we can look at the world's most famously good negotiations—the Northern Irish peace agreement—and quickly discern where Scooter Braun and Scott Borchetta may have gone wrong. Although it's too complex to get into here, Carrie Bradshaw summarizes the war in Northern Ireland as being like "the fight between marrieds and singles. . . . We're all basically the same, but somehow we ended up on different sides."

By this, I'm sure Carrie meant that everybody in Northern Ireland wanted the same thing—peace and prosperity—just as Taylor and Ithaca wanted the same thing—financial growth and success, which aligned heavily with Taylor's vision of being the most iconic brand in contemporary culture.

Despite the "what" being the same, they clearly disagreed on the "how," with Ithaca's side exercising what seemed to be a top-down show of power on Taylor. *You will do what we say, or else*, was the feeling Taylor reportedly received and which she resented.

In any negotiation, you have to give the other side a ladder to step down from their position gracefully in order to come to an agreement. In other words, find a way to make it *seem* like an agreement was a win-win, even if your side really won and the other side lost. Why? Because most negotiations are not won and lost because of the specifics being offered, but instead are heavily influenced by personal emotions and ego. There has to be a sense of alignment and at least a sense of commitment to the middle ground in order to remove the threat of any one party feeling like they are losing.

In this instance, given that a win-win strategy wasn't pursued by the private equity funds in favor of strong-arming Taylor, it is likely that she felt she had no alternative but to rerecord her albums. This meant that, even after Ithaca sold her catalog to Shamrock, Taylor was unlikely to walk away from her promise to her fans to reclaim her music.

Even Taylor suspected that she was moving both parties into a lose-lose situation: *You had to kill me, but it killed you just the same.* Yes, even Taylor likely knew it was highly unlikely that her rerecord strategy was going to work.

Taylor continues to allude to the sense of betrayal she felt as she was cornered by her ex-manager. She then goes on to lyrically describe being left with no other choice but to go to war, knowing that it was possible that all parties, including herself, would pay the price.

As we now know, Taylor ended up in a win-lose position; she

definitely won and private equity definitely lost. However, that result was far from guaranteed, and just goes to show the perils of leading a negotiation without considering that the person on the other side of the negotiation is, well, a *person.*

The Art of War, a treatise written by Sun Tzu, a Chinese general more than two thousand years ago, reflects on this issue in a way that is often used by the world's best business strategists in an attempt to avoid the potential lose-lose situation that both Shamrock and Taylor Swift found themselves in. For Tzu, the greatest victory isn't achieved in overcoming your opposition; it's in avoiding the battle altogether. "The supreme art of war," he stated, "is to subdue the enemy without fighting." Clearly, these are lessons that were passed on to neither Braun nor Borchetta.

It is no coincidence that Sun Tzu writes that should war come to pass between two tribes, it is important that when "you surround an army, leave an outlet free. Do not press a desperate foe too hard."

Ithaca, and then Shamrock, should never have tried to "win" in the first place by imposing such heavy terms on an initial transaction that left no space for negotiation. And through this ill-fated negotiation style, they ended up fighting against their own interests as well as Taylor's. They misunderstood the power dynamics to such a grave extent that the war, once started, was never theirs to win.

The big lesson here, about which entire books have been written throughout the long arc of history, is that the best way to avoid losing requires you to ensure that your enemy doesn't lose either. Because when your enemy suspects they are probably going to lose, they will die trying to bring you down with them.

The most successful negotiations that have ever come to pass in business, finance, and even Nobel Prize–winning peace agreements have come down to one thing: finding common ground where both parties can achieve a sense of "win" and starting your negotiations from there.

TAYLOR'S FOURTH TACTIC: DON'T BE A DEAD FISH

I remember one day meeting the former chairman of the luxury powerhouse LVMH's watch division, Jean-Claude Biver. His unnerving excitement made him quite unlike anybody I've ever met, and to this day I remember him talking at a race pace about how he transformed the (now massively successful) businesses of TAG Heuer, and, before LVMH, Omega, Hublot, and Blancpain, one after another. As he jumped around erratically, the last thing he said to me was by far the most consequential:

"Only dead fish swim downstream. If I had to give you one piece of advice, I'd say: Don't be a dead fish!"

Don't be a dead fish?

In other words, take the path of most resistance; go against the flow; and really commit to the hardships of being alive.

As I thought about other interactions I'd had with global executives, I started to realize: Oh my god. The world is *full* of dead fish. Just two weeks prior to meeting Biver, I had met with the CEO of a global airline to discuss why they had to cancel one of their highly popular airline routes: "because it just couldn't be executed profitably." I had heard a publisher explain that they turned down an exciting novelist because "we just couldn't prove there was demand for this new genre of writing," and I had spoken to an investor who had allocated over $100 million to a start-up because "our competitors were doing it, so we decided to do it too."

Nobody, it seems, wants to think for themselves. If the spreadsheet tells us to cancel exciting projects, then who are we to question the numbers?

Your ability to negotiate a position, especially if you're on the back foot, is exceptionally challenged if nobody is excited by the proposition of you winning the negotiation.

And given that there are dead fish *everywhere*, it's hardly surprising that industry after industry gets bulldozed by private equity.

Big finance and big business have created a world of homogenized *enshittification*. Everything in modern culture, business, and finance looks exactly the same, and everyone is too scared and tired to do anything about it.

Innovate? No, that's too expensive and private equity won't allow it. Take risks? Absolutely not, the senior vice president of the production company will only green-light projects that will be sure to create a box-office hit, even if it's boring. Release a new product? Nope, the stock markets won't like that either.

The $5 trillion industry of private equity has steamrolled the energy, life, and passion out of industries all over the world. And this is exactly why it's important to look at the people within the industry, to understand the industry itself. Causation and correlation mix heavily here: Was Ryan boring and an asshole because he worked in private equity? Or did he work in private equity because he was boring and an asshole?

Either way, it doesn't matter. Ryan was a dead fish who didn't have the energy or enthusiasm in life to swim upstream. And unfortunately, the world is heavily influenced, if not managed outright, by dead fish.

Taylor Swift, on the other hand, is decidedly *not* a dead fish. She is a woman who wakes up every single morning, gets out of bed, and says: Today I swim upstream.

Like Taylor, the most interesting, fascinating, and energizing people who create lasting, long-term change in our world are the fish who choose to swim upstream. And there are increasingly so few leaders, whether it's in business, finance, or culture, whom we can look up to for taking this difficult path, that when we do see them, we are attracted to them like magnets.

In the same way that the world was captivated by listening to Jean-Claude Biver talk about his obsession with the precision engineering of beautiful watches, the world stopped to listen to Taylor talk about her obsession with protecting the one thing that she is most passionate about: her music.

Why? Because Taylor knew that her music falling under the control of a dead fish would inevitably influence her ability to choose to swim upstream. Like the many artists who have had their catalogs bought and sold over the years, she would have no control over her existing work, and less control over what she created in the future.

There are some things in life worth fighting for, and in a world of increasingly dead-fish people—whether Taylor Swift fans or not—decided to back her ideological pursuit of something bigger than herself; they decided to back her war against the very thing that has *enshittified* our lives—private equity.

In her own words: "*And you say I abandoned the ship / But I was going down with it.*"

You'd be surprised at how often you see the people who choose to swim upstream getting support from unlikely places. People, it turns out, are human (see Power Move One, the world is full of humans, and Power Move Two, don't forget you're negotiating with humans). In the last millennium, at least one thing hasn't changed: Humans still crave deep connections with each other and with the world around them. And increasingly, the only people enabling these forms of connection are having to do so despite the many trillions of dollars that are trying to eradicate new, interesting, or fringy forms of art, music, and design. They are having to constantly fight against the momentum of capitalism and the army of investors who want to buy and sell our lives and our emotions in their portfolios.

The reason that private equity investors didn't foresee the sustained and high-impact retaliation from Swifties that may well continue to destroy the value of Shamrock's ownership is because the human analysts creating the spreadsheets, the human lawyers writing up the terms and conditions of the deal, and the humans putting forward the money for the transaction are dead fish.

And dead fish cannot even begin to comprehend the beautiful, daring, and emotionally alive people, like Jean-Claude Biver and Taylor Swift, who swim upstream.

* ◉ *

Sometimes, I look at the increasingly *enshittified* world that I am aging in and wonder: What happens to our society if CEOs and executives have to threaten to sink all the ships in the ocean just to protect the business they are so passionately in love with?

In the face of private equity, CEOs in all industries and in all geographies are looking at Taylor Swift. "How did she do it, and can we?" is what they're asking.

She turned up to a gunfight with a knife, yet still won the battle.

As private equity continues to roll out the same playbook of "buy, cut costs, sell, and make the world slightly worse" to every single business in its path, in every single industry available to it, Taylor Swift continues to build her empire, which is resistant to such short-term financial exploitation.

In an era where metrics and spreadsheets increasingly dominate decision-making by dead fish across industries, the "human" often gets sidelined in favor of cold, hard data.

However, Swift's management style, which was never considered for a single moment to have been threatening to private equity, showed that human-led strategies—prioritizing empathy, connection, and values—do in fact inspire and motivate people in ways that data and massive financial war chests alone cannot. And in a tough negotiation, she was able to bring stakeholders—*people*—with her much faster than private equity was.

CEOs like Taylor Swift, who focus on the *human* experience, pull in much stronger, more loyal followings of everybody who feels like they have been left out in the cold by the current capitalist system. Taylor's approach brought trust, loyalty, belonging, and purpose to the negotiating table, which motivated action more than $400 million ever could.

The business of creating and selling human connection, not just between Taylor and her fans, but in a decentralized and bottom-up way among her fans, is a new type of business that private equity hasn't figured out how to acquire and control. At least, not yet. And this is an asset that, at least right now, is pretty damn unique to Taylor.

She has shown us that there is an urgent need for finding and using the human connection as an overwhelmingly positive leadership style in an increasingly financialized, sterile, and metric-driven environment.

Indeed, in a world that so urgently needs change, the results are in: People are in desperate search of authenticity from the powers that be. And the fastest way to bring people with you? Well, it's to lean into the Taylor Swift School of Management negotiation playbook: Use your unique assets. Negotiate with human-led empathy. Create a win-win outcome. Don't be a dead fish.

POWER MOVE FIVE

BE ANTIFRAGILE

MANY YEARS AGO, WHEN I WAS AT GRAD SCHOOL IN ATLANTA, MY friend Adam very kindly doubled up as my running coach. I wasn't a serious runner, but I still pulled enough mileage in a given week to want to run in a more efficient way that optimized my still having kneecaps by the time I reached forty.

One of the things Adam used to say all the time that has stuck with me to this day: *Fast up the hills, slow down the hills.*

I guess this stayed with me because I, like a lot of people I saw when running, tended to do the exact opposite. Most people make the mistake of running close to their peak during the flat part of the course. And then, at exactly the point of needing the most momentum—when they're going up a hill—they significantly slow down.

As it turns out, and one of the reasons I still remember it, Adam's insight to run fast up hills and slow down them applies to nearly everything.

Including how Taylor Swift operates most of the time.

People, especially in their day-to-day lives, optimize their performance for the "flat ground," or the regular nine-to-five programming.

But the "flat ground" is not where opportunity lies; instead, in finance, business, and life, opportunity hides in volatility. The ups and downs. The hills. If you want to get ahead of the mediocre pack, in a race or in life, you need to optimize your strategy for the shortest but most important parts of the race.

A lot of this is psychological.

You can easily lull people into a false sense of security by letting them go at 85 percent of their max capacity on a flat road when you're only at 75 percent max, and then when they have no fuel left in the tank for the volatility of a hill, you'll find yourself operating at 95 percent when they're at 65 percent.

By timing your race (or career) strategy this way, you've created a 30 percent difference in functional capability when it matters the most.

My sister is an anesthetist, and she describes her entire job in a similar way—that most of the time, if everything goes okay, it's actually quite *boring* making sure a patient is fine during a surgery. However, her expertise is tested, and her career is defined, in the 1 percent (or hopefully less?) of cases where something might go wrong very quickly. Her job is nearly entirely about being able to run up hills quickly.

You actually see hedge fund managers working on this principle all the time. At least, the Unicorn equivalents of hedge fund managers tend to do this. During periods of low volatility in the markets, their portfolio returns will be lackluster. Maybe it'll look like they're underperforming. And they'll just sit there, doing nothing, while everyone else seems to be running past them on the flats.

Then, suddenly, the markets hit a hill. Inevitably, other fund managers will slow down to 65 percent when they run up the hill, and the Unicorn hedge funds ratchet up to 95 percent to win the game that is gambling on the financial markets.

Consider, too, the Michelin-star chef who has to perform during the high volatility of dinner service; nobody cares how well you can cook in your home kitchen if you can't execute on ninety covers of eight-course tasting menus at the same time to perfection.

Taylor Swift, like the world's best hedge fund managers, has been sprinting up hills since she was fifteen.

* * *

Taylor's ability to become the most-streamed artist in the world relates to a complex field of physics called chaos theory. Weird, I know.

Many years prior to 2012, when he released a book on the matter, Nassim Nicholas Taleb, a Lebanese American scholar of math and the financial markets, began to notice the same strange phenomenon occurring in systems and organizations across wildly different fields, including biology, finance, physics, urban development, and health care.

What he saw was that in an increasingly complex and seemingly random world, some systems perform *better* in chaos than others.

In fact, his work, which combined an exploration of the topics of Mathematical Uncertainty and Complex Systems and Statistics with the randomness of the stock market, pointed to something that seemed to be undeniably true: Where most systems, organizations, and people simply collapse under pressure, some not only remain standing but in fact *thrive*.

The idea of being "antifragile," as Taleb came to call such systems, changed the philosophy and the mathematics behind how we understand the world around us, from finance and business to the formation of stars and planets to the biology of evolution.

But the idea of antifragility is a hard one for us mere mortals to comprehend and is a pretty radical departure from the conventional wisdom that prizes stability and predictability above everything else.

Think about it like this: We've spent most of our lives telling ourselves that we need stability to function, and that instability is inherently *bad* for us. This is also deeply rooted in human psychology; evolution has taught us to be instinctively scared and distrustful of "different." Apart from the odd psychopath, nobody really *likes* when things change.

The idea of antifragility goes far beyond saying that uncertainty doesn't have to be bad. It actually says that uncertainty is *good*. Antifragility isn't just about surviving chaos; it's about flourishing in it. It's about flipping the script and turning adversity into opportunity, uncertainty into innovation, and chaos into creativity. It's about embracing the unpredictable nature of the world and using it to our advantage.

Antifragility is an invitation to embrace the inherent messiness and random nature of the world we live in and acknowledge that doing so may actually help instead of hinder us.

One good example of antifragility that Taleb outlines in detail is the entire human immune system, which actually becomes stronger and more robust, not weaker, when exposed to pathogens. As conventional wisdom tells us, exposing children to mild bacterial stressors in the first few years of their lives helps their immune system develop immunity, allowing the body to better fend off future threats.

In this example, it's easy to grasp that living in bacterial chaos actually helps the immune system, whereas stability and order do it a disservice.

Another clear example of antifragility can be seen in one of my (and Taylor's) favorite topics—winemaking. Counterintuitively, the best wine often comes from vines that are under water stress. In other words, dry conditions that create thirsty vines often produce the most flavorsome grapes, which are then turned into phenomenal wine.

This example often shocks people, who assume that regularly providing everything a plant needs will create the best outcomes. Au contraire, there's a reason Tuscany's rolling hills have led to its famous wine: The water rolls downhill away from the vines, forcing them to work hard to produce grapes. This also means that, with fewer resources, the vine will prioritize making smaller grapes with more concentrated flavor instead of big, watery grapes and big green leaves. The winemaker wants 100 percent of the energy of the plant to go into producing a great vintage instead of being wasted on the by-product—leaves.

Stress and uncertainty? Not only good but *great* for wine.

And a final example of antifragility? Taylor Swift.

* * *

A lot of people say that one of Taylor's strongest personality and business traits is that she is resilient. While this is undoubtedly true, it's not the full story.

Fragile people, businesses, and systems are damaged by disorder. Most companies, for example, had their share prices fall as the COVID-19 pandemic set in. This is because most businesses today are optimized for conditions that are *perfect*: supply chains that have no slack, products that are only released when customers have preordered them, and manufacturing in the lowest-cost locations. If these businesses were a material, they'd be glass. When COVID hit, they just *smashed* to pieces.

Some businesses, on the other hand, are resilient. COVID caused their share prices to fall in the early days, but they figured out work-arounds to supply chains and were able to adapt their businesses to new working conditions quickly enough for the share prices to bounce back to where they were before. You can think of a resilient business as being like rubber; there's a certain elasticity to it. Once it is stretched, it is able to return to its original shape.

A small number of businesses, however, are in a different category altogether. They are antifragile. They are less like rubber that bounces back to its original form under stress and more like the muscles in our body. When put under stress, they actually grow and get stronger. Resiliency is a component of being antifragile, but it is just that—one component.

The businesses that were antifragile during COVID didn't need their share prices to bounce back, because their share prices never really fell in the first place. Take Amazon, for example, one of the world's largest tech platforms. When people were scrambling to buy essentials in the supermarket amid empty shelves and fistfights over the last roll of toilet paper (doesn't this feel like it happened in another universe?), Amazon's online business massively increased its revenue because it had what no supermarket had: control over its supply chains.

Amazon is one of the few companies in the world with largely distributed global supply chain mechanisms, from product manufacturing and sourcing to holding warehouses and distribution centers. At Amazon, there is no single point of failure that would prevent toilet paper from being passed from millions of available sellers to millions of eagerly awaiting buyers.

In other words, while the rest of the world goes to shit (excuse the pun), Amazon's business actually gets stronger because the volatility wipes out its competitors.

Taylor Swift is like Amazon. She may not have been in the business of providing toilet paper during COVID, but if I had to make a comparison between her business and another, it would probably be this nearly $2 trillion company.

There are four key moments in her career when we can see that she took the path of most destruction because she either suspected or downright knew that the destruction would disable her competition and make her stronger.

DESTRUCTIVE PATH ONE: WITHDRAWING HER MUSIC FROM SPOTIFY

The first goes back to 2014, when Taylor Swift pulled her music from Spotify, the fastest-growing music streaming platform of that time.

In an opinion piece written for *The Wall Street Journal*, she explained that her decision was driven by her belief that the streaming service's compensation model for artists devalued their work. She criticized Spotify's "free" streaming tier, arguing that it remunerated artists and songwriters unfairly.

While I will dive into the specifics of her argument in a later chapter, suffice it to say that it was unfathomable at the time to have any music, let alone a brand-new album release, not appear on the platform that was fast becoming the home of global music distribution.

The last-minute decision to remove her music caused chaos for all streaming platforms, including and especially Spotify, which had taken for granted that artists would simply have to comply with the new business model that had been imposed on them.

As she rose to superstardom, many assumed that this decision was not "risky" but "fatal." When your goal is to become the most listened-to artist in the world, it seems counterintuitive to make it harder, not easier, for people to access your music. But being an antifragile entity defies intuitive wisdom; when she left Spotify in 2014, her music was in playlists of over nineteen million users, and the first week she returned in 2017, she amassed nearly forty-eight million streams.

This fatal move didn't kill her. And she didn't even need to bounce back from it. It actually made her *stronger.*

But if this would kill any other artist, why would it not kill her? Most artists become popular because we listen to them a lot. Taylor Swift, however, is just not normal. Because her relationship with her fans is "friendship first" and "music later," the economics of how her music disseminates into the world is the reverse of most mainstream artists.

In fact, in this respect Taylor Swift can be compared to a Rolex watch, not a Swatch. The harder it is for people to access her music, the more they crave her and are willing to follow her. By withdrawing her music, Taylor Swift became what is known as a "Veblen" or a "luxury" good; she essentially said, "I'm too exclusive for *free streaming.*" And instead of forgetting about her, her fans created an even stronger bond with her.

This is the very definition of being antifragile in action.

DESTRUCTIVE PATH TWO: BEEFING WITH OTHER MUSICIANS

In the world's most awkward awards-show moment of all time, the now infamous Kanye West sprinted onto the stage after Taylor Swift was awarded the Best Female Video award at the MTV Video Music Awards in 2009 for "You Belong with Me," telling her that he would eventually let her finish but that "Beyoncé had the best video of all time."

Mic drop.

This started a many-year feud between Kanye West and Taylor Swift against a backdrop of dizzying side feuds and interlinked arguments that you would need a map and a thesaurus to properly understand. I mean, as one example, the senior investor at the private equity megafund Carlyle, which supported Ithaca Holdings' acquisition of Taylor's music catalog via Scooter Braun, was a man named Jay Simmons, who later left that PE firm to start a new investment fund with Kim Kardashian. If this doesn't make you want to become a Konspiracy theorist, I don't know what will.

The complexity of the many feuds between Taylor, Kanye, and the cast of supporting frenemies aside, one thing became very clear throughout the ordeal: The more Kanye West beat down Taylor Swift, the stronger her fan base rallied around her, leading to extravagantly higher levels of emotional connection between Taylor and her fans within the Swiftverse.

After weaving a tapestry of feuds to serve as a backdrop to her rise to fame, one thing crystallized: Taylor Swift could eat beef sandwiches all day every day, and it would only serve to help her grow into the most listened-to artist of all time.

How is that possible, given that her entire identity is being the "cleaner-than-clean" girl next door? Because, at least from the outside, Taylor never starts the fights; she merely throws a clean right hook to finish them. She is, after all, the world's most successful underdog. I mean, who else could pull off "relatable" as a long-term brand strategy when they are a private-jet-flying billionaire? Taylor Swift, that's who.

But Swift's relatability, unlike every other "celebrity" or "rich, famous person," is not built upon what she owns or how she travels.

Her fans are all too aware of the weirdness and abnormality of her lifestyle, which Taylor openly discusses during interviews. She is relatable because, despite her money, she still gets picked on by the know-it-all men at work, who are dumber and less talented than she is but still get to call the shots.

In other words, the beef she gets thrown in her direction is the same beef that her core demographic of women deals with at their own, much less exciting, nine-to-five jobs. Her relatability is built upon a much more fundamental and intrinsic connection with her fans; and her feuds are just another way that she connects with the Swiftverse by saying: "I've got this one. I'm in the same arena as the rest of you. And I've got your back."

There are three main "vibes" to the feuds she engages in as a growth mechanism. The first category overwhelmingly resounds with her fans: "Powerful men taking advantage of less powerful women." This list includes John Mayer, Kanye West, Scooter Braun, Joe Jonas, Harry Styles, and infamously the DJ she sued for sexual assault for the sum of one dollar. The list goes on . . .

The second is a tightrope, and one that she realizes may eventually harm instead of help her: "Women who are bitchy and unkind." This list, which initially featured Katy Perry, Karlie Kloss, Nicki Minaj, and Miley Cyrus, has mostly been "resolved" over time, as even Taylor recognizes that there is more power, and a larger fan base, to be found in female solidarity.

The final feud category is simply "being on the right side of history." It includes fighting for artist compensation or refusing to play a stadium tour until her fans are given the water they need. This is the one she uses to appear to be "normal," even when Swifties universally acknowledge that she is *not* normal.

As Billy Joel sings, "We didn't start the fire . . . but we tried to fight it." Well, Taylor has become so good at fighting the fires that it actually helps her.

Because, you guessed it . . . she's antifragile.

DESTRUCTIVE PATH THREE: COVID-19

Concert halls closed, live venues were boarded up, bars were empty, festivals were canceled, and commutes were nonexistent. In 2020, due to the coronavirus pandemic, the global music industry fell on its knees.

Much like the broader economy, musicians and especially those mainstream artists who relied on stadium tours and performances as the bulk of their income canceled the release of music that they couldn't sell concert tickets for.

And the world got . . . weird. I've already revisited the panic over toilet paper, but what was even more terrifying than the thought of running out of bathroom supplies, at least to me, was the line going down the street to the local firearms store and the simultaneous hoarding of tinned goods. Meanwhile, some people's work, like mine, continued as if nothing had changed at all, except for a mandatory pop-up form that I had to sign to acknowledge I was not, in fact, still wearing my pajamas before I was allowed to present at my Zoom-based academic conferences.

Like, weird.

The world, both businesses and humans alike, was in total disarray—apart from Amazon, whose shareholders, as we've seen, experienced an insane return on investment as its global supply chains were kicked into action. Or Sophie Ellis-Bextor, who made an enviable comeback by drinking wine from the bottle on a Friday night and thrusting herself into her kitchen disco in the same sparkly gear that all midlife women have hidden in their cupboards, too scared to throw it away for fear it means their youth is coming to an end.

And, of course, Taylor Swift. Who, at the time, was getting ready for a summer tour of her recent album *Lover* at various music festivals. Crisis? What crisis? As artists canceled tours, delayed album releases, and couldn't figure out how to get into studios to collaborate with producers, Taylor embraced lockdown to make not one but *two* surprise full-length albums in the same year. And in doing so, broke every rule that exists around releasing award-winning albums.

When everybody else was fumbling to get a handle on their life, how was Taylor Swift able to Amazon herself?

Well, most of it comes down to the fact that, like Amazon, she has spent her entire career creating, buying, and owning her own "value chain," or the different parts of the music industry that she needs to engage with to release music.

So yes, she has unique access to a lot of the music supply chain because of her vast wealth and celebrity status—such as a music studio in her house and the ability to text A-list collaborators to join her. And like Amazon, she has also been painstakingly building by far the most important and valuable part of the supply chain—music distribution—so that she uniquely owns and controls it.

Remember, she's got the Swiftverse. And whether this was ever a strategic choice in preparation for a seemingly supernatural and catastrophic event like COVID happening or not, it turned out to be one hell of a strategic asset. It meant that she could do what nobody else but Amazon could do during 2020: keep delivering core products into the market.

She didn't need to rely on big events, third-party collaborations, or marketing her releases to the then-locked-down public, because she was able to seize upon the most unique period in history, a time when there was barely any competition for new material. She was able to release two of her biggest-ever albums so quickly without any PR because people were craving increased connection to the people and things they loved, and her music filled a once-in-a-lifetime (we hope) hole in people's lives.

By having full control of her own supply chain, she became incredibly strong at the exact moment when her biggest competitors became incredibly weak. Her ability to control her production and distribution meant that she was sprinting up a hill that nobody else could even crawl up.

And for the first time ever, Taylor didn't have to compete with other musicians, movies, or even in-real-life friends to win a deepened sense of friendship with her fans. As they sat at home with very little original or new content to consume besides hers, she had 100 percent of their time, energy, and money. And guess what? She leveraged the hell out of it—of course, making it an even exchange in the process.

DESTRUCTIVE PATH FOUR: RERECORDING HER MASTERS

Okay, so it seems dumb to even put it here, because duh. For many reasons, her decision to rerecord her albums after Big Machine Label Group was sold to Scooter Braun's Ithaca Holdings was a good one. It all worked out *massively* in her favor, right?

Some could, would, and even *did* say, as I have already argued, that it was unclear that this path was going to be successful for her. Did she get "lucky"? Could the outcome have been different, have failed to work in her favor?

Many people, especially financial analysts who have taken a stab at entering the Swiftverse because they feel they have some expertise to offer, will say yes. She was lucky. But her strategy cannot easily be copied.

These analysts, as I pointed out in the last chapter, are dead fish. They cannot comprehend the business she's building or the strategy she's employing, and therefore they are not in a position to comment on its replicability.

Can another musician who is in the business of selling streams rerecord her music successfully? Well, so far, we've seen that no, no other recording artist has been able to do it. But what if Barbie, or Harry Potter, or Marvel—all of which are building fan universes instead of selling streams—were to rerecord or rebuild their fan universes? Would *that* be possible? And while we don't have data that can back this up (yet), I suspect that perhaps, yes, this might be possible.

While analysts, reporters, and executives scoffed at Taylor's strategy and then declared her "lucky" on the other side, what they didn't really understand was that when luck seems to be running against her is exactly when Taylor is going to pull something big out of the bag. Because when her chips are down in the "real world," her chips are up in the Swiftverse, which only heightens her support.

Ironically, being antifragile, it's during the "good times" for her and her industry when she's most likely to lose widespread interest, streams, and fans. Rerecording her music gave her the ability to call upon, and in the process strengthen, the relationship she'd been building with her fans over the fifteen-plus years she'd been laying the foundations for the Swiftverse.

The music world assumed that rerecording albums—a lengthy, expensive, protracted, boring, and distracting affair—would suck the oxygen out of her career and be the end of her. For any other artist, this probably would have been true. But due to the way Taylor has organized her business, her fan base, and her relationships with her stakeholders, the opposite proved to be the case.

During a crisis, you should *never* bet against a system that is antifragile. As Taylor and Amazon both show us, that is exactly when their stock is going to rise. Investors who pay hundreds of millions of dollars to try to own what they *think* is "Taylor Swift's core product" (music) simply do not understand her empire as well as she understands it.

Taylor knows she is antifragile, and so knew the odds of successfully rerecording her albums were in her favor. She didn't need the hindsight that the rest of the industry needed to tell her so.

BECOMING ANTIFRAGILE

The most difficult thing about the strategy of running fast up hills and slow down hills, of course, is not learning how to run fast up hills. That is relatively easy with some amount of training. Instead, the hard part is being able to turn off your ego when it feels like people are running past you on the flat ground, and being self-confident enough to know that you'll overtake them when a hill arises.

While we can look at the examples of Taylor Swift, Amazon, and my sister the anesthetist, all of whom demonstrate just how powerful being antifragile is in their careers and in their ultimate success, becoming antifragile is not easy. There's a reason we look nearly exclusively to high-performing people to see real-world examples of it.

But increasingly, understanding the world of antifragility is becoming more and more important for one very specific reason: Our world is becoming more chaotic and less predictable than ever before.

We have more severe and unpredictable weather patterns, which are impacting our daily lives in new and unknown ways. The COVID-19 pandemic highlighted the world's vulnerability to global health crises, which are likely to increase in frequency and magnitude as our world's biodiversity declines and climate changes radically. Rapid advances in technology such as AI and automation are disrupting industries, labor markets, and social cohesion in unknown ways. Record levels of political polarization, the rise of populist movements, and unpredictable shifts in global leadership are changing our lives through the establishment of alternative supply chains. Conflicts, both within and between societies and cultures, and geopolitical tensions have become more complex, and unpredictability has become the status quo through the fog of war, which persists as I write this.

In short: If you are *not* antifragile, the likelihood of you, the business you run, or the society in which you live finding long-term success is greatly diminished.

Put another way, the business and strategy leaders of the future who will be able to lead organizations through globalized chaos will all be building antifragile organizations. Taylor simply happens to be ahead of the curve.

So why doesn't everybody become antifragile? Well, because as I've said, it's *hard*. It requires a strategic mindset, a willingness not only to embrace but to *love* uncertainty, and the ability to thrive in changing circumstances. Three components are tough but necessary to become antifragile.

ONE: EMBRACE UNCERTAINTY AND VOLATILITY

One of the key principles of antifragility is seeing uncertainty and volatility as an opportunity for growth and innovation instead of something that is straight-up terrifying and bad. Sure, this sounds like therapy-speak nonsense, but peel back a layer and you can actually see that CEOs of successful organizations do this all the time. However, it does require some mental rejigging of how we've been taught to think about the world around us.

When the future is unpredictable, conventional solutions that are optimized for a "steady state" are deeply inadequate—just look at supermarkets during COVID. Like vines that are under water stress, we're forced to use the few resources we have in a more creative way, and the necessity to adapt can lead to innovations. We are forced to explore uncharted territory and look at novel ideas that we would have ignored in other times.

This is one of the reasons why investors prefer to give start-ups too little money instead of too much; like the grapevines, it has been shown time and time again that resource-constrained founders create the best businesses.

As we now know to be true in a post-COVID world, volatility, more than anything, encourages experimentation.

In fact, in rapidly changing environments—like when Spotify moved the music industry to streaming instead of buying songs—the cost of not experimenting (and thus not learning or adapting) is way higher than the risks associated with potentially failing.

Rather than avoiding change and risk at all costs, we need to switch to a mindset of curiosity and adaptability. This is infinitely harder than maintaining the status quo and feels very counterintuitive to the human psyche, but when you speak to people who do it often, like athletes who compete regularly, they all say the same thing: By reframing a race or competition as "I will learn something today" instead of "I will either win or lose," we take bigger risks and the pressure feels way more manageable.

TWO: BUILD RESILIENCE

You can be resilient without being antifragile, but you cannot be antifragile without being resilient. Resilience is one of the hardest things in the world to teach yourself to be, which is probably why there are millions of published books about this very topic that line the shelves in bookstores endlessly, most of them going unread.

While "being resilient" is often described as a state of mind on a scale somewhere between "dusting yourself off" once you've fallen and "just hanging in there," it can also be useful to think of resilience in a more strategic way.

Resilience is the ability to bend, not break when you've had the spirit knocked out of you. It's when the supermodel falls over on the catwalk, gets up, and continues to walk as if nothing has happened. It's the ability to lose a big sales contract but still continue to raise funds for your start-up from investors, unfazed. It's losing your albums and then starting from scratch to rerecord them. It's kind of being a psychopath and turning your brain off, saying "fuck it," and continuing.

The mechanism underlying all of these "fuck it and move on" moments is decentralization. Whether for a person trying to do something hard, like run their first 5k race, or an organization trying to do something hard, like launch a rocket into space, the ability to be resilient comes from decentralization. Or in other words, not having all your eggs in one basket. Supermarkets during COVID had all their (supply chain) eggs in one basket, and so nobody could get toilet paper. Amazon, on the other hand, had decentralized supply chains, so if one failed, another could be used.

In the same way, one of the most fundamental but least understood parts of Taylor's business is the decentralized way in which the Swiftverse has been built. Fans grow their relationship with the Swiftverse not by having all their eggs in the Taylor basket and needing one-to-one communication with her, but by being decentralized and having relationships and communication with other Swiftverse inhabitants too. In the Swiftverse, there is no single point of failure. Not even Taylor Swift or whoever owns her master records can destroy the Swiftverse.

The need for decentralization in our personal lives is the core takeaway for most people who rush into relationships, abandon their friends, get rid of their rent-controlled apartment in favor of living in their new boyfriend's frat-like digs, and take up new hobbies like going to breweries and watching football on Sundays. When you break up, as most inevitably will, you are hit *sideways*. Your entire life has been balancing on one thing: a man with the emotional intelligence of a boy who will do something dumb that will make you leave him.

Never be reliant on one person, one supplier, or one outcome for success. Decentralization, in every way, underpins our ability to be resilient. And being resilient is how we become antifragile.

THREE: ACCEPT WEIRD AND BAD THINGS

While the benefits of being antifragile are clear, you realize that becoming antifragile is hard specifically because of this final point: the need to accept what you cannot control. Antifragility is about digging deep and finding the inner stoic in yourself and your organizations.

The Serenity Prayer, attributed to the Protestant theologian Reinhold Niebuhr in the 1930s, found widespread popularity when it was printed in *The New York Times* and embraced fully in spirit by Alcoholics Anonymous. Although various versions of the prayer exist, one prominent form is: "God grant me the serenity to accept the things I cannot change, courage to change the things I can, and wisdom to know the difference."

Heck, yeah. Accepting things happening to you, however, is not the beginning, middle, and end of being antifragile. Instead, antifragility comes from the ability not to spend your time freaking out about what has already happened and wishing that a different set of outcomes had been laid at your feet, but instead getting to work and dealing with the cards you've been dealt. Being antifragile is not merely withstanding hard things, but actually going further and being able to bring something *positive* out of the negativity.

A lot of musicians, when COVID-19 lockdowns occurred, said "Ah, I can't tour anymore. My label has decided to delay releasing my album. This SUCKS." Taylor, on the other hand, showed us: *I can't change the pandemic. But cool, here's an opportunity to absorb market share from other artists who aren't releasing anything right now—better get to work quickly!*

So how do you train yourself to feel stoic about things that happen to you when they're not desirable? Well, perhaps we can look to wine again for the solution. And no, I don't mean *drinking* it, although on bad days that can certainly help . . .

There's a reason winemakers say that they are "training the vines" when, to outsiders, it may seem as if they are merely "growing" the vines. The idea behind training vines comes from the fact that as the vines grow from a seed through to a grape-producing plant, you are literally training them directionally on a trellis, and you are also training them to produce grapes under a certain amount of water stress.

Learning to be mentally antifragile requires the same type of training we give our muscles in the gym—subject ourselves to stressors every now and again so that we get used to the existence of "different" and "weird" and "bad" and "uncertain." Over time, this creates the kind of resiliency that enables us to say: Who cares? And to move on quickly to finding solutions to problems.

○ ● ○

The seemingly "overnight" success of Taylor Swift can largely be attributed to the fact that, when times are good, casual observers of her music and her fandom declare that she's *nearly* like the Beatles and other wildly successful music leaders, but never in a way that suggests she has redefined an entire industry herself.

Most of them, including the investors who spent hundreds of millions of dollars buying her catalog, did not understand that they were observing her running on flat ground. But Taylor and most antifragile companies, executives, and Unicorns are not optimized to deliver excellence on flat ground; they have optimized every part of their lives and their businesses and their craft to do one thing, and one thing alone: excel in small moments of crisis when everybody else is failing.

Antifragility is as much a frame of mind as it is a business model that can be leveraged to compete in the small moments that separate winning from losing, whether it's trying to get a podium position in Formula 1, rerecording albums, or simply trying to get over a bad breakup.

As the world becomes more chaotic and our systems continue to be hit by seemingly random events driven by politics, climate, new technologies, or a changing economy that is out of our control, some analysts are going to look at Taylor Swift in the same way that they look at hedge fund managers now, and say: That was a fluke. They got lucky.

But other people, like me, believe there's no such thing as luck.

POWER MOVE SIX

ENGAGE IN
WHITE PSYOPS

U MM, ABE, WHY IS EVERYTHING COVERED IN BLACK TAPE?" I WAS standing in my friend's East London kitchen, and every product I could see was covered in black tape or blacked out with marker. When I went to the bathroom a few hours later, I noticed the same there—even the toothpaste was covered in black.

I had met Abe in Boston, and before he moved back to London, he studied at Harvard Kennedy School. It sat opposite to Harvard Business School, both physically (with a river between us) and ideologically. Students at Harvard Business School were learning how to be the next cohort of the capitalist elite, whereas students at Harvard Kennedy School were learning how to use politics and policy to rein in the next cohort of the capitalist elite.

When I was at Harvard working with executives and business leaders trying to figure out how to increase their share prices by making the most of tools such as marketing, strategy, and more, Abe was at the Kennedy School feeling disgusted by the new-age corporatization of our lives.

"I am sick of my life being influenced by branding and marketing.

It's everywhere. I don't want to see brands anymore, so I've hidden the packaging. We still don't really understand how it influences us subconsciously, and I value my freedom of thought enough to want it to remain unhijacked by three or four global corporations that own nearly everything we buy!"

Like most people at Harvard, Abe is quite intense, so I thought nothing of the black tape episode other than it being one of his quirks.

But every now and again, then at an increasingly higher rate, I began to think: Maybe Abe was onto something back then!

Every single day, the average person sees around six thousand to ten thousand advertisements. Now, assuming the average person sleeps about eight hours a night (a big assumption for many, I know), that means that the person sees between 375 and 625 ads an hour. An *hour*!

This number should shock you because, well, it is rather shocking. We are being flooded, all day, every day, with commercial branding and marketing and advertising, and at an accelerating rate. I mean, back in the 1970s, boomers only got five hundred per day, not per hour.

I've actually stopped writing and am trying to figure out which of them I can remember. Given that I haven't left my house yet today, it's hard. Sure, I doomscrolled this morning and read the news and turned on the radio while I ate my breakfast.

But can I recall any of the fifteen hundred ads I've been exposed to? After a whole five minutes of thinking, I remember one. For Prada. I saw it on my Instagram doomscroll. It strikes me as a weird one to remember, given that it's unlikely I'll be dropping a few thousand dollars on a Prada handbag anytime soon.

So what about the other hundreds of brands or products I have unknowingly come across this morning? Who knows, and who cares? I clearly don't, since I can't remember any of them. But more interesting, what about the money that these hundreds of brands have paid to advertise to me, who can't even remember seeing them, never mind buying their products?

The global advertising market is just *enormous*, with the total spend reaching nearly $750 billion in 2023, an amount that seems to grow every year. Yet regardless of how big this number gets, there is one universal constant that inhibits how much large (or small) brands can sell us stuff. And that is? How much attention a human brain can pay to absorbing the advertising that is placed around us every day.

Even today, I feel like I have personally reached my saturation point for being able to even see, never mind remember or act upon, a brand's plea for me to buy its stuff. Human attention is quite the opposite of a marketing budget, in that it can't grow exponentially. It is rather static, and, in cases like mine as I get older, it feels like it is diminishing.

This means that you have a limited pie, with each corporation trying to buy bigger and bigger slices of said pie, for larger and larger amounts of money.

So let's run some back-of-the-envelope numbers. Although the figures are extremely hard to calculate, let's imagine that Taylor Swift's Eras Tour created $5 billion of consumer spending in North America and $5 billion for the rest of her global tour, a number that is far too hard for me to try to guess, but that I've seen economists use often enough to trust.

That's $10 billion of consumer spending. If you want to compare Taylor Swift (the brand) to a company, you could easily compare her to Nordstrom, a leading US fashion retailer with a market capitalization of roughly $10 billion.

How much does Nordstrom allocate to its marketing budget? Well, typically a corporation of that size will spend somewhere between 2 percent and 4 percent of its revenue, which equates to between $200 million and $400 million.

How much did Taylor Swift spend on marketing her Eras Tour, which generated such high revenue streams, not just for her, but for the wider economy? LOL. Nowhere near half a billion dollars.

But how is that possible? Think back to her tour, when you couldn't watch TV, pick up a magazine, talk to friends, or read the *Financial Times* without seeing her name ten times. How did she manage to spend way less money than Nordstrom but manage to take up an infinitely higher percentage of our brains and conversations and daily lives?

It's because Taylor doesn't engage in traditional marketing, which seeks to get us to buy something in the short term by using direct and often manipulative tactics. Instead, she engages with what I'm going to call "white psyops." White psyops, short for white psychological operations, is a form of psychological and social influence principles that Taylor uses to be more than just an artist whose name we remember; she uses white psyops to quite literally become a part of our lives.

To consider just how impactful Taylor Swift (the brand) has been, think about the fact that Abe may be able to stick black tape over his Colgate toothpaste, but no matter how hard he tries, he cannot tape out an entire conversation happening among millions of people for many years in a row.

WHAT IS TRADITIONAL MARKETING AND WHY DOES TAYLOR NOT DO IT?

Our ability to influence people is one of the most foundational elements of human society. It underpins everything from our own personal relationships and social structures to whom we vote for, what we buy, and how the stock market moves.

Being able to influence people in our personal lives is a strategic skill that is so important that it consumes nearly everything we do, all day, every day. In fact, it plays such a huge role in our lives that we often fail to even notice it, just like the fish swimming in water who says to his fish friend, "Water? What's that?"

This skill may allow us to convince someone out of our league to date us. Or impact whether or not we get chosen for a job, win over our mother-in-law, or come across as the most interesting and charming person at a dinner party.

Trying to influence outcomes is hard. Really, really hard.

Branding, marketing, advertising, and PR are other forms of influence that corporations, brands, and products engage in heavily, usually to try to convince people either to start buying their products or services or to increase the number of products they buy.

To understand why Taylor Swift is so incredibly unique in the mechanisms of her success, you first need to understand how 99.99 percent of brands and products attempt to influence.

The task of influencing consumers is usually given to somebody at a company called the chief marketing officer, or CMO, and the activities that CMOs do are usually a mix of the following:

Branding: The process of creating a unique image and identity that leaves the consumer thinking, "I want this product."

Advertising: Directly telling people over and over again, "You want this product."

PR: Managing the reputation of the brand, usually through community relations. It's about getting *other* people to say, "Trust me, you'll want this product, because I already have it."

Marketing: A broader strategy that includes advertising, market research, product development, and distribution tactics.

In the music world, the record labels want consumers (us) to buy the products they are selling—music streams, concert tickets, and merchandise. Influencing people to become "fans" of artists is really, really hard and expensive in equal measures, and here's why.

Brands use widespread advertising to make a ton of people aware that their brand or product exists in the first place. Because, you know, if you don't know it exists, you can't buy it. Think of the advertisements you see in subway stations or at airports. They're not trying to get you to buy those products right there and then; they just want you to know they exist. They want to pique your interest. They'll want you to see the brand somewhere else and think, "Ah! Yes! I've seen this logo before," even if you can't remember where. And if you see it enough times, it becomes familiar. Nearly even trustworthy.

Eventually you'll begin to desire it. Maybe you'll see other people using the product. Your favorite Instagrammer will be discussing it. Zendaya was papped wearing it. It seems to be everywhere, but nowhere. "If I wanted it," you begin to think, "where would I even be able to get it?"

This is the hardest part of the marketing funnel—making a person go from "Yes, I would like that" to "Okay, my laptop is open and my credit card is out, I'm going to buy it."

The second hardest part of the marketing funnel? Making you want to buy more, and more, and more from that brand because you are now a "fan."

This is the goal of all musicians, and especially Taylor Swift—to have as many "fans" or even "superfans" as possible.

In fact, these last two steps are so hard to achieve that CMOs end up spending billions and billions, and even, collectively, nearly a trillion dollars a year, trying to convince you to buy their stuff. And how do they convince you, exactly?

What you're about to read has essentially become the crux of our contemporary consumer economy.

They buy data from weird places to try to figure out how old you are, how much you earn, and where you live. They track the cookies on your phone to see what websites you go to and then try to guess what brands you like. They follow your location to try to figure out what your schedule is like and whether you prefer to buy online in the mornings or late at night. They know who your friends are, whether or not you paid your rent on time last November, and if you are on your period or, surprise!—they'll know before you do that you're pregnant. They know if you're going through a breakup and are emotionally unstable enough to book flights to Tahiti. They'll suspect you have cancer before you've had your annual medical because, well, why else would you be so tired and be buying so many supplements?

The advertising-branding-PR-Instagrammer-digital-marketing universe is so big, so complex (so toxic?), and deemed so extremely necessary for bringing in revenue to nearly all businesses that it's like a corporate drug. Once you get onto that escalator, there's no getting off it. It is simply impossible to increase revenue and to become a highly valuable brand without it, so much so that the common spend of a US business on marketing is anywhere from 2 percent to a whopping 10 percent of their revenue. Marketing spend is, sadly, the main source of revenue growth for most global businesses.

That is, unless you're Taylor Swift.

MI5 AND TAYLOR SWIFT HAVE AT LEAST ONE THING IN COMMON

There are two ways to think about influencing. First, there is direct influencing, which is what I think of when I think about the nearly trillion-dollar advertising-industrial complex predicated on Google, digital cookies, TikTok influencers, Instagrammers, and more. It's what feeds the consumer-driven economy.

Then there is another less concrete, little bit weirder form called indirect influencing, and this is not at all associated with consumer products or the corporate world but has been perfected by governments, spy agencies, and more recently, Taylor Swift.

In early 2024, Taylor Swift was very strangely accused of fronting a US government–backed plot to help President Biden win the 2024 election. From the outside, the concept seemed a little bit . . . crazy? But when you understand how Taylor Swift engages in marketing and influence, it may not actually be quite as crazy as it sounds.

(May I suggest that now is the appropriate time to get your tinfoil hats ready.)

Psyops are used to convey piecemeal information to audiences in order to indirectly influence their objective reasoning. Psyops campaigns are usually used to sway the behavior of governments, organizations, groups, and large foreign powers. Oh, and Swifties.

In fact, psyops are so great at influencing large numbers of people that achieving the ability to orchestrate psyops within a marketing department is seen as an Olympic-size feat.

There are some very famous, albeit dark, psyops campaigns that have been used in recent history. During the Vietnam War, the

American-led Operation Wandering Soul involved playing upon the Vietnamese belief that a person's soul is trapped for eternity on Earth if they do not receive a proper burial. The US military, knowing this, repeatedly played tapes with recorded messages of Vietnamese "ghosts" telling the northern fighters to "go home" or "stop fighting." Thus, the Americans were able to reduce the number of people they were fighting against.

Yes. Weird and evil.

More recently, large-scale psyops campaigns have been shown to have emanated from the Internet Research Agency, a Kremlin-backed Russian company that dealt with online propaganda and influence operations on behalf of Russian political and business interests. This agency was investigated and ultimately indicted by lawyer-turned-FBI-leader Robert Mueller's team, with charges including "impairing, obstructing, and defeating the lawful functions of government." Or, in plain speak, election interference.

Psyops, relative to directed marketing campaigns, are seen as a far superior, albeit mysterious and notoriously difficult, act of influencing people and moving them toward certain ideas and outcomes.

The goal of psyops is not simply to get Person A to buy Product B; it's to get Person A to believe in a set of values that are espoused and enshrined around Action B. For a government, that action may be how you vote. In consumer marketing, that action will be what you buy.

It involves deeply engaging with the emotional state and inward psychology of the audiences and consumers in question. And thus, once audiences are engaged, they can be used to accomplish the lofty goals of the psyops instigator, whether it is voting for the incumbent in an election or running all over the world in an Eras outfit and exchanging friendship bracelets with strangers.

There are two big differences between a successful digital marketing campaign and a successful psyops campaign.

The first is that digital marketing is organized in a top-down and centralized manner, whereas psyops campaigns work in a bottom-up and decentralized manner. The second difference is that digital marketing is legal, whereas psyops is usually illegal. Or, like, at least a little bit in the *gray* zone.

So right about now is the time to forget and dismiss everything you've ever read about Taylor Swift being a queen at traditional digital marketing, because that's just not how she runs her marketing campaigns. In fact, she rarely even engages with traditional direct marketing, because she's too busy doing something much more effective: indirect psyopsing.

NOT ALL PSYOPS IS EVIL

Psyops has a reputation for being bad because, well, it usually is. It is the use of behavioral psychology and propaganda against us (or "them"?) such that control of our own minds and actions is essentially relinquished to some other person, organization, or even government. It is usually associated with deception and lying, and the reason we distrust the idea of psyops so much is very simple: If someone has to "trick" me into doing something that I wouldn't otherwise do, surely this adopted behavior is not in my own best interests, but in the interests of somebody else.

It gives credence to the idea that our minds are being hijacked and stolen, the very thing that Abe is sure that brands are trying to subconsciously do to him through their packaging, and goes against our most basic right: to enjoy the freedom of our own thoughts. And indeed, they *are*, but just not very well!

However, not *all* psyops use deceit and malice, just as not all computer hackers are bad. In the same way that there are "white-hat" hackers, who hack into systems to try to find their weaknesses before an ill-intentioned hacker can get there, there are white psyops. These do not try to hide the source of the propaganda, tell lies, or manipulate the entity being influenced.

Allow me to make it very clear: What Taylor Swift engages in is very much the latter—the *not* illegal and *not* bad psyops.

Infiltrating people's minds is hard, so much so that I've already outlined the nearly trillion-dollar value of the traditional media marketing ecosystem. But I think about psyops in the same way that a friend recently told me she parents her toddler.

"If I tell her to wear something, she'll scream, say no, and throw a tantrum. But if I ask her, *Would you like to wear this?* she'll usually just say yes."

The difference between these two types of parenting is nearly identical to how regular brands engage with consumers versus how Taylor Swift engages with her fans.

Regular brands engage in top-down marketing, which constantly inundates us, the consumers, with information on why we *should* or *must* buy their products. Maybe they don't specifically use those words, but it is often implied that if we don't, we will become worse off (less hot, or less beautiful, or less popular). And if we do buy the products, we will become better off (hotter, more beautiful, and more popular).

Modern marketing essentially tells us that we have two choices: to do what the brand says, *or else.* Or else we're not cool. Or else we're not fun. Or else we're not hot. Or else we're not skinny. Or else nobody will date us. Or else we'll have no friends. Or else we won't be successful.

It's not really that different from my friend telling her daughter: You will wear this outfit, *or else*.

The thing about "or else" marketing, regardless of how subtle it may be, is that it just doesn't work. At least not in the long term. We may end up buying the mascara to "look good." We may end up buying a Prada handbag to "fit in." But eventually, the consumer will get tired and say, Fuck it. I'll accept the "or else" and take my chances. Because I give up. I have run out of money to pay brands, I have run out of attention to give to Instagrammers, and I have run out of mental capacity to worry about being thin.

I give up.

The problem is that this kind of marketing is based on an aspiration that has been curated by somebody above you, in a marketing department, who decides what "better" looks like or just how thin "thin" should be.

And guess what? There's only so long you can scare people into believing whatever bullshit you're shouting at them, even through the lovely and fun and sexy and colorful ads that chief marketing officers put on the internet. Just as our brains are saturated with ads, they are saturated with being told what "good" looks like.

So if the Consumer Advertising Complex™ is so saturated, tired, ineffective, and unsustainable for marketing budgets and our human brains alike, why isn't everybody doing this white psyops thing instead?

What is it? How come Taylor Swift is one of the only executives who has figured it out? And how can this be replicated across our own spheres of influence, whether they be professional or personal?

WHITE PSYOPS RULE ONE: HAVE SKIN IN THE GAME

It's kind of impossible to believe that nearly a billion dollars of heavy-weight corporate machinery, the international tinfoil hat brigade, legitimate terrorist organizations, and global political cartels are trying to figure out how to run an effective influence campaign, and yet it's a young woman who wears friendship bracelets to work who has figured it out. Alas, here we are.

So how does she do it? Well, definitely not by telling us, in a top-down chief marketing officer way, that we should listen to her music or buy her concert tickets. Consider that if Taylor were our mother (an outcome many of her fans already openly discuss their desire for), she would ask us when we wake up: Would you like to wear this dress today?

Or even better, she would say: "Wear whatever you want. *You do you.*"

The core difference between a psyops campaign and a modern marketing blitz is the fact that psyops engages in peer-to-peer decision-making that makes it *feel* like there is no campaign at all. There is no apparent chief marketing officer who will decide what the optimum behavior is, or the best way to dress, or the right way to vote.

This kind of rings true with Taylor. To my knowledge I can't ever remember seeing her music, shows, or merch actually being advertised.

In many ways, this is why psyops often *feels* nefarious, or at least is discussed in so much more a nefarious way than traditional marketing: The seeming lack of a mastermind, or a hidden one, means that you cannot discern for yourself how much you want to adopt the belief or behavioral system that is being imposed on you. At least with traditional marketing, you can decide whether you subscribe to a mainstream belief, such as beauty standards, or not.

Like Abe, who can decide whether or not to tape over the brands in his kitchen.

But when a psyops campaign is done properly, you have no way of discerning whether the beliefs you hold on to are the ones you have curated in the freedom of your own thoughts, or whether someone has very subtly and very subconsciously made their beliefs your own.

This is exactly what Abe has been thinking about for years: What if we can't even tell when we're being marketed to effectively anymore?!

In short, a psyops campaign does not insist that you enroll for the specific beliefs of those higher up than you, but simply merges you into a pool of people who have similarly held beliefs, regardless of where those beliefs came from.

A pool of people like . . . the Swiftverse.

Another example that quickly comes to mind is the 2018 Nike campaign "Dream Crazy," which featured the controversial NFL player and social justice champion Colin Kaepernick. The campaign slogan, "Believe in something. Even if it means sacrificing everything," cleverly positioned Nike as a brand that not only aligned with social justice but actually lived out its own slogan, adding insane authenticity kudos to a brand that, in its products, seems to take fewer and fewer shareholder risks, making the brand appear bland at best, stale at worst. At the time, Nike lost a lot of public support from consumer demographics who were not aligned with the ongoing Black Lives Matter protests that summer, which Kaepernick supported, resulting in Nike sneakers actually being set on fire across the United States by anti-Kaepernick protest groups.

Which, naturally, did one thing: It allowed Nike to be the de facto sneaker of choice among pro–social justice campaigners. No single campaign at Nike ever discussed the Black Lives Matter protests directly, just as no white psyops campaign will use a hierarchy to tell people what they should believe. Instead, Nike acted as a brand that simply merged people into a pool of others with similarly held beliefs, uniting extremely strong communities around belief systems, not products. The fact that this community probably bought the Nike product afterward was a second-order (but still intentional) consequence of the psyops campaign.

Nike told you to Dream Crazy, and then somehow people bought their sneakers. Taylor tells us that we're all best friends, and then somehow we all ended up (or at least desperately tried to end up) at her show.

The basis for each and every white psyops campaign is authenticity. There was a real chance that Nike could have come across as being inauthentic, that it was using the #BLM protests as a way to advertise some upcoming sneakers. However, the campaign *didn't* feel inauthentic because Nike at the time supported social justice campaigners, who had a lot on the line to lose, by putting a lot on the line to lose in brand value. And Nike did lose a lot of support from certain groups. In other words, Nike was actually willing to believe in something, even if it meant sacrificing everything. Just as Colin Kaepernick did, alongside a massive list of other protesters.

Like all psyops campaigns, Taylor's job is to create a peer-to-peer, bottom-up system of moving ideas and beliefs. And it just so happens that she is one of the only people in the world who has already created an incredibly strong and prolifically successful peer-to-peer network of people who engage very strongly in similar ideological ways: the Swiftverse.

Swift's psyops campaign is predicated on the same type of authenticity we saw with Nike, with an equal amount of her own skin in the game. She has shown Swiftverse inhabitants time after time that she is not asking them to do something that she herself is not willing to do. A small but incredibly effective demonstration of this throughout her Eras Tour was the fact that she repeatedly stopped playing and left up to ninety thousand people waiting in stadiums while she asked for assistance for fans that she could see were struggling in the audience.

This idea that "we're all in this together" is one of the most effective ways to demonstrate skin in the game. If one fan was going to feel uncomfortable, well damn, the whole stadium would have to feel uncomfortable while they waited.

And while most organizations try to instill belief systems into groups of people, like corporations with their workers, for example, most fail simply because of the lack of that first but most important ingredient of authenticity.

I mean, if you ever listen to CEO interviews, you will hilariously often hear them talk endlessly about how they are trying to create an "emotionally safe" workplace environment, and never was this more true than after the #MeToo movement. And yes, most people like me will roll their eyes and think about how ironic those statements are, given that most times, people's direct bosses are total narcissists, meaning that there is very little truth to what the CEO is saying. What a company *says* and what a company *does* are sometimes very different things.

But why do authenticity and safety matter when trying to move people on beliefs? Why do CEOs care about an employee's emotional safety so much?

Well, the basic science behind this tells us that when you feel like you are safe, emotionally or physically, you are much more mentally open to trying new things, being creative, meeting new people—and most importantly, *adopting new beliefs.*

This is why my friend, the two-Michelin-star chef, says that he runs his kitchen differently from most other Michelin kitchens in one big way: He does not scream at the junior chefs. "They simply cannot feel like they can be creative or excel when they are too scared of making mistakes," he told me.

Also very important is that in his kitchen you will find him working alongside his line cooks every single day from the crack of dawn until after dinner service is finished, doing the same tasks as even the most junior of his chefs, despite his decades of experience and fame. Peeling hundreds of potatoes every day and cleaning the floor is, essentially, the chef version of having skin in the game alongside those he is trying to influence.

Taylor, through building the Swiftverse, has used several mechanisms to build trust with her fans, somewhat notably including the "beefs" she has involved herself with over the years. As you saw in the last chapter, there are two flavors of beef sandwiches in particular that helped to engender a strong sense of ideological belonging, trust, and authenticity between Taylor and her fans: coming together against the "powerful men taking advantage of less powerful women," and coming together to "be on the right side of history."

Plus, you know, the fact that she wears her heart on her sleeve and openly divulges emotionally painful events in her life that we actually have all been through.

Whether you're a billionaire pop star trying to create superfans, a $120 billion company like Nike trying to create a viral sneaker campaign, a chef trying to develop a strong pipeline of talented chefs, or just a person trying to figure out how to become a better member of teams at work and play, being authentic matters. And there's no better way to actually show this, rather than just saying it, than by having skin in the game and demonstrating that your expectations for your own behaviors match or even exceed the expectations of those you're trying to garner support from.

At a very basic and human level, this is most often exemplified by standing by relationships in the long term, even when they are difficult; acknowledging responsibility for the good outcomes as well as the bad; and being vulnerable and honest with those around you.

But while being authentic and having skin in the game are critical key ingredients in mass influencing those around you, by themselves they are not enough to accomplish goals such as psyopsing your way to being the most iconic brand in contemporary culture or the most highly esteemed chef in the world.

For that, you need two more things: running a community in a decentralized manner and bringing that community together through a "unite and lead" strategy.

WHITE PSYOPS RULE TWO: DECENTRALIZE

As I've alluded to already, one of the weirdest things you'll read about Taylor Swift being a marketing genius is that she "communicates frequently" with her fans.

Well, yes . . . ish. Actually, in traditional media terms, she communicates far, far, far less frequently directly with her fans than other celebrities. I've said it before, but allow me to say it again to double down on this point: Most of the time it feels like Taylor is constantly communicating with her fans, but she's not. This feeling is generated because the fans are constantly communicating with *one another*.

This is the beauty of the Swiftverse being a decentralized network; it does not rely on Taylor's Main Character Energy™ every day to exist. In fact, I wouldn't be surprised that if she disappeared entirely, the Swiftverse would continue without her for quite some time.

Unlike other celebrities, we do not know what she wears every day. Or what workouts she does. Or where she goes. She doesn't post TikToks or Instagram stories about "What I eat in a day" or pictures of her "feeling cute, might delete later."

In fact, the weirdest thing about people constantly saying that she's a marketing genius because of how well she communicates with her fans is that there was a period when her fans barely heard from her in the years during the lowest points of the Kanye–Swift beef sandwich, yet her audience grew massively anyway. Further, consider the fact that her most blockbuster of all her blockbuster album releases, *The Tortured Poets Department*, was released with a complete lack of interviews or personal appearances (apart from her choreographed Eras Tour concerts).

Decentralization, by which I mean when the planning and decision-making in a group are distributed or delegated away from a central, authoritative point, is absolutely crucial for a successful white psyops. And this is where the Swiftverse just shines.

Why? Because in the Swiftverse, there are ten million people you can speak to who will make you feel like you're engaging with Taylor Swift, when in fact you are not. While I never see her name advertised, there are several times a day when I see a Swiftie post a video about a new costume they've made to mimic her; a new song a fan has written in her style; a new tweet-thread about Easter eggs that may have been missed; a Reddit forum discussing the importance of the number 13 to Taylor. Each of these posts will interact with hundreds, if not thousands, of other users, and the net impact of the decentralized web of Swinfluence will be just *enormous* compared to a single advertisement telling you that her album is amazing, go and listen to it.

So clearly, not only does decentralization allow for authenticity (because no, Taylor Swift did not pay for these people to spend hundreds of hours making outfits to copy hers) but it also does another really important thing: It gives you reach that traditional marketing cannot.

When people receive information from diverse and decentralized sources such as TikTok, Billboard, Instagram, Radio One, and pretty much anywhere and everywhere Taylor's album was reviewed to be her best yet, it appears more organic and credible than Taylor saying: Hey guys, this album is my best yet.

In this manner, white psyops couldn't be more different than traditional marketing.

So now that we know that 53 percent of the US population of voting age are inhabitants of the Swiftverse, let's look at the strategy that Taylor uses to influence these people in her direction. Just like everything else she does, it's the exact opposite of mainstream marketing.

I already made the point that marketing, especially in the age of *digital* marketing, is becoming increasingly expensive as large corporations try to steal more of your attention from their competitors. But what do you tend to remember more: seeing six thousand different brand names a day, or a friend telling you about their new favorite lipstick?

Exactly. The latter. And word-of-mouth influence among Swifties in the Swiftverse is not only a thousand times more effective at moving strong ideas across large numbers of people—it's . . . free.

She does not gain any influence advantage by singling people out to tell them to "buy my product, or else . . . you won't be cool enough, hot enough, or thin enough."

We know that trust and authenticity are key elements of effective white psyops, and therefore a centralized narrative through direct marketing is nearly always viewed as untrustworthy propaganda on behalf of a brand (uh, hello again to my friend Abe). A decentralized approach, on the other hand, makes the message seem more grass-roots and genuine.

In our own lives, at a very basic level, it works in exactly the same way. If you want to be known among your professional network as the expert in your field, there's really no point in writing this into your bio on your LinkedIn profile and posting about it every day; this feels inauthentic to the extent that people may literally start to assume the opposite.

However, the people I've worked with who have indeed been the most successful in their field have usually been the quietest about their knowledge. Not because they are humble; in fact, it has nothing to do with personality, but rather with the fact that *so many* people are able to discuss their talent *for them* that they do not have a need to discuss it on their own behalf.

And taking this one step further, it is precisely true that the most successful people are the ones who have painstakingly created a wide, decentralized network of their peers. Usually, they have been central in "connecting" lots of different people to each other without seeking anything in return.

Indeed, my Michelin-star-chef friend told me that he recently suggested that one of his most senior chefs leave his restaurant to work in a competitor's three-star restaurant. When I asked why he would do that, especially after having taken so many years to train this chef, he said: "It's simple. I want him to go over there, and be successful, and continue and grow the network of great chefs that I am connected to. He doesn't need me to become great."

Decentralizing the organizations, communities, and relationships in our lives, whether personal or professional, can feel risky. How did Nike know what the protesters and the antiprotesters would do with its new slogan? They didn't. It could have been catastrophic. But because it was led with authenticity, as in most risks we take in life, there was a community behind them willing to support them.

WHITE PSYOPS RULE THREE: UNITE AND LEAD

Unlike rogue political candidates' pursuit of dark psyops campaigns, Taylor does not seek to use traditional methods of divide and conquer, in which a psyops campaign gives information, usually fake, to one side to isolate them in their beliefs.

Instead, she uses a specific strategy that has been used before, and that, in very rare cases, has led to the biggest and most impactful political, social, and economic movements in history, causing the end of apartheid, the formation of the postwar European Union, and the American Civil Rights Movement.

And that strategy?

"Unite and lead" is, if executed properly, an extremely strong, long-lasting, and powerful way to spread influence very quickly. Instead of dividing groups and communities of people, it brings together people who may already feel alone or marginalized and who are seeking a home. It requires actively working to integrate different groups of people and communities into something cohesive and diverse under a particular belief system.

And Taylor's belief system? That everybody belongs. That everybody deserves a friend. That everybody is welcome.

She has demonstrated this belief system over decades, through numerous albums and via her global tours, through her actions and advocacy. Just look at the deep connection with her fans and the random acts of kindness she offers them, yet never discusses. I mean, in 2018 she bought a fan who had been homeless through eight months of her pregnancy a house! She is known for hosting secret sessions at her home and inviting fans to be part of her journey. She writes to them, back and forth. Furthermore, her activism extends to social issues, including speaking out against racism and urging her audience to vote and stand up for equality. She uses her music to promote acceptance and create a sense of community. In short, Swift has made it her North Star to ensure that everyone feels included, valued, and seen.

In fact, it is entirely possible that the steep rise of both the number of her superfans and the depth of their relationship with the Swiftverse could be entirely down to the fact that the Swiftverse is one of the few remaining corners of positivity on the internet and in real life. The values that Taylor espouses—of trust, authenticity, friendliness, and kindness—are so highly regarded simply because they seem to be so hard to find anywhere else.

This is not because she is the only billionaire in existence who happens to be "nice"; rather, it's been a long-standing strategic choice of Taylor's to remain steadfastly aligned with her tenacious kindness because this is the belief system that underlines the entire Swiftverse; it's the carrot at the end of the stick that brings hundreds of millions of people to Spotify, Instagram, Reddit, TikTok, and more to listen to her, discuss her, and make friends while doing so.

She is unique in her ability to provide safety while everywhere else feels like it's becoming darker and more dangerous. As the level of perceived threats in the world increases drastically, perhaps the

Swiftverse feels like the last haven of hope, with the appeal of positive values and beliefs.

So now that Taylor has this Swiftverse with an army of fans and superfans who are enmeshed in her belief system, what should she do with it? What is Swift's *goal*?

As mentioned, a typical dark psyops campaign will use the beliefs of the community to generate an actionable outcome, such as voting for a president or buying a particular product, by dividing communities and exploiting their insecurities.

In the "unite and lead" strategy favored by Taylor Swift, beliefs are transferred through positive, not negative, reinforcement. The focal point is not division but something else that the Swiftverse naturally has in abundance: collaboration.

And oh my god, do Swifties in the Swiftverse collaborate. In fact, if you consider that the Swiftverse is a decentralized system that, with or without Taylor's input, does its own emergent things by itself, you'll see that "collaborate" is the strongest emergent behavior to come out of this collection of Taylor obsessives.

And what do they collaborate on? A lot of very weird, and some less weird, things. I mean, I have seen Swifties record and release entire albums of what they think Taylor's future album will sound like. And because it's in the Swiftverse, it has become famous. I have seen Swifties meet each other through the Swiftverse and fall in love. I have seen strangers from the Swiftverse mail one another beads so they can complete one another's friendship bracelets. And I have seen them make someone's life hell because that person may have hurt Taylor's feelings. I have seen them protest en masse against perceived injustices. I have seen them try to inflate or destroy company share prices.

I mean, after the release of *The Tortured Poets Department*, hundreds of small, decentralized communities organized "TTPD marches" across villages, towns, and cities all over the world. They brought boom boxes, made huge banners, and formed human chains as they marched through the streets playing the album. For no apparent reason other than to show their solidarity with . . . Taylor? And each other?

This is demonstrative of the power of spreading ideas and actions through belief instead of advertising.

Would Nike have been able to become a significant channel of discussion throughout social justice protests in 2018 had it simply created an advertising campaign instead of bringing together decentralized and geographically distant people who had a strong emotional connection with one another, as well as a "higher cause"?

Would the Michelin-star chef be able to retain junior chefs for years on end in the physically and emotionally demanding environment of a kitchen without giving them the promise of achieving something that is bigger than any of them individually?

There is just no end to the power of collaboration in a successful unite and lead strategy, because much like the divide and exploit strategy, it attaches itself directly to the belief system of the individual being targeted. But the difference between these two strategies is that unite and lead will enlist "superusers" with a common, not different, belief system, to instill the idea that they are working together for a higher purpose in a community of like-minded collaborators.

I'd like to emphasize this point a little more, because here is where the white psyops campaign differs so much from the global advertising industry.

Unlike a brand that decides it wants to penetrate the market of all females between the ages of fifteen and twenty-four with an income of twenty thousand to forty-five thousand dollars a year, Taylor's Swiftverse is attractive to *anybody* whose belief system is predicated on the notion that *everybody belongs*. That everybody deserves a friend. That everybody is equal. Age, gender, geography, and income no longer matter; the target market for Taylor Swift becomes massive.

Unite and lead is a strategy that feels like one hell of a strong emotional drug to those who experience it, which is why the difference between "Swiftie" and "not Swiftie" is so binary; Swifties can be somewhat . . . cultlike. (I say that from my personal experience of being one.) This is why white psyops campaigns, especially for those products or brands that have gone viral, are envied so much by chief marketing officers who try to replicate the results through lackluster traditional marketing.

As Taylor says herself, *"Put narcotics into all of my songs / And that's why you're still singing along."*

I asked the more junior chef, who was interviewing for the job at the three-star restaurant, why he still did the years of sixteen-hour days and no vacations. Unlike his boss, he wasn't even famous and had no restaurant of his own.

"I dunno," he told me. "I guess because I believe in it?"

Exactly.

Bringing a community together through collaboration is the easiest and fastest way to ensure that *everybody* has skin in the game that you're playing and asks those in the community to double down on the shared belief. Which ultimately means creating a shared purpose, encouraging and fostering collaboration, and guiding those relationships, whether personal or professional, toward common goals.

This is true whether it's with a global superfandom, a social justice movement, a culinary team, or the person that you're dating; unite and lead strategies consistently prove to be the most effective means of bringing people together to achieve outsize goals.

One of the most interesting facets of understanding the seemingly never-ending power of the Swiftverse is the question that naturally follows the question of how she has become so powerful.

Which is: Exactly what does Taylor want to *do* with all this power?

And this is one of the Big Questions about Taylor's career. In terms of traditional marketing, she does not sell to her audience in the same way that many celebrities do, and she really limits the brand partnerships that she engages in. To the extent that she does monetize her tours, she tries to do it as fairly as possible to her fans so that she does not gouge them on ticket prices; for example, she declined using Ticketmaster's dynamic pricing strategy, which prices tickets depending on the size of the queue of people in the waiting room ready to buy them.

Because, you know, at the end of the day she is still a businesswoman. In theory, she *could* fill a stadium with an average ticket price of fifteen hundred dollars. But in the interest of accessibility for her fans, she *chooses* not to. Not a lot of people would turn down the additional revenue to give their fans a chance to see them. Oasis, for example, opted to use dynamic pricing for their 2025 reunion tour, much to the disgust of their long-term fans.

In many ways, she is above brand partnerships. She did not create her own line of beauty products or hair care, like Lady Gaga (Haus Labs), Rihanna (Fenty), or Blake Lively (Blake Brown). Neither will she try to sell you other brands using "buy this or else" tactics. She doesn't design lingerie or other accessories like Kim Kardashian. To most marketing and brand partnership experts, she is an enigma. She is "leaving money on the table." She is . . . weird.

So if she's not fully monetizing her lightning-in-a-bottle power, then what is she doing with it? What does she want, if it's not making a ton of money by monetizing the Swiftverse?

This question is precisely why conspiracy theories ran amok about her political ambitions, and why some groups are suddenly wary of her white psyops capabilities: because people realized that she had accrued an absolutely enormous amount of financial, economic, business, and *cultural* power that she could theoretically use to break down governments, install new presidents, enrich herself and her friends, sway Super Bowl outcomes, and more.

Perhaps if she was obviously monetizing her brand and her business to a greater extent, the tinfoil hat brigade would feel satisfied that her power wouldn't impact their own lives too much. But if she wasn't even using it to enrich herself, then something very, *very* sinister must have been happening . . .

But what if the creepiest answer to this Big Question is the real one: that she doesn't want to do *anything* with this influence that has turned to power? That all she wants to do is make good music, potentially write good books and produce good movies, and live in the Swiftverse being comfortably happy with her life?

The fact that this could even be a plausible explanation for the lack of Swiftverse monetization is, rather ironically, what continues to increase the value and influence of the Swiftverse so much.

It doubles down on the two things that sit at the very heart of her success: that she is authentic, and that all she wants is to be the most listened-to artist in the world.

• • •

As Abe had indicated several years ago when I opened his kitchen fridge to see an army of black-taped food containers, we increasingly exist in a hypercapitalist economy, where our hopes, dreams, fears, and anxieties are constantly being exploited, directly or indirectly, for the purposes of influencing our behavior in one way or another.

Some of it is dark and illegal, as we can see with dark psyops. Some of it is downright depressing but nonetheless legal, as we can see with direct and targeted traditional marketing. And some of it is extremely powerful in an overwhelmingly positive way, which most Swifties can attest to.

One lesson we can learn from understanding the shape and movement of influence and, subsequently, power, is that everybody wants it, yet so few people have figured out how to get it.

Another lesson we can learn is, in many ways, similar to what you've already read in this book: that everybody is an individual who just wants to be treated with respect and care. Taking a decentralized and unite and lead approach to relationships, friendships, and community building in our lives has proven to be one of the most successful ways to influence your way to the top.

POWER MOVE SEVEN

CHALLENGE AND EMBRACE CHANGE

WHEN I WAS FIFTEEN, MY FIRST BOYFRIEND GAVE ME A CD MIX-tape that I incessantly listened to for the entire duration of our two-week romance. When love turned to hate because he cheated on me with a prettier girl in the year below me, for some reason I continued to listen to it. The Cure's "Friday I'm in Love" will, unfortunately, always be a great song stolen in my mind by a guy whose last name I can no longer remember.

Flirting through illegally downloaded music on mixtapes was not the only form of what now feels like weirdness about life when I was a young teenager. For example, none of us really had any makeup or hair products, and so we largely relied on our natural beauty and frizzy hair (cough) to shine. I remember once giving a boy called Michael whom I met on the school bus my home landline number when he asked for it (no, he never called). And the only way I had any clue as to what may have been happening in the real world outside my rural town in Ireland was when I watched *The O.C.* religiously every Sunday morning, hoping that if I prayed hard enough I could become Marissa.

And apart from The Cure, the other sound that signified my ill-fated attempts at teenage dating was the harsh, 2600 Hz internet dial-up theme tune on the family computer in the kitchen when I unplugged my landline phone to see if my crushes had signed into MSN Messenger.

Back then, life was *analog*. And not just for me and my rural friends, but for teenagers all over the world. Mobile phones had just started to become a thing, and although I had one, I didn't really know what to do with it. I had nobody in my phone book with whom I could exchange an "SMS." If you were lost, you'd have to ask somebody to give you directions. For this reason, cars had encyclopedia-size map books in them, and most people knew how to use them. If I was hanging out with my friends, I would either be home at or (ideally) before the deadline set by my mother, or I'd desperately try to find a pay phone to call her and tell her I'd be late.

If you wanted to go shopping, you would drive to the nearest mall (which, for me, was well over an hour away) and physically look inside the stores to see what was happening in the world of fashion. If you missed the big movie release at the cinema, you'd have to wait for at least six months for the VHS to become available at the local video store, and then another few weeks for it to stop being loaned out. If you wanted to find new or interesting music, you would listen to "alternative" and sometimes illegal radio stations in the middle of the night to hear what was coming through the airwaves, before traveling to a music shop to order the CD, which would take several weeks to arrive. Only then, you'd learn that this "exciting and new" music was in fact already six months old in America, from where it was generated.

Around the same time that my boyfriend dumped me and the boy from the bus never phoned me, Taylor Swift had just moved to

Nashville, and instead of complaining about the guys who weren't interested in her, she was writing songs about them. Just maybe, Taylor Swift was not all that different from me?

And at this time, though, the world around us started to change. And not just for teenage girls, but for everybody.

Dating habits aside, the world when Taylor and I were teenagers was starting to be drastically reshaped by the introduction of a new technology that would come to move the fundamental axes upon which global corporate power and competition were built.

Our *analog* world started to disintegrate, and was soon replaced by a totally new and different paradigm: the *internet*.

In many ways, it splintered the worlds of society, business, and finance into two groups: those who could adapt to the algorithmic age, and those who could not. In other words, those who could survive and . . . well, we'll never know about the ones who didn't, because the world has moved on and forgotten them.

Fast-forward to today, and it is really impossible to understand the magnitude of not only the success that Taylor has created for herself but the sheer tenacity it must have taken her to get there without fully comprehending the environment in which she was trying to accomplish this, and how radically it changed during (and after) her rise to fame.

Sure, there's that famous line in *Miss Americana* where she speaks out about the music industry's double standard for women: "*Everyone is a shiny new toy for like two years . . . Constantly having to reinvent, constantly finding new facets of yourself that people find to be shiny.*" What she doesn't mention, however, is that the music industry—like so many industries and creative fields—is reinventing itself, too, and constantly.

We live in an age of what economists call "creative disruption," where new innovations and technologies are displacing and replacing old ones at an unfathomable speed. Creative disruption is the move from renting DVDs at Blockbuster to streaming on Netflix; from calling your friends on the landline to DMing on TikTok; from going to class in person to pretending you're not still in bed during your Zoom lectures.

The music industry, like many of the creative industries, was completely blindsided by the introduction of the internet in the early 2000s, just as it was by its subsequent loss of control over the global creation and distribution of songs and albums.

The world of Big Music™, as Taylor was starting to define her name, her brand, and her style in Nashville, operated on a very different model from the one seen today. Back then, a small number of music labels controlled the entire industry. They got to pick who became famous, a dynamic described by Taylor in the *TTPD* song "Clara Bow" as "*All your life, did you know / You'd be picked like a rose?*"

They got to decide what type of music the musicians wrote and performed. They got to decide which magazines a performer would grace the cover of. They allocated a marketing budget to the artists they thought would be the *next big thing*. And by far the most important thing, they controlled the distribution of the music from the artist to the record shops, and eventually into the hands of fans.

It was an entirely top-down system, controlled by who you can only imagine were fat men in big suits with evil laughs surrounded by cigar smoke.

Only if artists behaved themselves by fitting into the mold of what was desired by the men in suits would they have a shot—just a *small shot*—at making it big.

In the same way that we saw a young Taylor performing for fans, she would have been performing for music executives, trying to make herself seem nice, pretty, young, talented, and something that they could shape into whatever or whoever they wanted.

WHAC-A-MOLE

So, yeah. The internet happened. And that kind of changed all this. *Drastically.*

Remember Facebook? Well, one of the earliest executives at the high-growth start-up was a guy called Sean Parker. Parker's original claim to fame was setting up a start-up called Napster: a peer-to-peer file-sharing application primarily associated with digital audio file distribution.

Or, more to the point, Napster was a way for teenagers sitting at their family computer in the kitchen to illegally download songs for their mixtapes.

Illegal music downloads facilitated by an entirely new wave of websites on this thing called the internet were causing chaos for music executives. *If people are downloading music illegally instead of buying our CDs, how do we make money?!*

The answer was simple: When people steal music, you *don't* make money.

In a complete role reversal from today's music business model for performing artists, back when Taylor was getting started, she toured around the United States pretty much for free, using her tour as a way for people to find her music, decide they like it, and buy the CDs. She made money from selling albums, not from touring.

Today, it's totally the opposite: Taylor's billionaire status is driven in large part by her tour revenue, and . . . yes, you guessed it, she makes relatively little money from streaming. But more on that later.

Music execs, in a vain attempt to stop the music sales revenue from hemorrhaging, sued Napster and eventually got the site to shut down. *Great!* they thought. Until up popped LimeWire, its replacement. So legal proceedings started once again and shut the site down. And then came FrostWire and LuckyWire and eDonkey and eMule and Kazaa and site after site that facilitated music thievery.

Eventually these executives realized, *Damn.* We're playing Whac-A-Mole. With the *entire internet.*

TIL SPOTIFY DO US PART

By the time a Swedish entrepreneur called Daniel Ek approached the music men in suits, they were desperate. At the rate they were going, the entire music industry would be decimated in a few years. Far from their earlier position of being able to direct everything and everyone in the industry, they were spiraling out of control. They could not get people like me—teenagers in far-flung countries—to stop downloading and to start buying music instead.

Sure, they could control individual artists, even chains of record stores. But they could not control the more than two billion people who had internet access by 2010.

The music industry was centralized from the top down. The internet was completely, totally, and utterly decentralized from the bottom up. They knew what faced them was potential extermination.

So, with this in mind, the big labels signed deals with Daniel Ek and said, *Sure.* Go ahead and put all of our music catalogs on Spotify, where people can listen to them for free and advertising revenue can pay our artists for their music instead.

If this seems like a bad deal for the music industry, well, that's because it was. But executives were hoping that Daniel Ek was right about one thing: that people were more interested in the "download" part of free illegal downloads than the "free" part of free illegal downloads. People, he said, would be okay with paying for music if they could download it. And Spotify would be the intermediary platform controlling the downloadability.

Now, if you're Taylor Swift, what do you reckon you'd be thinking? Probably something along the lines of "I'm killing myself touring for free to sell CDs. I have dedicated my whole life to music, and I didn't go to college; I *need* to make this work out. My music is really good, and it shouldn't be free. I need to pay my own bills and make an income somehow. Oh, and did I mention that I'm killing myself touring and you want to remove the only part of this that makes it worthwhile: selling CDs?"

Apart from allowing people to download music, Spotify changed the industry revenue model in another very important way: It moved music from being something that people *owned* to something that they *used*.

You have bought a Taylor Swift album for fifteen dollars, and whether you listened to it once, ten thousand times, or not at all, the labels received fifteen dollars of revenue. Spotify's proposed model paid artists on a *per stream* basis instead. Every time someone listened to a song, the artist received $0.0035. So to make fifteen bucks per album, you needed people to listen to your songs 4,286 times. That's an impossibly high number.

Whatever way you look at it, Taylor was being screwed over. Under this new model, she would not make money from touring. And also under this new model, she would not make money from streaming music. The existence of the entire profession of singer-songwriters and performing artists was under threat; the business model had become no longer commercially viable.

So in 2014, in protest, she withdrew her music from Spotify right before the release of her fifth studio album, *1989*.

THE BEGINNING OF THE END, OR THE END OF THE BEGINNING?

Taylor often gets criticized for what people perceive to have been a "flip-floppy" stance on music streaming. She left Spotify, only to join Apple Music. She struck a deal with Tidal and then fell out with Apple. And then, all of a sudden, she came back to Spotify.

To understand why Taylor's stance on music streaming may have seemed a little all over the place, it's useful to zoom out and look at what was happening to other industries, creative and not, at the same time.

Just as private equity is a multibillion-dollar financial asset class that completely consumed everything in our lives before transferring these so-called assets to a dead fish's investment portfolio, in the early 2000s there was a remarkable rise in another form of financing that has had an equally large impact on the world we live in: venture capital.

Venture capitalists, or VCs, are investors who allocate capital to start-ups. The idea is that they fund the start-up in order to help the company go from not existing to being worth billions of dollars in a few short years. The company is then sold to another, much bigger company, or is floated on the stock market, and the VCs get their money back, plus a *lot* more.

This form of financing famously arose from the Silicon Valley area of California, and most of its metamorphosis to notoriety was predicated on its being able to generate a lot of value by replacing "real world" assets with "digital assets."

This is a simplification, of course, but to illustrate this point, consider the following start-ups that were backed by VCs:

Uber, a digital taxi platform that owned no cars.

Airbnb, a digital hotel platform that owned no buildings.

Twitter, a digital news-sharing platform that had no journalists. And?

Spotify, a digital music platform that had no musicians.

The most important feature of a venture-capital-backed start-up is one that I've already mentioned: *scalability*. These start-ups could scale so fast because they were all predicated on outsourced, decentralized, and bottom-up digital networks on the internet, resulting in entire industries being eaten alive.

In fact, one very famous VC called Marc Andreessen, whose VC firm today has nearly $50 billion of capital, published a blog post called "Why Software Is Eating the World," in which he described the different ways that technology would transform the entire world.

This post, in turn, formed the ideological basis of the now $500 billion VC investment market, which goes something like this:

If the internet is going to transform every single industry that exists, then as an investor, I would like to own the start-ups that are in turn going to own the new world.

Investors saw a once-in-many-generations opportunity to transfer the ownership and control of the dominant companies in every industry to . . . themselves. Andreessen, in his blog post, wrote this about the music industry:

"Today's dominant music companies are software companies, too: Apple's iTunes, Spotify and Pandora. Traditional record labels increasingly exist only to provide those software companies with content. Industry revenue from digital channels totaled $4.6 billion in 2010, growing to 29% of total revenue from 2% in 2004."

While it was hard for Taylor to understand what was happening in Silicon Valley, far away from Nashville, as she tried to figure out what she would do about music's new streaming model, one thing became clear:

Like the music execs playing Whac-A-Mole with illegal streaming websites, if she wanted to try to fight Spotify, she'd be fighting something much bigger that seemed to be emerging. She realized that to win the war on music streaming, she would have to go to war with the new revenue model of the entire *internet*. Which was, essentially, becoming the new model of the global economy.

THE PIVOT

The hardest thing for a company to do is pivot its business model, the reasons for which become more clear when you compare a business pivot to what seemed to play out as Taylor's relationship with Joe Alwyn was coming to an end.

I mean, you never really quite know: Is the problem me, or is it them? Should I try to change, or should they? Are they even *capable* of changing? How much more time should I give this?

And the most difficult question of all: If I leave, how will I ever know that it was the *right* decision?

As I explained in Power Move Two, creating a strategy is hard.

But just as hard is executing said strategy. However, what seems to totally perplex executives are the age-old questions: I'm not sure if this is working. Should we change the strategy? And if we wait around to see whether or not we need to change, will it be too late to change?

As the internet was in the early stages of changing the way consumers interacted online and offline, there were no firmly established business models, ways to generate revenue, or cultural norms associated with the new world. Taylor, understandably, would have asked herself, the label, and her management team: What if this is a passing phase, and we kill our business model for a new way of listening to music that doesn't really take off? Why would we *do* that?

They're fair questions. And we should remember that hindsight is twenty-twenty. Now that the moment has passed, people often discuss Taylor's beef sandwich with Spotify as being opportunistic: She said her boycott of the streaming platform was to further musicians' rights and fair compensation, but then she famously ended up back on the platform after all.

What's difficult to communicate, though, is just how hard it is to make big, important, industry-defining decisions when you have little to no information about which direction the (brand-new) global digital economy is moving. Being one of the biggest musicians at the time, although it feels weird to say that given just how much bigger she is now, she had significant influence on the way that the deals between tech companies and music executives were being shaped. If she didn't take a moral stand, then who would? After all, she is decidedly *not* a dead fish. And this is precisely what not-dead-fish *do*.

Her decision to go back to Spotify, however, was clearly justified by the fact that during her hiatus from the platform, tech companies, including creative streaming platforms like Netflix and Spotify, had coalesced around a specific business model.

And in this decision to put her music back on Spotify we can see the single point of inflection where Taylor went from being a singer-songwriter to being the entire music industry.

For at this time, artists had two choices: They could either not stream their music on tech platforms and make precisely zero money, or they could go ahead and stream their music on tech platforms and make slightly more than zero money.

Well, Taylor Swift decided that there was a third option, and her pivot back to Spotify was an all-encompassing strategic change of direction to a new business model predicated on this option: to stream her music on the tech platform and to use its tech and business model to her advantage to become the most iconic brand in contemporary culture.

Brave, insightful, smart, courageous, and strategic don't even begin to describe how well the queen of bait and switch maneuvered this lose-lose situation to turn it into a win-win.

DRIP, NOT DROP

What became very clear leading into the mid- to late 2010s is that tech companies, backed by deep-pocketed venture capitalists, had a very specific business model, which included:

1. Raise millions of dollars of investment.

2. Create enormous "network effects" using the decentralized technology to bring hundreds of millions of users onto the platform.

3. Use algorithms to serve them content, keeping them addicted to the platform 24-7.

4. Then sell the billion-dollar business with its millions of users to someone—*anyone*—else.

Taylor realized that this model made businesses, music, literature, products, movies, brands, even *culture*, binary. A movie either did really, really well because the algorithm pushed it to virality, or nobody heard of it.

Just like the businesses themselves, which became worth either billions of dollars or nothing, these tech platforms forced the same economics onto the music and TV shows that people were streaming.

If Taylor was going to go all in on the new streaming model, she knew that there was a very large chance that, should she continue with her previous business model, her music would not get picked up by the algorithm, and she would not be discoverable by hundreds of millions of fans all over the world.

Thus, she did what very few brands or businesses were able to do back then, mostly because of a lack of foresight. She changed her business model to mirror that of Spotify and tech platforms.

Elon Musk, Jeff Bezos, Mark Zuckerberg, and Taylor Swift all have one thing in common: They drip, not drop.

* * *

Nobody became a billionaire by selling secondhand books until Jeff Bezos. Nobody made billions of dollars by launching rockets until Elon Musk. And nobody became a billionaire by selling music until Taylor Swift.

The old, predigital models of industry, especially in a world where you were *creating* something, whether that was a start-up, a rocket, or an album, followed the *drop* model. As in, once in every creative cycle, you drop a release. Not more often, and not less often.

When building rockets, the drop cycle is extremely long and involves a process of designing, building, testing, and launching that could take decades. For example, at the time of this writing, development of the American Space Launch System (SLS), which NASA is hoping to use to bring a crewed payload to the moon within the next decade, has cost $25 billion, has taken thirteen years, and has not yet had a proper launch test. Will there be an SLS drop within the next decade? It's hard to tell.

Prior to Jeff Bezos and Amazon, building and establishing peer-to-peer businesses took decades, if it was possible at all.

In fashion, large luxury houses had collection drops of their fashion lines twice a year, typically in Spring/Summer and Fall/Winter collections.

In music, there are album drops, and actively performing artists typically drop an album every eighteen to twenty-four months. Then we consume said album before the six-month album tour concludes and work on a new album begins.

These drop cycles are tales as old as time.

What billionaires have in common is that they reduced the time between each drop of their product. Elon Musk built SpaceX iteratively, testing new rocket advancements all the time. In a sharp departure from traditional car manufacturing, Musk's Tesla releases software updates constantly. Fashion houses still have their two-collection-a-year drops, but in between they now release micro collections and collaborations. And seriously—Taylor Swift has released *eight* albums since 2020. Nine, if you count the *Tortured Poets Department* double album as two.

Taylor's business-model pivot incorporated one of the most fundamental truths of the new technology stack upon which our lives are built: Algorithms do not like "big drops"; in fact, they prefer content drip, drip, drips.

This new algorithm-led world made venture capitalists successful. It made start-up founders successful. So Taylor knew there must be a way for it to help make her successful too. Maybe even *the-most-iconic-brand-in-contemporary-culture* level of success.

She realized what others didn't, very early on: If you're going to be successful in the postanalog world, your business model should be drip-centric. Which involves releasing content, lines of code, software updates, Instagram updates, fashion collaborations, or rocket testing results *all the damn time.*

The venture capitalist Katherine Boyle, a partner at the firm that Marc Andreessen founded, has described this phenomenon as "constant shipping." "Ship" means to "send," just like a parcel. In the context of software development, though, it means "put into production." Successful founders like Elon Musk, she says, ship *constantly.*

At the same time, in the world of luxury fashion houses and consumer fashion strategy, we can see the same phenomenon occurring. Ana Andjelic, the luxury brand executive we met earlier, created the very term I'm using now in a Substack post titled "Drip Is the New Drop."

As described by Ana, "A drip is a continuous stream of products, signals, content, incentives, rewards, tokens, points, interactions, events or access. Perennial newness gamifies the brand experience and makes it more individual and unique. . . . Drips reward the long game over short-term gains. Drips also galvanize communities, incentivize collaboration and membership, and decrease competition. Drips are the opposite of winner takes all: they are decentralized and governed by activity in their communities."

The drip, not drop model is a clear breakaway from the preinternet, pretech platform era in which a musician could, if they worked hard enough, get a few number one hits and fill the pockets of the men in suits who controlled them, along with the rest of the industry, from the top.

Now, algorithmic curation has moved the power to make or break an artist away from executives and directly into the hands of fans. Fans, may I add, whom Taylor Swift has made a twenty-year effort to gain a monumental market share of.

To understand exactly how Taylor pivoted her business, it's useful to do a comparison of some of the elements of her pre- and post-Spotify model.

COLLABORATE, DON'T COMPETE

The status quo for, like, *ever*, had always been for a business to compete against everybody else in its category. This is probably because the size of the market, until the age of the internet, had been pretty fixed at a small number. Let's say that there are only one million people who can access your product as they are constrained by geography. Then you find yourself in a position of needing to compete with everybody else in your category to win over as many of those one million people as possible.

However, what the internet did was increase the size of a market to the entire global population who have internet access. Now that there are *billions* of people who could become your customers, you don't really need to compete anymore. In fact, it becomes mutually beneficial for you to pair up with other businesses that have similar values, share a similar mission, and could help you reach into previously untapped parts of the market where you'd like to grow your customer base.

Collaboration has become a key part of the go-viral-or-die, winner-takes-all mentality of the internet age. It's the reason that Mattel's Barbie movie had so many collaborations with shoes, food, jewelry, credit cards, and every other imaginable type of business, and that our entire reality was rebranded Barbiecore for a period of months, to some people's delight (and others' horror). And yes, Barbie was a viral, home-run success.

Taylor Swift is no stranger to collaborations, although the Swiftverse has yet to establish itself in the real world as Swiftcore. While her collaborative form has historically taken the shape of corecording or cowriting music with a diverse range of musicians from differing genres, Taylor seems to have branched out more recently into unofficial collaborations through an ongoing relationship with her contemporary Beyoncé. For example, where Taylor and Beyoncé may have once been pitted against each other, each of them was in attendance (and part of the main attraction) of the other's global stadium tour movie releases. Aware that there is likely a considerable overlap of their fan bases, they have leaned into each other not just to provide the kind of celebrity-level endorsement only they could engender but to help each of them grow their market share.

And then we have one of the most successful, unspoken collaborations of our time: Swift x NFL. Okay, so this is absolutely not, as far as the public is aware, an organized collaboration, endorsement, or partnership. But it's hard to deny that, intentionally or not, Taylor

Swift brought hundreds of millions of fans to the NFL who were from age, gender, and geography demographics that would have been impossible for the NFL itself to have brought in. Just as Swift fans all over the United States started googling "Who is Travis Kelce," Taylor made significant progress in claiming a more significant share of the "bro-dom" NFL fandom, resulting in over $300 million of additional brand value for the NFL and a lot of Super Bowl–size media attention for Taylor.

TIME AND ATTENTION, NOT MONEY

The preinternet era was defined by big drops creating big increases in revenue, and Taylor would tour in a bid to sell the CDs that she had just dropped.

As the internet economy grew and the start-ups like Google, Facebook, and Spotify matured, one thing became very clear: The monetization model of digital platforms was drastically different from their analog counterparts. So much so, in fact, that to this day there is still a lot of uncertainty around whether or not a tech company with a multibillion-dollar valuation is really worth that much.

Nevertheless, platforms like Facebook made it very clear that the most important dimension of a person's assets that they could give a digital platform was not their money but their attention and time.

And the so-called *attention economy* was born, whereby a person's attention and time are treated as a resource more valuable and scarce than their money. And it was often monetized in the following way: through advertising. That's right, the attention economy by way of these digital platforms started to fuel what is now the insanely huge, multitrillion-dollar digital advertising industry I discussed in Power Move Six.

Traditionally, companies would have considered ways in which to make their consumers spend more and more money on their products. But digital platforms have no products to sell, other than keeping you busy. So now, these digital behemoths spend a considerable amount of time contemplating ways to make you spend more and more of your time on their platforms.

Instagram, TikTok, Twitter, and Facebook rather famously try to use the algorithm to serve you addictive, endorphin-fueled content. Netflix tries to make you binge-watch your way through your weeks, months, and years. And Taylor? Well, she releases album after album full of Easter eggs that place her fans into never-ending, yearslong unsolvable mazes of the Swiftverse.

And just as every additional user on Instagram or TikTok makes the whole experience more fun and interesting for everybody on the platform, the Swiftverse also experiences this phenomenon, better known as "network effects." As more people come into the Swiftverse, it becomes more fun, and people want to stay there, trying to figure out together which song was written about which villainesque character in the Swiftverse and why.

There is, however, one big difference between Swift's attempt to consume her fans' time and attention versus, let's say, social media. Whereas Instagram seeks to monetize a user's attention by pushing increasingly addictive content in the hope that it can make the user watch more advertising, Taylor doesn't need to do this. Given that her revenue model is predicated on the sale of stadium tour tickets, the time and energy her fans dedicate to the Swiftverse is not seen in the same nefarious light as the advertising-centric model of social media.

In fact, far from Swift's model being bad for users, Taylor has actually created a model that rewards her fans with friendships and deeper relationships instead of advertising. Which, as always, leans into her mission of bringing people together through culture by way of friendships.

GROWTH THROUGH DEMAND, NOT SUPPLY

The traditional model that existed for cultural media content was built on a top-down, centralized model for how artists were managed (hello, men in suits), and also for how work was *created*.

Since every eighteen to twenty-four months an artist would drop an album, as a fan, you'd have to hope to enjoy it, because that was all that you would be given until the next drop eighteen to twenty-four months later. I mean, Beyoncé, who is one of the biggest music industry heavyweights after Taylor Swift, didn't release a single album for six years between 2016 and 2022. So if you didn't enjoy her *Lemonade*, you had a long time to wait before you heard *Renaissance*.

What we can see from looking at the fashion industry, however, is that even if you do not love the biannual Spring/Summer and Fall/Winter collection drops, you can always pursue the brand that you stan by acquiring pieces of smaller, collaboration-based drips that occur between the big drops.

Likewise with those in the Swiftverse, a drip allows you to hedge your bets. Don't love *folklore*? Well, thankfully there are *1989* "Vault" tunes coming your way soon.

Apart from hedging the fans' expectations, dripping means that they are constantly engaging with the creator, in dialogue about what they want and how they are anticipating it. Releasing an album eighteen months after the last means that an artist is creating hype from nothing. Releasing an album a month after a previous release means that you are not starting from scratch with fan momentum. Rather, you can build on existing hype to double your exposure, your popularity, and your market penetration.

It also means that the demand for your music is there, waiting in excited anticipation for you to give them something. They have not *forgotten* about you.

Demand-led growth plays on the same economics behind the lucrative model of luxury goods. Look at Rolex, for example. Because there are more people who want to buy Rolexes than actual Rolexes in circulation, the pent-up demand for the brand can be used to increase the time, energy, and money spent by consumers, and intensify the emotional relationship between the consumer and the brand.

It is exactly the same with Taylor Swift. Unlike other musicians who do not have the same close relationship with their fans extending back several decades, a demand-led growth strategy does one other very important thing: *It guarantees success.*

Consider that most artists put music into the world and hope (and pray) that people find it via the algorithm so they can listen to it. Unless you are aware of the fact that an album is coming out, nowadays it is often impossible to organically find it (again, the algorithm). So what happens when you release an album? Well, it may or may not become successful. You're not sure, because you can't be certain about how many people will find it.

In a demand-led model, however, people are already waiting for the drip to drop. You can be guaranteed that a certain percentage of your fan base will engage with the album upon its release, and plan accordingly. Having the ability to somewhat predict the future success of creative output is incredibly valuable to a business and to a brand. And this is exactly what Taylor Swift has done—created never-ending, pent-up demand that is constantly waiting, like a dog unsure of when he will get a treat, for something to drip.

• • •

Writing a book is a hard thing to do if you're somebody who is easily distracted. When I write, I try to leave my phone in another room and tell lies to myself about my ability to use the internet on my laptop, which I hope my brain doesn't detect.

iMessages, WhatsApps, Facebook Messenger, Instagram DMs, Twitter notifications, emails to several different email addresses, news alerts from the million news subscriptions I have, phone calls, voicemails, product notifications from the brands I shop, and, weirdly, Uber telling me that I should order a cab soon if I want to avoid surge pricing, despite currently being in rural Ireland.

There are hundreds of times a day that I think: I wonder if I could change my phone number and go off the grid. It's usually in these moments that I remember my brief first relationship, the mixtape CD I was given, and yearn for something that feels like it could never exist again: an analog world.

I, and de facto Taylor Swift, lived through the biggest global economic restructuring of the modern world, which reorganized everything from how we shop to who we marry, in ways to the same extent that the Industrial Revolution did in the late 1800s. A lot of businesses did not make it through this restructuring, and a very tiny number of them grew to sizes that were previously thought to be impossibly large.

Will this trend of tech dominance continue, and will some brands continue to get bigger and bigger, aided by algorithms and drip, not drop business models?

Well, I'm not sure. While the momentum behind the new-age tech platform's domination seems like it's on an unstoppable path, back in the early 2000s, music executives in big suits were saying the same thing about their own business model. After all, they owned the entire value chain of the music industry in a way that was once impenetrable from the outside.

But they were penetrated, and eventually they lost all power. So, does our immediate future look like our immediate past? It's hard to tell. I recently acquired a "dumbphone," which was a surprisingly expensive gadget with an intentionally low number of features. Pharrell Williams, both a creative genius and a business strategy guru, dropped an album with zero marketing on his fifty-first birthday, called *Black Yacht Rock*, which could be listened to only from a dedicated, one-page website.

I can imagine a world wherein the future looks a lot like my early adult years—technology exists, but we control it, instead of it controlling us.

Regardless of what the future may or may not look like, my point is that it remains uncertain.

And while there are lots of things that we can learn from Taylor's move into a full-fledged algorithm-dependent, decentralized business model, perhaps the big takeaway here is not that she and her brand and her music should probably be valued more like a highly scaled tech platform than as a singer-songwriter. Instead, the takeaway may actually be that she was one of very few brands and businesses globally that was able to say the following:

Okay. I've gone away and thought about it. And yes, you're right. This streaming revenue model is here to stay. And it sucks for the music industry, and it sucks for me. But I can either sit here and let it destroy me, or I can get on board with it. Spotify, you say you want me to come along for the ride? Okay, fine. But I'm going to use your technology to make myself so damn big that you're going to be riding on my coattails. Now, let's go.

Despite the controversy caused as the news of her rejoining Spotify disseminated, there is no shame in Taylor changing her mind, because that is simply what good executives do. They assess the situation and make changes to their business model, their strategy, and their execution of that strategy as they see fit. The key, though, is having the ability to know that a pivot is needed and to be able to commit to that pivot entirely.

Her "So Long, London" lyrics about going down with the ship amid a white-knuckled grip were likely written about her ability to remain steadfastly committed to a relationship instead of a strategy, but: When Taylor is in, she is 100 percent in. There are no dead fish around here.

However, and perhaps more directly applicable to her late 2010s business model bait and switch, she also sings: *Sometimes, walkin' out is the one thing / That will find you the right thing.*

Taylor's decision in 2017 to rejoin the streaming platforms was the most consequential decision she made that can be directly tied to her current status as an iconoclastic contemporary musician, worldbuilder, and billionaire. And this is the power of Taylor's ability to engage with strategy: She used it to turn what for many was their downfall into the very thing that propelled her.

POWER MOVE EIGHT

BRING PEOPLE WITH YOU

I N JANUARY 2019, AN EXTREMELY CHARISMATIC TECH START-UP FOUNDER was on top of the world: He had raised nearly $13 billion of venture capital financing at a $47 billion valuation for his start-up, which had promised to change the nature of how people worked together in offices. He was idolized by employees, investors, the media, and the world of celebrity entertainment. He flew around the globe in a private jet, hired a famous rapper to perform at staff parties, and met with the world's top political and economic elite.

But by August that year, everything had changed: The CEO and founder of the company was forced to resign, and the business eventually declared bankruptcy. I am, of course, talking about the now infamous founder Adam Neumann and his ill-fated start-up WeWork.

Fueled by a blend of charm and eccentricity (to say the least) that was initially engaging, it all began to unravel as WeWork grew. His tendency to make sweeping, often impractical decisions without any scrutiny or strategic foresight created a volatile environment—like randomly firing staff or making big budget decisions on a whim.

Overall, it was clear that Adam severely lacked Power Move Two—there was no strategy in sight.

But the problems at WeWork went much further than just a missing strategy. In fact, it was Neumann's personal brand of leadership that was ultimately responsible for the loss of the nearly $50 billion company.

Characterized by grandiose promises that were too big to be kept, in tandem with a relentless pursuit of expansion even at the loss of investor capital, Neumann directed WeWork to a vision that was not sufficiently grounded in reality.

In other words, and in as plain English as I can put it so that we're all on the same page, Neumann was full of shit. And eventually investors realized that the wool had been pulled over their eyes.

So what went wrong exactly?

Well, Adam Neumann's WeWork shenanigans created a furious debate among the investment (and wider business) community.

In one camp, you had all the stakeholders who insisted that a visionary founder *had to be* a narcissist who is removed from reality to achieve greatness.

Starkly in the opposite camp, you had the investors and corporate czars who believed that nothing but operational excellence mattered; the "vision" amounts to little more than a bunch of lies that are told to keep employees and investors happy.

And somewhere in the middle were the people who assumed that leadership probably needed a bit of both: a dogmatic adherence to a vision that is somewhat unattainably large, with an ability to actually execute on building a business sustainably.

Okay, so what do Adam Neumann and a now-disappeared $50 billion have to do with Taylor Swift, or with *us*?

Well, the first takeaway from the Neumann debacle is quite clear:

Leadership matters. Leadership was the reason that WeWork became a multibillion-dollar company in the first place, and leadership is the reason that it later went bankrupt.

The second takeaway was that for investors, executives, and academics alike, it became apparent that there is no clear consensus on what "good leadership" actually looks like. Most investors walked away having lost money and vowed never to work with Neumann again; on the other hand, one large investor later decided to give Neumann a further $350 million for a similarish but different start-up idea in 2021.

In fact, *defining* leadership alone is challenging because it encompasses such a wide range of behaviors, traits, and contexts. For example, do you want your boss to be a leader like Elon Musk or Barack Obama? Because they are two wildly different flavors. For what it's worth, I've had this exact conversation with very talented people who have argued extensively and heatedly about their choice here. If you're a highly creative engineer with too much energy and an intrinsic desire to crash and burn a few ideas, you may prefer the former. If you're a trained diplomat with a lower risk tolerance and a need to solve problems through mediation, you'll definitely prefer the latter.

"Leadership" can be defined in many ways, especially in academic literature, from *transformational* and *transactional* to *servant* and *situational.* Each theory emphasizes different aspects, such as vision, motivation, or adaptability, making it difficult to pin down a single definition that fits all contexts.

In some instances, Taylor is clearly a servant leader. In others, she's a transformational leader. Some situations require a person to increase the level of motivation of their team; others require more adaptability.

But regardless of the exact type of leadership being employed, we know that leadership is extremely important. It is the process of influencing and guiding individuals and groups toward achieving common goals—like growing a business, finishing an assignment, winning the presidential election, or scoring a goal at your local five-a-side soccer tournament.

It involves setting a vision, inspiring others, making strategic decisions, and fostering an environment that allows yourself and others to grow into success. Leadership is crucial for several reasons, like creating a sense of direction and purpose, whether personally or professionally; building relationships, whether it's a professional network or a friendship; managing and resolving conflicts; and setting (and upholding) a standard of behavior and culture.

If I were to make a list of the people that I would deem to be "leaders," it would almost certainly include some of the big names that are rather obvious, like the Unicorns: political leaders like Nelson Mandela, Nobel Peace Prize–winning leaders like Martin Luther King Jr., and science leaders like Jane Goodall.

But it would also include names that very few people have ever heard of. My stepfather, who volunteers relentlessly for a charity in my hometown that provides services for vulnerable people; my high school classmate who now campaigns endlessly for those with the deadly disease of cystic fibrosis; my friend who looks after her aging parents.

Leadership is not one of the most important skills for achieving Unicornness; rather, it is *the* most important skill. After all, it is not enough to be really, really great at something if you cannot use that greatness to motivate change or to shape the world in some direction. The world's best artists do not want to create beautiful pieces of work simply for the sake of completion; they want the people who see their work to feel inspiration and awe. Likewise with Taylor Swift, who writes hundreds of songs that may never be heard. The reason she curates some of her best music into albums that are subsequently released is because she wants her music to make an impact on the world.

Translating "being great" at something into "inspiring change" is done through leadership. Like in cooking, where salt and fat are used to transport flavors from one food to another, leadership is used to transform great talent and effort into positive societal impact.

The equation is pretty simple:

Unicorn + Leadership = Influence + Power

Which immediately begs the age-old question that is the focus of one of the most-taught subjects at Harvard Business School: How does one "do leadership"?

And unfortunately, there are so many classes on this topic because it is very difficult to be prescriptive about how to Become a Great Leader. Every person is different, every situation is different, and every culture is different. There is no unified theory of how to translate your effort into impact.

However, most leaders who inspire change and transform the world for the better (in both big and small ways) have certain leadership tactics that, while they may not *define* the leader, are used over and over again to gain enough popular support to be able to bring people with them.

GAINING POPULAR SUPPORT

The premise of leadership is the belief that the leader will bravely choose a path while everybody else follows behind them. Therefore, having the ability to get people behind you is in many ways the crux of what it means to adopt a leadership position; it is an idea that extends far beyond the notion of popularity.

In fact, if you think about high school, you'll probably quickly realize the huge disconnect between the people in your school who were the most popular and those who had the most positive community impacts through leadership. In most cases, and certainly at the all-girls high school that I attended, the two groups of people were definitely *not* overlapping in any Venn diagram.

On March 7, 2024, the founder of the world's largest hedge fund, Bridgewater, which has more than $150 billion to its name, became a Swiftie. Ray Dalio, a total finance shark, declared at the Eras Tour concert in Singapore that he would like Taylor to run for the US presidency in 2024.

Now, Taylor Swift is clearly a very popular musician—arguably the most popular musician *ever*. But would massive popularity alone be enough to make a normally very level-headed fund manager express his interest in a President Swift–run United States? Or did Ray Dalio experience something more than popularity at the Eras Tour, when he sat among fifty-five thousand Swift disciples?

I want to dive a little deeper into the weeds on how interconnected, complex, and context-specific terms like leadership, power, likability, and popularity really are.

Because if we are to learn anything from Taylor's leadership style, it is a twofold lesson. First, it is downright *hard* for nonwhite males to tap into the conventional wisdom on how to amass power through leadership that is taught at the world's top business schools. Second, we can also see that the type of leadership that Swift demonstrates may be harder to achieve, but it is absolutely more powerful than traditional methods employed by the majority of Fortune 100 CEOs.

Let's start with an example that picks up where we just left off, by considering the perception of Swift's power. Of course, we know that she's extremely popular, which is loosely linked to the idea that she is "liked." Yet for women, it's extremely difficult to transform "being liked" into "being powerful," because, unlike for most men, the more powerful a woman is, the less likable she is deemed to be.

Years of speaking to influential women in positions of power has anecdotally confirmed to me: This wild paradox is unfortunately true.

As Taylor has often pointed out, there are two distinct vocabularies that are used when discussing power—one for women and another for men. But you don't just find two vocabularies in leadership; there are two sets of acceptable behaviors as well.

Many years ago, during my MBA program at Harvard, I took a class on leadership, during which I happened to be sitting next to a Black friend who had long dreadlocks. So, sure. An Irish woman and a dreadlocked man are not the typical movers and shakers in a post-MBA finance world.

During a class discussion on "approachable leadership," we watched a video interview of Jeff Bezos that showed how he engendered support and created rapport with people by making himself seem more approachable. Bezos self-deprecatingly told the audience how, upon his admission to the undergraduate physics program at Princeton, he felt he wasn't as smart as his peers, opting to graduate in computer science instead. He added that he wasn't as good at physics as his peers who went on to study for a PhD.

If ever there was a humble brag . . .

Listening to this interview was supposed to make the audience feel like "Wow, this guy has $200 billion in his back pocket, and despite his desire to colonize Mars and own the entirety of humanity, he's just so *down to earth*!" And sure, it kinda worked. If you weren't as cynical as I was watching the interview, you may have thought, "This guy is just as insecure as the rest of us."

This, my professor told us, was one of the best ways to seem both powerful *and* likable—making other people feel like you are just normal, even if you aren't. By downplaying your success. "I may be the world's richest man, but damn, I wasn't smart enough to do what my friends were all doing."

My Black friend and I exchanged glances. "When," we asked each other after the class, "was it ever possible for a Black person or a woman to outwardly tell people 'Hey! I suck at these things!' and appear *more* powerful, not less?"

While this leadership strategy may work for men, for whom there is an assumption that they are naturally smart and powerful, for minorities it only reinforces or even confirms any subconscious beliefs that we are less intelligent in the first place. If you are Taylor Swift, this strategy does not help you gain popular support; it does the opposite.

Suffice to say, sources and strategies of power are very, very different for white men versus minorities—which in business and finance includes women like Taylor Swift. And me. And approximately 50 percent of the global population who are female. And roughly 85 percent of the global population who are not white.

Instead of appearing "likable," women and minorities in business instead have to co-opt a much more complex strategy: They must disarm the people who may feel threatened by their perceived power by making themselves appear smaller, and simultaneously appear strong and powerful enough to be considered objectively worthy of holding power in the first place.

If it sounds tough, well . . . it is. And female executives have been discussing just how difficult this is for a *really* long time.

Taylor has outwardly, and rightly, recognized that this is an impossible tightrope to walk. However, despite the difficulty, she has managed to achieve power in ways that Jeff Bezos has just not. Okay, perhaps Bezos is infinitely more financially powerful than Swift. But nobody has even joked about wanting Jeff Bezos to run for president. Bezos doesn't have an army of hundreds of millions of Bezoites willingly waiting to defend him if he faces public criticism.

And here's why.

At some stage during the interview we watched in class, Jeff Bezos obviously felt the need to try to tell the audience how they should perceive him. He essentially leads the audience to think that he's smart enough to get into a top science program, but he is too commercially savvy to want to stay in academic research like his peers. While Bezos might outwardly say "I wasn't smart enough to do a physics PhD," what the audience will subconsciously take away is that "he was too successful at a young age with Amazon to start in a PhD program."

Subconsciously manipulating people to engender support? This is a very top-down, centralized way to think about leadership.

Which makes sense, I guess, because Jeff Bezos's entire success has been predicated on starting and running organizations for which there is one boss with one huge ego.

Nobody on this planet could possibly believe that somebody who slips in and out of the Richest Person in the Universe spot, who is hoping to control the whole of civilizations in outer space, and who builds himself megayacht after megayacht, believes his peers at college, most of whom probably went to work for him at Amazon later, were "smarter than him." I'm sorry, but this is clearly a man who, deep down, truly believes himself to be the smartest person alive.

Taylor Swift, on the other hand, doesn't tell people how they should think about her. You'll never hear her say: *I sucked at math; my classmates were so much better at math than I was, so I dropped out of high school to pursue music instead.* Her song "Shake It Off" was, indeed, an anthem that attempted to make precisely this point: Think what you want about me. I don't care.

But very unlike Bezos, her power is created not through top-down centralization but through peer-to-peer empowerment. Therefore her likability is decided not by what she *says*, but by what she *does*.

People, brands, food, memes, or music that get large grassroots support are usually popularized because of how they make people *feel*, from the bottom of the community up, instead of because they are told they should like it, whatever it is.

There was more than a grain of truth in what your parents told you: Actions speak louder than words. In fact, it's absolutely true. In the Swiftverse, where Taylor's power is predicated on her authenticity, being "just another Swiftie," and being a peer instead of a boss, there is only one possible strategy for becoming more likable: being yourself and hoping it's enough for everybody.

No amount of interviews espousing faux modesty is going to make people like you. In fact, it is probably going to do the opposite.

Unlike for white men who make up the vast majority of the public-facing leadership ranks, there are very few established playbooks for women and minorities to gain popular support. But there is one that *nearly always* works. Moreover, it's universal. It doesn't work just for women and minorities but for *everybody*.

The best way for people to become powerful is by asking for and demonstrating over time that you should be given people's trust, respect, and support. Not by telling them that they should give it to you.

It's a leadership playbook that relies entirely on authenticity and uses it as a cornerstone for connecting with people to gain support.

This is why, I suspect, the perception of hatred that Taylor felt after the Kanye West incident impacted her so deeply. When most leaders get knocked down, the aspect of themselves that people are rejecting is often an outward-facing façade that has been created to portray an image that may not necessarily reflect all of who they are. Once that façade has been rejected, they can easily create a new, slightly different one.

Taylor, on the other hand, felt the rejection to the deepest crevices of her core because she has only one strategy for engendering the support that keeps her career not only in existence but thriving: to *be herself* and to hope that it's *enough*.

Because when people stop liking her, she cannot rebuild the Swift-verse on a different persona. She cannot tell her fans, after twenty-odd years of them feeling like they intimately know her, that she has changed.

Garnering public support is one of the most important aspects of being a leader, because having support means that you can access the resources you need to change the world. But achieving that in the first place is hard, and especially for women like Taylor Swift, who cannot employ the multiple generic tactics often used by men to manipulate or convince people that they're worthy of their support.

Building peer-to-peer popularity is incredibly hard but, as we saw in Power Move Seven, can be magnitudes more effective at moving ideas and accomplishing goals once it exists. However, it is an *extremely* high-risk strategy given that it takes so long to become effective, given that power bestowed in this way cannot easily be "bought and sold" in a top-down manner.

This is also one of the main reasons that women and minorities in leadership positions always discuss how much emotionally harder it is for them to lead compared to their white, male counterparts. Because once attacked, as happens more frequently to minority leaders, the values that constitute their very essence are brought into question, not just a "leadership mask" they happen to be wearing.

Gaining popular support through authenticity is not the fastest, easiest, or cheapest strategy to become influential. But here's the thing: When it's done properly, it is *really* successful.

While there are many ways to be an authentic leader, as I've already mentioned, each dependent on the person, the context, and the situation at hand, there are four tactics that Taylor consistently uses that largely seem to fulfill the most important criteria of "doing leadership" at the highest levels.

TAYLOR TACTIC ONE: GET OFF THE FENCE

One of the core tenets of leadership that successful Unicorns hold is being able to make decisions quickly, even when they don't have all the data they would like, or they don't know enough about the situation.

I remember once during a strategy class at Harvard, the following question was posed: You are the CEO of a large auto manufacturer. It's 2015, and Tesla's electric vehicles are growing in popularity. Do you pivot your company away from combustion engine cars to compete with Tesla, or remain steadfast with your current strategy?

Most of the student responses? Let's wait and see. We still don't have enough data to know whether it'll be worth the investment to pivot and compete in the electric vehicle space.

They mostly decided that the "doing nothing" strategy was the best course of action in an industry that was being disrupted at an alarming pace.

In general, most people default to making no decision, or to carrying on with the status quo, for as long as they possibly can. This is a totally normal human reaction: We are biologically predisposed to hate change, and we avoid it for as long as we can.

Indeed, picking a side and getting off the fence is one of the hardest things for anybody to do, because diverging from the status quo carries a far greater risk. "Ah," you could argue, "that may be true, but the rewards are also much bigger if you're on the winning side!"

While that is very true, it has been shown time and time again that most people live their lives, whether it's how they choose jobs, romantic partners, or even invest in the stock market, by minimizing the downside (i.e., following the status quo) instead of maximizing for the upside (i.e., taking a risk).

Leaders, on the other hand, are so called in part because of their unique ability to get off the fence. They acknowledge that if they are waiting for a perfect understanding of a situation or a complete set of data about a fast-changing world to make a decision, they will never be able to do so.

The ability to make a decision, especially one that is made quickly and in the face of uncertainty, demonstrates knowledge, experience, judgment, and clarity of thought. When we're around people who can make decisions, we feel reassured.

At a very basic level, think about what happens when you organize a first date. Can you imagine if you asked your date what they would like to do, and they said, "I dunno, what would *you* like to do?," to which you replied, "Uh, I dunno. What do you think?," and this pitiful conversation went back and forth into eternity? Would you be excited to meet this person? Or would you rather meet someone who said, "I have an idea: Why don't we go to this bar, or do this thing, at this time, on this day?"

At a more complex level, imagine if Taylor said, "Geez, guys, I dunno about this whole album rerecord thing. It might not work, and it might in fact be career suicide, but I guess I might just try it and find out if it'll be successful? I'm not sure if I'll do all of them, so let's just start with one."

Nobody, and I mean *nobody*, is happy to get behind indecision. It's exhausting, it's nauseating, and it's a buzzkill.

When Swift decided to rerecord her music, she didn't have any data that told her she was going to successfully pull off a coup. In fact, as we've discussed, the only data that existed lived on the laptops of the dead fish who bet against her. And it all suggested she was going to lose.

However, she got off the fence and made a decision to move ahead, full steam. Not a little bit of a rerecord. Not "let's try it and see if it works." She wasn't standing with one foot on either side of the fence. Instead, she went all in. Had she been in the Harvard strategy class, she would have raised her hand and said, "If I were the CEO of, say, Ford, I would be pivoting to compete against Tesla; sure, the data may not be there *yet*, but by the time the data exists, it'll be too late. Tesla will have killed us anyway."

Leaders decide with speed and conviction, because they know a bad decision is infinitely better than no decision at all. And over time, with real-world experience, the best leaders I've worked with seem to have an astonishing gut sensory system that will tell them in mere moments what entire teams of strategy consultants will tell them after "running the numbers" for months.

A young CEO might look at a business they are in the process of acquiring and ask the chief financial officer to create more spreadsheets that outline more and more ways in which the acquisition can go badly. It is not uncommon, however, for a seasoned CEO to be buying a multibillion-dollar business with some back-of-the-envelope math, at best. "Those numbers feel good to me" is something you hear often.

Taylor Swift, it appears, is exactly that seasoned executive who is very much in tune with her business, her industry, and her gut feeling about when things may work or why they may go wrong.

You see, real leaders don't live on the fence; in fact, they are very much nowhere near the damn fence.

TAYLOR TACTIC TWO: BEND WHEN YOU HAVE TO

The world, and especially the music business, is unrecognizable today compared to when Taylor Swift released her first album. There are new technologies, new business models, new politics, new genres, changing demographics, and changing tastes. Each of these, on their own, would be difficult for a business leader to navigate. But together? It's catastrophically hard.

Which is why so few companies in the United States, one of the most competitive markets in the world, "make it." In fact, 20 percent of new businesses fail during the first two years of having started, 45 percent during the first five years, and 65 percent during the first ten years.

Leaders who adapt proactively don't just react to changes in the big and small pictures; they anticipate shifts, seriously plan a range of possible scenarios, and seize opportunities to innovate and lead change. At its core, adaptability, just like antifragility, is about being able to withstand the things that put stress on and change the whole system. It is about seeing the *opportunity* in change, rather than perceiving it as a threat.

And just like antifragility, there is a biological and scientific link between systems that are adaptable and those that are successful.

Charles Darwin had a name for this, which formed the basis of our understanding of the field of biology: evolution. Darwin suggested that organisms that adjusted the best to their environment are the most successful at surviving and reproducing.

Likewise, the famed theoretical physicist and cosmologist Stephen Hawking, whose work hugely impacted the study of general relativity and the human place in the universe, was quoted as saying, "Intelligence is the ability to adapt to change."

If adaptability is so good, then why has Taylor Swift so vocally been *against* it, especially when it comes to her wanting or needing to change her artistic and performance style?

In *Miss Americana*, Swift remarked, "Everyone is a shiny new toy for like two years. The female artists have reinvented themselves twenty times more than the male artists," something that was highlighted again in two songs on her *folklore* album. In "This Is Me Trying," she sings, *"I had the shiniest wheels, now they're rusting,"* and in "Mirrorball," *"I'm a mirrorball / I can change everything about me to fit in."*

Her complaint, in short, is more often about gender than about survivability—that women have to reinvent themselves as artists, executives, and leaders more often than men because there is a much more narrow and acceptable view of what is deemed an appropriate framing of a woman's existence. Sexy, but not too sexy. Smart, but not too smart. Not too young, not too old. Just right.

While I agree with her that women *are* in fact pushed much harder than men to use all the tools available to them to keep consumer interests alive—their bodies, their dating lives, their sex appeal, their looks, their gossip, and somewhere deep down on that list, their talent—I would also argue that Taylor learning how to constantly reinvent herself is exactly why she has become as big as she is today. Yes, she has had to do this more than any man. But is it not also true that in doing this, she has become bigger than any man, dead or alive?

And just as Taylor's leadership style is infinitely harder to execute and maintain, isn't it also the leadership style that will help her gain the most popular support and influence?

All systems, whether biological or physical, or in business, finance, and economics, must constantly adapt. Those that don't will die. Those that do will have the ability to become stronger.

Taylor often alludes to the emotional difficulty of constantly changing in her lyrics, from discussing the circus that is her life as she performs for us—*"I'm a mirrorball / I can change everything about me to fit in"*—to describing the exhaustion when one artistic phase, boyfriend, or way of living is over, and a new one begins—*"I was dancing when the music stopped . . . I can't face reinvention."*

The art of leadership is as much about the art of reinvention as it is about getting really good at doing your one thing over and over again. It's about being able to bend when you have to.

TAYLOR TACTIC THREE: BE RELIABLE

One of the weird and not at all predicted outcomes of the COVID pandemic was that more people would start to drive, and fewer people would use public transport. The result? Well, if you're like me and rely on public transport to get around, your life has become utterly miserable. And I'll tell you why.

As more people began driving, traffic increased massively. Sure, driving was great during COVID when most people didn't leave their houses. But now, when you're stuck on a bus that sits at an intersection for ten minutes, it is grim.

The worst part isn't that you end up sitting on a bus endlessly when you could be doing *anything* more interesting. It's that you never know how long it's going to take you to get somewhere. So if you have an important meeting at 9:30 a.m., you may need to leave the house two hours before the meeting. Maybe it usually only takes forty minutes to get to your destination, but on at least two occasions it has taken nearly two hours. Therefore, you have to assume that the journey may take the longest time it has ever taken.

This is the curse of *variability*. The wider the range of expected outcomes, the less that system is trusted to do anything. So what happens? The system enters what is called "terminal decline"; people will be forced to seek alternatives such as driving or taxis to get around instead of buses, making the problem worse.

It turns out that we behave in nearly identical ways when we experience variability in other people. Let's say you go on a date with a guy who is a total gentleman one day, then totally forgets your name the next. You need to ditch him ASAP.

Reliability may sound like the world's most boring aspect of leadership, but it's hard to overstate how important it is as a competitive advantage. That's because it's hard to be reliable, and very few people, systems, or processes are reliable.

Reliability is, in fact, the entire backbone of my friend's two-Michelin-star restaurant. The Michelin stars are awarded based on covert judges coming to the restaurant at unknown days and times, and most often when you least expect it. They might come during a slow Tuesday lunch or a busy Saturday dinner. They are testing the ability of the chef to deliver outstanding excellence every single day, during every single meal service, to every single customer. Without fail.

Very few people, businesses, or leaders can achieve reliability, which is why it's one of the biggest down selectors when considering whether someone has leadership potential.

Does this person actually turn up to coach the soccer team every Wednesday evening, come rain or shine? Is this hostess always really nice to our diners, regardless of whether they're going through a personal existential crisis? Does this guy text me back within normal response times?

You'd be surprised how few people are able to be consistently reliable, especially across all aspects of their lives.

On the other hand, unlike the guy who texts you ten times in one hour and then forgets you exist, Taylor Swift is what I like to call a Reliability Machine. In fact, there's very little difference between her and my 2005 silver Škoda, which has nearly half a million kilometers on its clock, despite having been driven into a few ditches. In twenty-odd years, neither Taylor nor my car has ever let me down (although one looks significantly better than the other).

In fact, as of 2024, Taylor Swift had only canceled a handful of shows over the decades she's been performing. She canceled a show in Thailand back in 2014 because of a government coup (out of her control), the freak weather episode in Buenos Aires on her Eras Tour forced her to reschedule the concert for the next day (out of her control), and the Eras Tour shows in Vienna were canceled because of a terrorist threat (out of her control). In fact, she only ever canceled because of sickness *once*, back in 2011.

The math on this is rather extraordinary. Of her 1,150 shows, she has a 99.7 percent reliability rate. Compare this to the MTA's data on the New York subway's F line, which had a 72 percent reliability rate in 2023. And to the US's most reliable airline, Delta? Only 82.9 percent.

So no amount of MBAs, operational consultants, or world-famous executives can come anywhere close to Taylor's ability to do the most insanely over-the-top performances and to do them *reliably*. As my chef friend told me, it's not that hard to get a Michelin star. *But keeping it is nearly impossible.*

It may feel like ultrareliable people like Taylor Swift are just built differently, but they're not. You or I could, in theory, be just as reliable. But—and maybe this is just my age starting to talk here—everybody has those days when they're supposed to go out for a drink, but they want absolutely nothing more in life than to lounge in pajamas with greasy hair and takeout.

The difference, I guess, is that Taylor—in between her multiple ten-thousand-calorie-burning shows, and with full-on jet lag—still washes her hair, puts on her makeup, and goes out on the town in Manhattan. Her good friend Zoë Kravitz had this to say about her in 2021: "Nobody works harder than her. It's this beautiful ongoing journey. And she's driven by her love of music. She's just never gonna stop."

Being reliable is one of the most important, but also the most exhausting and challenging, aspects of leadership. It's always one of the least appreciated characteristics, and it only becomes apparent when it is gone. For example, I often took the public transport that I had before COVID for granted. Now, I miss it dearly. In the same way I take for granted that my lifelong quest to see Taylor Swift perform the Eras Tour will be realized because I have tickets to her show. Statistically, unless lightning splits the stage in two, Taylor will be performing.

I imagine the response Taylor would give to the question "What if you're sick?" is similar to what the chef said. "Sick? You're not."

If popular support is what you're after, reliability is crucial to getting people behind you. Be the person that shows up to coach soccer in the pouring rain. Be five minutes early to meetings. Never fail to turn up, even if it kills you. Because once people realize that they can rely on you, they will reward you with their trust.

TAYLOR TACTIC FOUR: GET SHIT DONE

I used to work with a guy who spent a lot of time, and I mean a lot of time, trying to figure out how to climb the ladder to success.

He wasn't spending his time getting work done in order to be successful, as one might think. The problem was that he was spending most of his time trying to figure out how to be successful without doing the work.

He spent 99 percent of his time trying to figure out how to "cheat" his way to the top.

This mentality of trying to be successful without having to do any work is more pervasive than you may think. Not too long ago I had a meeting with a student I'd met while he was an undergrad at MIT. "I'm trying to figure out how to map my career in a similar fashion to yours," he told me during this meeting. When I asked him to be more specific, he replied: "I want to do what you did: be successful without having to work your way to the top."

I nearly fell off my chair.

"Just because I am young," I responded, half wondering if a recent undergraduate would consider me to be young, "doesn't mean I haven't worked eighteen-hour days seven days a week for the last decade to get where I am today."

I'll tell you what I told both these people, and what Taylor would likely tell you if you asked her:

If you want to be a leader, you have to do the work.

Some (very lazy) people might think that graduating up the

ladder into positions of leadership is something that happens *to you*, and not something that you *actively do*. This framing, though, tells us a lot about their perception of leadership.

Sure, the recent graduate that I spoke to might think that a senior job title enables you to tell other people what to do at work. In reality, the more senior a position at work, the more leadership is a part of that job, and leadership is not merely telling people below you what to do. On the contrary, it is about finding ways to help the people who are working their way up behind you. And it's simply not possible to help somebody else do something you've never done yourself.

One of the most powerful facets of leadership is being able to bring people with you through the act of doing the same hard things you ask of others. You'll find that leaders are extraordinarily capable of doing a hell of a lot of really hard things, most of the time without even thinking twice about it; they have a psychological indifference to the pain of hard work or to doing things they hate doing.

Every Saturday morning, for example, I do a volunteer-led running race in my local park. Long after the runners have gone home, the race volunteers are still collecting the signs dotted along the course. One day, in the freezing cold and pouring rain, I watched one of the volunteers putting the signs into a shared storage shed. When he saw how messy the shed was, he was faced with two options: throw the signs on top of everything else and go home, or clean out and tidy the whole shed.

Although nobody had asked him to do it, I watched him choose the latter option, and I'm sure he never mentioned that he had been the person who had done the hard work.

This is Taylor Swift. Authentic leadership grows on the back of an insane amount of energy that people dedicated to getting hard stuff done, often without it being asked or required of them. The Eras Tour was a two-year demonstration of Taylor's relentless dedication to getting shit done. Rerecording music? Done. Releasing her tour movie? Done. Working insanely hard so that her fans could have the best possible experience of her music? Absolutely.

I've already discussed having skin in the game being a way to build trust and deepen relationships within communities. Being able to get shit done, all day, every day, is a similar tool for showing your community that you are reliable, dependable, and trustworthy.

It's turning the guilt you feel every time you think, "Ugh, I feel bad, I should have just done that!" into actually getting it done.

It's being the person on the team who is extremely competent, capable, and in the trenches with everybody else, whether they're the CEO or the intern, and whether anybody is watching or not.

. . .

There are two things that really make me cringe when people talk about themselves. My first pet peeve is when people self-label as a polymath, a fancy name for someone who is brilliant at everything. My second is when people self-label as leaders.

What do most people actually *mean* when they say they're a leader? The label "leader" has become a filler word for those who aspire to have the title, without actually doing the hard work of demonstrating leadership qualities. If you go to an industry conference, they will introduce a CEO panelist as a "leader" out of common courtesy. However, many could (and would) argue that a CEO who earns $10 million a year while their company loses market share to an innovative start-up technology is likely not a leader in any capacity.

Was Adam Neumann a leader? And if so, was he a *good* leader?

Unicorns who pair their extraordinary skills, talents, and efforts with leadership are able to become hugely influential and powerful.

They can create $50 billion corporations, seemingly as easily as they can destroy them.

If they're leaders like Taylor Swift, they can irreversibly change the music industry.

If they're leaders like my high school friend, they can offer hope to the thousands of people with cystic fibrosis.

If they're the volunteers at my weekly running club, they can bring communities of people, who may never otherwise meet, together.

I've already noted that leaders are not just people who are popular. In fact, leaders are sometimes decidedly not popular, either because they are forced to make tough decisions that go against the grain or because their leadership style is so quietly understated that they never draw enough attention to themselves to be popular.

However, what all leaders have in common, even if they are not all popular, is the ability to gain popular support from those around them. This nearly always comes in the form of bringing people with them on a common mission.

The strongest leaders are those who grow their power through authenticity, and usually in a bottom-up manner, meaning that their leadership strengthens when the people in their communities are encouraged to grow over time. This creates a strong peer-to-peer foundation of followers that a leader can influence, like the Swiftverse.

The four tactics employed by Swift—as well as the world's most famous leaders—are the ability to get off the fence and make fast decisions with conviction; the ability to adapt and bend as context requires; the ability to be the most reliable person in any room; and the ability to be the person who gets shit done without complaining or without being asked.

As varied and complex as the subject of leadership is, gaining community support and being able to accumulate power to influence such communities is pretty simple: Just do what Taylor Swift does.

Ask yourself this simple question when making a decision: What would Taylor do? Because even though Taylor is a billionaire CEO and superstar rolled into one, there's nothing that she does in terms of her leadership that we can't all do as well, even if it is hard.

She would make a decision and stick with it. She would realize that the direction of the wind has changed and bend with it accordingly. She would be the most reliable person in the world, even in the face of government coups and terrorist threats. And yeah, anytime she thinks, "I dunno if I can be bothered to do this," she just goes straight ahead and does it anyway.

POWER MOVE NINE

DON'T EAT THE MARSHMALLOW

I N THE 1970S, A GROUP OF PSYCHOLOGISTS AT STANFORD UNIVERSITY, led by Professor Walter Mischel, got a group of kids and, one at a time, left them alone in a room for fifteen minutes. A marshmallow was placed on the table at which they sat. Before the psychologists left the room, they told the children:

"You are free to eat the marshmallow, but, if you wait for fifteen minutes until I come back, you can have two marshmallows."

The experiment was the first aimed at understanding the age at which delayed gratification develops in children, which seems a bit crazy, since I'm not entirely sure delayed gratification exists in adults.

How many children do you think waited for the two marshmallows? Or more to the point, would *you* have waited for two marshmallows?

The idea that the "today" version of us would sacrifice for the "tomorrow" version of us encapsulates nearly every aspect of our being, yet is so seldom talked about that usually only during a midlife crisis does it occur to people that they have been making trade-offs their whole lives, and that they were unsatisfactory.

I mean, several times a day our ability to delay gratification is tested. As I write this, it's 11:00 a.m. and I'm starting to feel peckish. My mind wanders to what I know is downstairs in my kitchen: leftover cake. Like many people, my delayed gratification signals are jarred and can be broken by just the thought of food, my weakness. Of course I want soft, sugary sponge cake for breakfast! And while I'm at it, why don't I dig into the cheese box too? In fact, if I'm going to get out the cheese, I may as well have a glass of the chilled white wine I've been saving for a few months.

There is a reason why at eleven o'clock on a Tuesday morning, and despite being Irish, I am not high on sugar, dairy, and alcohol: Very boringly, I have things to do later. And in fact, I have things to do right now—like writing this book. After I finish today's work, I'm going to have meetings, during which it would be useful if I was not drunk. And this evening I plan to go for a run, since I promised a friend I'd run a race with him in a few weeks, and it would be less than useful if I ate half a cake before that.

But the weird thing about not eating the cake and cheese and popping open the wine is that I'm refusing to eat the marshmallow in favor of what? Boring meetings and something that probably seems pretty hellish—exercise?

The difficulty of choosing to be sober and sugar-free on a Tuesday morning is that the reward is some weird mixture of not feeling like my life has come off its tracks, knowing that I can stick to a routine even if nobody is forcing me to, going to bed and sleeping well because I'm healthy and relatively fit. But none of these things, by themselves, is better than cake, cheese, and wine. At least on first inspection. Navigating these trade-offs is so complicated, in fact, that I suspect it's why it's never taught, never really even *mentioned*, in schools or universities as part of the regular curriculum.

Think about the career services that you may have interacted with in your life. Has anybody ever told you that one of the biggest drivers of success for you will come down to whether or not you have the ability to say no to the marshmallow? Whether you can forgo what is conveniently staring you in the face right now in order to pursue a better long-term future?

No. Unfortunately, career guidance counselors focus on helping you firm up your résumé, giving you weird tests to see which daily tasks you'd enjoy doing most in a job, and then providing you with a list of companies you should consider applying to.

All the decisions that we make, from what and when to eat, to the jobs we apply for, where we decide to live, and even who we decide to date, have monumentally huge impacts on our lives, and they all come down to one thing: Are we eating the marshmallow now, or are we waiting for two?

One of the most glorious, refreshing, and inspiring aspects of Taylor Swift's character, both professionally and from what we can see of her personal life, is that the woman isn't waiting for two marshmallows, or even three. She's waiting for hundreds.

RIGHT HERE, RIGHT NOW

The world, whether we like it and choose to believe it or not, has now been fully optimized for grabbing the marshmallow and running. In fact, I don't think there's a single industry that favors long-term thinking over short.

Consider that our clothes, which used to be made for lifelong use, have been chewed up and spit out by the consumerism of fast fashion, whose "or else" marketing tactics tell us that we should buy, buy, buy every fashion drop as they are pushed in front of us. After we have worn cheap synthetic materials that we now know to be dumping microplastics into our bloodstreams, we throw them away. Because clothes are so cheap now, we can easily buy more as the fashion retailers "drip" through our lives.

In fact, clothing-store apps have made it so easy to buy clothes that you can do it in the same way you play a game. Like it? Swipe right. Automatic purchase. It'll arrive at your door the next day. Can't afford it? Doesn't matter. For the price of three coffees a week, you can pay for it over time.

Entertainment has gone the same way with the rise of streaming. There's a chance you may be too young to remember the days when you went to school and talked about what might happen between Marissa and Ryan in this week's episode of *The O.C.* because, unlike today, back then you couldn't "binge" on a whole series of prime-time TV without moving from your sofa. With access to vast and never-ending libraries of content, how we watch TV reflects a broader shift toward needing immediate access and consumption over, I dunno . . . needing patience and the buildup of anticipation we used to experience?

And don't even get me started on social media platforms, home to hungry algorithms that are meticulously designed to get you to eat your marshmallows by prioritizing immediate, physiologically triggered feedback loops through likes and comments, all in the name of short-lived engagement with "friends" or, as they're better known today, "followers."

All of this, by the way, usually takes place on our phones, our laptops, and our devices that are specifically designed to be used and then thrown away within a single design cycle so that we can buy the next even more expensive model. And when I say "we *can* buy," what

I actually mean is "we *must* buy," because while the former version makes it seem like we have a choice whether to discard what may be a perfectly fine phone, in fact, we don't. Because the tech companies that design, manufacture, and control our devices through software engage in what is called "planned obsolescence," whereby when companies want us to buy a new model to increase their revenue, they purposefully make our devices feel like they're not working, through regressed software or poor battery performance.

And this, I'm afraid to tell you, is the hypercapitalist-optimized, short-term hellscape in which we find ourselves today. Dopamine is one hell of a drug.

In fact, after writing these depressing statements, I am rethinking the wine downstairs.

It is nearly impossible, you see, to live in a world that is optimized for short-term gain yet still try to engage with longer-term, slower, and more intentional thinking, doing, and buying. And if you think that the politicians or business folk are going to rein in this behavior, think again.

Half the problem with the overdominance of capital markets in our lives is precisely that political leaders are trapped in the same short-term crises. Facing reelection every few years, they usually prioritize policies that give immediate benefits to secure votes in the next election rather than implementing long-term solutions that will actually create the society we want and need. This has led to a cycle of short-termism in policymaking, which has totally eroded the ability to address long-term challenges like, I dunno, health care or climate change.

And don't think you can look to CEOs for answers either, because they have their hands tied in trying to keep their masters, the Wall Street traders, happy. You see, corporations are under constant pressure from shareholders and financial analysts to outperform their competition with strong quarterly earnings reports *every single quarter.*

Think about that—CEOs of publicly traded companies have to realize their ambitions and generate increasingly higher levels of revenue *every three months.* Clearly, they are forced to emphasize short-term performance at the expense of long-term investments in the technologies and infrastructure that our world needs.

If you're unsure why all of this is necessarily a bad thing, consider the following questions:

Don't bridges, motorways, houses, and energy systems take years, not quarters, to build?

Doesn't it feel good to have a friend that you have known for decades?

Isn't the item of clothing you've had the longest the most important piece in your closet?

Aren't the best brands, like Chanel, Jaguar, and Louis Vuitton, the ones that have built up their reputation over more than a century, not just a single quarter? The things we want and need that are built in the long-term, it appears, seem to be juxtaposed with the short-term nature of the modern world we live in.

However, all hope is not yet lost.

There are two people in the world of business and finance who are, against the odds, operating on the principle of long-term, *don't-eat-the-marshmallow* thinking, and it has catapulted them into the value creation Hall of Fame. They are also two people who, on the outside, couldn't be more different.

One is ninety-three years old, lives in Omaha, Nebraska, and eats a bacon, egg, and cheese McMuffin for breakfast every day. The other is slightly more than a third of his age, significantly better looking, and sings self-written songs for a living.

Warren Buffett, one of the best investors in the world and the CEO of investment fund Berkshire Hathaway, and Taylor Swift are nearly identical when it comes to their marshmallow strategy for business and life.

• ⊚ •

Known as the "Oracle of Omaha," Buffett's reputation is built on his superb, nay *extraordinary*, track record of generating consistent, long-term returns for himself and his investors through insanely high highs and insanely low lows of wider economic periods.

Unlike a lot of investors who, especially during the 2017–22 wild and exuberant market rally, made a ton of money in short-term, "pump and dump" strategies, Buffett has chosen to do the opposite. In fact, I'm about to describe Buffett's investment style in the same way that you'll have noticed me discussing Taylor Swift's personal and professional style: value-based, intelligent, ethical, and durable.

Like Taylor, he has become a celebrity not only for what he does for a living but for being a beacon of wisdom and guidance in other areas of his life too. I mean, there aren't many men worth nearly $150 billion who have been living in the same modest house in Nebraska that he purchased for $31,500 in 1958, with his wife of nineteen years, whom he married after his previous wife of more than fifty years passed away. Despite his immense wealth, he is famed for the authenticity with which he lives the gospel he preaches about being frugal and slow-moving in business and in life.

Buffett, deemed by most to be the world's greatest and most legendary investor, has been able to consistently beat the market by pursuing this simple strategy and philosophy: Follow a long-term, disciplined approach to investing.

And it is really no coincidence that Taylor Swift has become the world's most legendary singer-songwriter, beating all records, including her own, by pursuing the same simple strategy of maintaining a long-term, disciplined approach to building her brand.

LONG-TERM INVESTING

The fundamental building block to their success is predicated on leaving the marshmallow well alone.

We can see that Swift has diligently focused on creating and maintaining long-term value through her music, brand, and relationships with fans. One of the most interesting aspects of the Swiftverse, especially when considering her branding and partnerships portfolio, is how she does not use the relationship she has built up with fans to monetize her position among them.

That wasn't always the case, however. I want to take a moment to argue that before Taylor returned to Spotify, and therefore moved her entire business over to a drip, not drop strategy to build upon her Swiftverse engagement, she did participate in extensive brand partnerships: Coca-Cola, Keds (shoes), CoverGirl (cosmetics), and L.E.I. Jeans. "Love Taylor? Buy this random stuff!"

Back then, her goal was to monetize her relationship with her fans. However, as of June 2017, when she returned to Spotify, fully embracing the decentralized model, she optimized instead for increasing fan engagement, not increasing monetization.

This led to partnerships and collaborations that enabled, not distracted from, the experience of the Swiftverse. For example, with Capital One, whose credit cards enabled easier access to and purchase of Eras Tour tickets; AMC Theatres, which showed her Eras Tour movie; and Target, which stocks her physical CDs, records, and merchandise.

Although it's hard to believe, she could be making a lot more money today than she already is by engaging in a broader range of brand partnerships. But she's not, because her long-term vision is to become the most iconic brand in contemporary culture—something that takes a long *time*. And selling random stuff to her fans will do nothing but prioritize short-term revenue over her long-term goal.

Similarly, Buffett's investment philosophy centers on identifying companies with enduring and long-term competitive advantages that will generate long-term value. Anything that seems overly "sexy" and "hot," like self-driving cars, rocket launches, and artificial intelligence, where prices are driven up on a short-term basis to enrich investors, is a total no-go area for him.

Like Taylor sticking very rigidly to a small range of brand partnerships, Warren Buffett forgoes making a quick buck because the long-term risks to his business, including the very real risk of being distracted from his goal of being history's most successful investor, are not worth it.

Both Buffett's and Swift's strategies reflect a commitment to long-term value rather than taking advantage of a short-term opportunity.

STRATEGIC PATIENCE

My mother always used to tell me, "Patience is a virtue, keep it if you can; always in a woman but never in a man." This was usually a good (and rather constant, in my house) reminder of the societal and moral value of waiting to get what I wanted until a better or more advantageous time.

Taylor Swift's career is an absolute testament to strategic patience.

Consider that she could be in a math olympiad for her carefully timed album releases and how they tie to her meticulous crafting of narratives around them, all dripped into the Swiftverse, of course, as Easter eggs. Her patience is also seen in managing her brand and public image, particularly through controversies, legal battles, and in her interactions with audiences.

In 2013, Taylor accused the DJ David Mueller of groping her; he then filed a defamation lawsuit when he was fired for sexual assault, claiming damages for his lost earnings. Not only did Swift win the defamation case two years later, but in her countersuit in 2017 she was awarded damages of one dollar. That is a whole *four years of hell*. Most CEOs, executives, or businesses would settle the lawsuit to save their time, which could be better spent running the business; to save their money, because, goddamn, do you have any idea how expensive lawyers are?; and to save their emotional state from combat that will not advance their business or personal interests.

Taylor? Not a chance. She endured the long-term pain so that she could send a strong message to the world, and especially Swifties, that she would use the power they gave her to better the world (part of her "be on the right side of history" psyops campaign), and a strong message to anybody who might want to throw legal shade at her again in the future. That message? "I have deep pockets to pay for a better legal team than yours, and all the time in the world to make sure that I fuck you over right back if you come anywhere near me."

Patience, for Taylor, is a tool used to open her up to new fans, ideas, genres, and creativity, while also being the very thing that protects her.

Buffett, likewise, is the OG of patience as a strategy, known for stating that "the stock market is designed to transfer money from the Active to the Patient." In other words, his success is often realized by patiently sitting and doing nothing while very active investors who may be running around trying to make a quick buck end up losing to him. He is happy to wait for the right opportunity to invest at a fair price, and while other people are rapidly buying and selling as conditions change, he does not; he holds on to his investments through market volatility, doubling down on patience as a virtue in building long-term wealth and success.

And that's not to say, of course, that "patient" is synonymous with "sluggish" or "status quo"; when Buffett or Swift *do* make decisions, they make them at lightning speed and with conviction. As I said, Buffett is patient in waiting for the right opportunity to arise. But when it does, he moves so damn fast to own that investment space that his competitors can't keep up. Similarly, we've seen with Taylor that she has been patient with her long-term strategy of building her empire while simultaneously engaging in rapid-fire decision-making, such as when she pulled her music from Spotify.

FOCUS ON QUALITY AND AUTHENTICITY

Maybe my favorite thing that Swift and Buffett share is their focus on genuine human relationships, doing business ethically, and using authenticity not only as a way to become successful and wealthy but to build a good life.

Of course, I don't need to outline again the details of Taylor using authenticity as her core strategy for building long-term relationships, but also consider that she has a relentless emphasis on high quality and perfection, for the sake of Swifties. Combined with her authenticity, and the heart-on-her-sleeve relationship with her music and her fans, she has cultivated a staunchly loyal fan base and enduring brand that see her not as a billionaire celebrity but as the girl next door, the sister, the mother, the best friend who has been in their life for the last two decades.

In a nearly identical manner, Buffett's investment criteria include not only the economic prospects of a business ("Make money through any means possible!") but also the quality of its management. Sure, just like any investor he looks for the companies he invests in to be sound. But more than that, and unlike the majority of Wall Street, he is unwilling to overlook bad corporate behavior, CEOs and management teams that are not trustworthy, and companies and technologies that seem to make the world worse.

His investment philosophy seems to be closely linked to the question: "If I invest in this company, and it does take over the world, is that a world I would want my grandkids to live in?" If the answer is no, he won't invest.

Which sounds an awful lot like: "If I allow my music to make these men more money than they've ever had before, the same men propping up the patriarchy that keeps women like me beholden to their misogynistic interests, would the world be a better place? No? Okay. I'm out."

It's hard to fully explain how rare this sort of long-term optimization by ultrasuccessful people is. The entire world around them, including the business, financial, and legal infrastructure in which they operate, is built around the opposite of what Unicorns are optimizing.

They are, truly, one in a billion in how they think, operate, and live their lives.

But they don't *have* to be. Sure, it's easier to get sucked into dopamine-driven, algorithmic, short-term overconsumption and underambition. But it's never too late to escape the wormhole of our modern economy in favor of a better, more sustainable, and clearly, as Taylor has shown us, more successful way to live.

In the same way that the infamous Professor Michael Porter created Porter's Five Forces, which were a method of analyzing and creating optimal strategies across industries, from Taylor Swift we observe Taylor's Five Forces for moving our lives—professional and personal—from short-term misery to long-term hope.

In other words, if you're totally clueless as to how best not to go near the marshmallow today in favor of multiple marshmallows tomorrow, here's how Taylor has done it.

TAYLOR'S FIRST FORCE: COMMIT TO THE FUTURE

You don't have to tell me that people are becoming increasingly bad at committing to things, whether it's upholding plans that were made a long time ago with friends or, you know, actually deciding to stop dating ten other people even though you're convinced you've just met "the one."

I probably don't have to do much to convince you that we're living through a multigenerational commitment crisis.

In fact, one of the best talks I've ever heard was at the 2018 Harvard graduation ceremony, where a Harvard Law School graduate named Pete Davis gave a talk called "A Counterculture of Commitment." In his speech, he called out what we all know to be true: Our endless swiping across the infinite number of things that are available to us is not only harming us but it's harming the future we're failing to build.

Why spend an hour watching a movie on Netflix when you can

spend an hour trying to decide which of the available ten thousand movies to watch?

Why give a person an honest shot at dating you when you can date several other people simultaneously?

This resonates pretty strongly with a conversation I had not too long ago. I asked my friend which of two luxury items of clothing she thought I should buy as a long-term investment. Her response? Both.

Quite movingly, Davis went on to explain that while there are infinite choices on Netflix, Tinder, and even for your career after graduating from Harvard, there are negatives to constantly swiping through life:

> But as I've grown older here, I've also started seeing the downsides of having so many open doors. Nobody wants to be stuck behind a locked door, but nobody wants to *live* in a hallway either. It's great to have options when you lose interest in something, but I've learned here that the more times I do this, the less satisfied I am with *any* given option. And lately, the experiences I crave are less the rushes of novelty and more those perfect Tuesday nights when you eat dinner with the friends who you have known for a long time, who you have made a commitment to, and who will not quit you because they found someone better. . . . That is why, in this age of liquid modernity, we should rebel and join up with a counterculture of commitment consisting of solid people.

There is no doubt that thinking, acting, and living in a long-term way is better for us and the world. But the first thing we have to do if we want to unlock this superpower, as Taylor has shown us all too often, is to commit to the future we want.

We saw this in 2017, when it looked like Taylor had drastically shifted her business model to focus on long-term growth and building her fan universe instead of monetizing album drops. We also saw this in 2023, when her relationship with her then boyfriend Matty Healy ended amid scrutiny and pressure from Swifties who felt that he did not represent the values and ethics that she did.

Unless you have a vision and desire to prioritize the "tomorrow" version of you over the "today" version of you, and commit to that vision deeply, you will spend every minute of your life in a constant battle with yourself over whether you should eat the cake and the cheese downstairs.

TAYLOR'S SECOND FORCE: ALIGN YOUR LIFE TO YOUR GOALS

One of the really important findings of the marshmallow experiment at Stanford was that the kids found it infinitely harder to delay gratification and wait for two marshmallows when one marshmallow was right in front of them, practically *teasing* them.

In fact, the children ended up having to come up with all sorts of distraction tactics to force themselves not to think about the marshmallow they could see. They had to go out of their way to change their behavior in order to get the two marshmallows.

This is true of nearly everyone I know who engages in long-term strategy, whether it's personal or professional. As an easy example, consider that "You are what you eat," meaning that if you only eat unhealthy food, you will be unhealthy.

Where this is perhaps even stronger, yet is somehow less frequently discussed, is that you, as a person, are in large part a combination of the five people you spend the most amount of time with. You become enmeshed with their personalities, their values, how they dress, what they read, and generally how they live their lives.

This is one of the biggest reasons that high-performing people tend to spend most of their time with . . . you guessed it, other high-performing people. Likewise, when you see celebrities hanging out with other celebrities, it is mostly because celebrities live really, *really* weird lives compared to normal people. And it's just hard for normal people to relate to that or to understand and adapt accordingly.

I recently rewatched *Notting Hill*, starring Julia Roberts and Hugh Grant, and was very surprised to realize that the entire premise of that movie, like so many of my other favorites, is built upon an impossibility. No, the megafamous star cannot adapt to your life as a bookshop owner. And nor will you ever adapt to hers. And the bakery shop owner will never actually be able to marry the secret Prince of Aldovia, Maldavia, Astrovia, or wherever they're from.

If the entire world is geared up to convince you, everywhere you look, that you should *go on, just eat the damn marshmallow*, then like the kids who developed distraction tactics, you need to remove yourself from that world as much as you can.

They say that systems beat motivation, and it's true. Building a system of people and preferences into your life that reflects your bigger, better, long-term goals is going to make it far easier to achieve them than trying to do it by motivation alone.

Why? Because it is hard trying to make trade-offs in your mind all the time. Should I go downstairs and drink the wine, or should I keep writing and go for a run later? Now, imagine if the wine wasn't in my fridge, chilling to be opened, in the first place. It wouldn't even occur to me that I may *not* write and run.

Taylor's friends are ultrasuccessful business executives and investors (Ryan Reynolds), performers (Lana Del Rey), and, well, I don't know enough about American football to comment on who she may be dating. The point being that surrounding yourself with excellence will force excellence to be your minimum acceptable standard.

Don't commit only to a vision, but commit to making the changes in your life that will serve the vision you have committed to by favoring your long-term interests.

TAYLOR'S THIRD FORCE: PRACTICE THE PAIN

As I outlined in Power Move One, you often see that someone who is a high-performing person in one field is a high-performing person in another field. Look at Taylor Swift. Sure, she's going to be, if she isn't already, the world's most listened-to artist of all time. But I strongly suspect we're about to see TS Act II come into play, whereby she branches out more fully into other creative areas where she's also a superstar.

Let's not forget that she's a Unicorn in a singer-songwriter capacity, but as I've already noted, she is also a top investor, as well as a top adviser and thought leader.

So, how is it possible that one person can be so good at so many things?

I strongly suspect it's because people who have learned how to block out short-term pain in one area of their lives can easily apply this in several other areas of their lives. I'll use myself as an example here. Anybody who met teenage me would likely agree that I was a bit of a wild child. I loved to participate in and to conjure up shenanigans more than nearly anything else. However, when I went to university to begin my undergrad, a lot of that changed. Why? Because I joined the rowing team.

Rowing is up there with swimming, cycling, and being a jockey in terms of self-flagellation. It takes complete, total, and utter dedication to force yourself to endure numerous painful and long training sessions each day. In particular, my least favorite training session consisted of being stuck on the rowing machine for a ninety-minute period, rowing mindlessly and repetitively into the void, with each stroke taken as painful as the last, for what seemed like ten eternities. No amount of music, daydreaming, or wishful thinking could have made those sessions less torturous.

But you know what? I did, eventually, get more used to them. Did they get easier? Physically, no. But mentally, I guess so.

However, the real impact of those gym and water sessions was outside the rowing team. I found that after only a year of training in this military-style regime, a lot of "hard" things just felt easier. I found that when it came time to study for exams, I could sit at my desk and concentrate for eight, nine, ten, or more hours straight without needing a break.

In fact, I had actually come to really enjoy the discipline.

Despite the fact that I had less time for studying, my grades actually got better, not worse. And I found that in all aspects of my life, I became totally unafraid to tackle "hard" things, because they just didn't seem that intimidating anymore.

I see this among my friends who are Unicorns, and likewise among the HPPs I do not know personally. They all have an endurance mindset that, over time, has made the "pain" part of the short-term pain nearly disappear.

This, rather obviously, makes the short-term pain versus long-term gain trade-off sound stupid, or even obsolete. Long-term thinking and acting becomes a win-win situation.

I am convinced, having seen it myself firsthand, that the ability to no longer feel inconvenient pain is something that can be taught and learned over time. The reason that Olympic athletes don't just hit the snooze button at 5:00 a.m. and go back to sleep like the rest of us is not that they possess superhuman qualities that are beyond our reach. Rather, and perhaps more boringly, it's just that they're used to it.

In what felt like a bit of a comedown, I remember my Olympic athlete friend Paul O'Donovan, an HPP both in rowing and in his "main job" of being a doctor, telling me something that shocked me. When I asked him how he deals with the constant pain, sacrifice, and trade-offs, he simply said:

"I really don't like doing hard things. If I found this hard, I wouldn't do it. I'm lazy, just like all humans."

If you're like me, this will make absolutely no sense to you at first. But what he really meant, I presume, is that he has already trained himself not to feel the pain. Because engaging in pain, all day, every day, for long-term benefits is just not feasible or sustainable.

Swift herself says that she ran on a treadmill for the length of her show for six months prior to starting her Eras Tour, all while singing her tracklist. All I'm going to say about her ability to tolerate pain is that none of the professional runners I follow on Strava or Instagram who tried to do the same thing could do it multiple days in a row.

People who engage in long-term mindsets, especially HPPs, find mental and physical ways to train their mind and body not to notice the pain anymore. ·

TAYLOR'S FOURTH FORCE:
KNOW WHEN TO SAY NO

Closely linked to Taylor's Third Force is the Fourth, that nobody—and I really do mean *nobody*—can do impossible things all day, every day, without a break. I mean, even Taylor Swift, the queen of doing eight thousand things in a single day, discusses how she takes her downtime as seriously as an Olympic sport.

If you were an alien, and you came down to Earth for one day, I strongly suspect the strangest thing about our society that you'd tell your off-Earth friends about is our diet culture.

Never eat meat.

Only eat meat.

Eggs give you cancer. So do milk and dairy.

Don't drink red wine. But also, drink red wine.

Not eating eggs gives you cancer, by the way.

Now, I'm never going to be a Victoria's Secret model myself, so my advice here will probably be disregarded. But there's strong anecdotal and even scientific evidence that says: *You gotta know when to pull back from the extremes.* In other words, you have to know your own limits so well that you know how not to breach them.

Although the world seems to be full of people, usually influencers, preaching all sorts of extreme diets, clean living, and utterly bizarre daily rituals that are supposedly going to turboboost your health, wealth, and happiness, I'd be curious to see how many of these people who have recently popped up are still living by these standards in five, ten, or fifteen years' time. It is possible to do anything to the extreme for short bursts, but impossible to do it over the long run.

In fact, the desire to engage in long-term ambitions while forgoing short-term wins is only possible when you know your own limits well enough to reduce the pressure that comes along with such ambitions. For example, while many people who sign up for the gym in January as part of a New Year's resolution will turn up twice a day for training after not having seen a treadmill in a year, an elite athlete will never overtrain. They are so in tune with their bodies that they can mentally quantify the harm that pushing themselves too hard will incur.

It turns out that optimizing to be "the best," or "elite," means acknowledging that you will have periods when you are at 100 percent of your max, mixed with very necessary periods when you exist at 2 percent of your max.

As any athlete will tell you, downtime is one of the most important parts of your training schedule!

You'll be delighted to know that it's the same with food. Last year, I went to one of the world's five "Blue Zones," regions where people live much longer than elsewhere. In Sicily, I found that people's lives seemed to be the exact opposite of what efficiency-obsessed career optimizers online suggest. They drank lots of wine, ate lots of fish, and consumed lots of carbs(!). They spent a lot of time walking around, being sociable, and visiting their friends. They put family ahead of career and . . . honestly, they were just *happy*.

They were not journaling at 4:30 a.m. before going to the gym at 5:00. They did not drink bone broth for breakfast, lunch, and dinner, followed by Pilates and breathing work. They did not automate their emails, avoid seeing their friends, or have a ten-year ban on booze.

Taylor, as far as we can tell, is an ultrasuccessful "when I'm on, I'm on, and when I'm off, I'm off" kinda CEO. Because when she's working, she's producing multiple albums and on a global tour. And when she's off, it's taco takeout and a bottle of wine. This is eerily similar to Warren Buffett, who, despite being a seemingly healthy ninety-three-year-old who has yet to announce his retirement, seems to live his life somewhere between being the most knowledgeable person alive about the industries he invests in and taking his time every morning to have a McDonald's breakfast.

As Taylor said herself in a commencement speech at NYU in 2022 when she was awarded an honorary doctorate:

"Life can be heavy, especially if you try to carry it all at once. Part of growing up and moving into new chapters of your life is about catch and release. What I mean by that is, knowing what things to keep, and what things to release."

In other words, be comfortable living in the gray zone, where you cut yourself some invaluable slack between the black and the white.

TAYLOR'S FIFTH FORCE: NEVER BE BEHOLDEN TO OTHERS

There is very little point in killing yourself to do any of the above in order to optimize for delayed gratification when you don't actually have control over your life in the ways that are important in the first place.

Let's imagine that you have set yourself up, in every possible way, to refuse the one marshmallow. You are *determined* to get two. You are willing to wait it out. You have your strategy in place.

Then, all of a sudden, the experiment is changed; the professor at Stanford tells you, Sorry, you actually have to eat this. There won't be two down the line. And in fact, you're only going to get *half* of this marshmallow.

One of the least obvious pitfalls about trying to change from dopamine-based careers, relationships, and lives to being driven by long-term purpose and sustainability in pursuit of success is that, a lot of the time, we don't actually have enough control over our own lives to make that decision.

Being beholden to other people's interests is, actually, more often than not an outcome of pursuing short-term gain and is a hard cycle to break out of.

It's like the story that's commonly told about the guy who works in finance and goes to work every day saying: "Only ten more years of this before I can afford to be a fisherman in the Caribbean!" Of course, the sad irony is that the financier obviously has a lot more wealth than the fisherman, begging the question that I asked of my private equity friend who wanted to open a French bakery: Why do you need so much money to go live your dream?

People who think this way will never, unfortunately, realize their dream. Why? Well, one reason is because they are a dead fish about to join other dead fish swimming downstream. But the main reason is that by the time they end up earning a million dollars a year, they will find it impossible to go back to earning and being happy on much less than that.

To this day, I have yet to meet a single person who was able to step out of the short-term corporate lifestyle optimized for quarter-to-quarter earnings in order to switch to long-term, values-based existence. Mostly because, as Taylor's Second Force tells us, you are who you surround yourself with. Eventually, these people's friends will all be living lifestyles based on annual bonuses that are determined by quarterly, or even weekly, profits and losses. Their spouse will either be someone who does exactly the same thing or whose lifestyle relies on that culture. To chase a dream in France, they will have to leave behind family, friends, and pretty much their entire existence.

As people get older, they forget about their dreams, which suddenly feel "too hard" to pursue because they didn't follow Taylor's Third Force of practicing the pain. Instead, they gave in and gave up.

These people are, for better or worse, beholden to the status quo, and in due course will become beholden to every algorithm that uses their data, every private equity investor who owns everything around them, and every chief marketing officer who "or elses" them into buying so much stuff to prop up share prices that they can't afford to ever leave their job in search of happiness.

There's a reason Warren Buffett, despite being worth a cool $150 billion, lives in a house valued at only 0.0009 percent of his wealth. And there's a reason Taylor Swift nearly killed herself to re-record her masters.

Unlike politicians to their voters, and CEOs to their shareholders, and investors to the stock market, the key to reaching the two marshmallows is being able to control your life and avoiding the short-term trap that prevents most people from getting there: being beholden to those who benefit from you staying down.

That's not to say, of course, that people like Warren Buffett or Taylor Swift don't have somebody, somewhere, that they're at least in small part beholden to. I mean, Taylor wrote a whole damn song about the Swifties who protested her relationship with Matty Healy so strongly that, as some commentators noted, it may have caused the relationship's demise. In "But Daddy I Love Him," she goes as far as to say: "*I just learned these people only raise you to cage you.*" The very fans that granted her the position as the most celebrated female artist the world has ever seen were now trying to dictate the terms and conditions of her life.

Likewise, Warren Buffett has some incredibly important stakeholders who influence his actions: the investors whose money he is investing! And if they don't like the way he is doing that, they will stop giving him money in the same way that Swifties can stop streaming Taylor's music or buying her tour tickets.

Ultimately, there's nobody in this world who doesn't have to consider at least *someone* when they make decisions, personal or professional. But the ultimate Power Move is being strategic in who you ultimately decide you are beholden to, and why.

* ● ●

Pete Davis, in his Harvard commencement speech, added:

> When Hollywood tells tales of courage, they usually take the form of "slaying the dragon"—it's all about the big, brave moments. But I've been learning from these heroes that the most menacing dragons that stand in the way of reforming the system or repairing the breach are the everyday boredom and distraction and uncertainty that can erode our ability to commit to anything for the long haul.

The quick Instagram scroll. Casually flicking through dozens of movies but never watching any of them. Buying both coats because you couldn't figure out which one you preferred.

Can you imagine Taylor Swift endlessly doomscrolling on Instagram? No, neither can I. And not because she's superfamous and has people who likely could do that on her behalf. The reason you cannot imagine Taylor swiping endlessly through short-form, brain-numbing content that distracts her from her life is because that's just not how people with long-term vision and purpose spend their days, weeks, or lives.

And success, especially one-in-many-generations success, is nearly entirely predicated on leaving that marshmallow damn well alone.

POWER MOVE TEN

DON'T LET SUCCESS KILL YOU

TAYLOR SWIFT HAS PEAKED. TAYLOR SWIFT REPRESENTS EVERY-thing that is wrong with the world. Taylor Swift is monoculture. Taylor Swift is over. Right?

There is a famous scene in *Jurassic Park* where the two kids are hiding out in their car in the park at night. The water in two cups on the car's dashboard starts rippling. Suddenly, they hear a noise so loud that it reverberates around them. As it gets louder, it is clear that the thuds belong to a dinosaur approaching them.

The water on the dashboard of the car serves as a visual indication of the closeness of the dinosaur—small vibrations on the surface of the water at first eventually lead to the two cups shaking.

An enormously monstrous dinosaur is among them and about to make its presence known. The question for the kids in the car is: Is it a *good* dinosaur or a *bad* dinosaur?

I thought about *Jurassic Park* as I sat in Boston's Gillette Stadium with my gin in a plastic cup perched on the stadium wall in front of me, as the clock on the stage was ticking down the seconds to "midnight" to begin the Eras Tour show.

Ten seconds. Rumble rumble rumble.

Five seconds. Rumble rumble rumble.

I look at my glass, which is vibrating.

As the clock strikes "midnight," the stadium explodes into a deafening roar.

The question for the Swifties in the stadium is: For how much longer will Taylor be allowed to be seen as a *good* force to be reckoned with, instead of a *bad* one?

· ● ·

Since civilization began, people have been trying to predict the future.

Long before technology existed, sailors came up with rules of thumb to try to predict the next day's weather conditions. After all, their lives depended on it.

"Red sky at night, sailor's delight. Red sky in the morning, sailors take warning."

Similarly, farmers desperately tried to predict the weather in order to manage their crops as their (and their families') livelihoods depended on it. For example, old wisdom will tell you that the time just before the full moon is considered particularly wet, and is best for planting during drought conditions.

Today, we also try to predict the future. Economists try to predict whether inflation is going to go up or down. Stock traders try to predict the direction of stock prices at certain times. Political analysts try to predict who will vote for which candidate.

The thing about predicting the future, however, is that you *can't*. And the thing about people who *try* to predict the future is that nine times out of ten, they end up looking like complete *morons*.

"Inflation *has to* go down next quarter. It is guaranteed. Therefore we should decrease interest rates," says the economist, who "predicts the future" with a spreadsheet that is wrong far more often than it is right.

Apart from the fact that it's impossible to predict the future, we seem to take a lot of comfort from listening to people who try to.

In Ireland, for example, hardly anybody "checks the weather" before starting their day. I mean, there's just no point. When you live on an island in the North Atlantic Ocean over which cool westerly weather systems from North America and the Atlantic mix with hot easterly weather systems from the European continent, anything is possible. But rain is guaranteed.

I remember an American friend visiting Ireland. As we ate breakfast, he "checked the weather" and told me that, miraculously, it was not going to rain today!

"I think you're wrong," I told him dryly.

"No, seriously! Look. Zero rain! We can do a hike today!"

"Umm. Look out the window behind you," I replied, and he turned around and saw that it was already lashing down rain.

But people check the weather and read stock market forecasts and pay a lot of money for the opinion of people who look to the future because it makes them at least *feel* like they have more control over our wild, unpredictable, and increasingly chaotic universe.

It should come as no surprise to learn, then, that the business of predicting the future is booming. We just can't consume *enough* content that predicts the horrifying, morbid, euphoric, ecstatic, deathly, murderous, elated future of ours.

And there's nothing that people like to predict more than the demise of a great icon.

"Taylor Swift fatigue," said *The New York Times* when *The Tortured Poets Department* was released, in an album review that went viral.

Just how much Taylor Swift is too much Taylor Swift? The article reflected,

> Four new studio albums. Four rerecorded albums, too. A $1 billion oxygen-sucking world tour with a concert movie to match. And, of course, one very high-profile relationship that spilled over into the Super Bowl.

They say that there are only two certainties in life: death and taxes. Well, I'd like to offer up a third certainty for contemplation:

That the global media will always piggyback off the positive momentum of a rising star, building them up in a symbiotic relationship that benefits both parties, before unanimously deciding that the rising star has risen too far, and further enriching itself by cutting that star down.

The media's current mandate is to generate revenue—*any* revenue at all—in a world in which traditional media is being consolidated, people are no longer engaging in traditional formats, and market share has been utterly decimated by online social media platforms like Instagram and TikTok. The media is incentivized, at any and all cost to the truth, to make a quick buck.

The easiest way to do that is by selling predictions that, right or wrong, engage people in surface-level "hot takes" that are controversial. It's called clickbait. It's called *Taylor Swift Fatigue.*

This begs two questions.

The first is, Are we not allowed to critique Taylor Swift without it being viewed as a lie-embedded, clickbait-focused, nonsense piece of content? To which the answer is that we emphatically, absolutely can.

In fact, I've just spent the previous nine chapters of this book explaining to you how powerful she is; how smart she is; how rich she is; how much she influences the minds and actions of hundreds of millions of people, global corporations, the European and US federal banks, and elections; and how she is the cultural icon of our decade.

It would be incredibly and horrifically negligent *not* to allow for important discourse around Taylor's so far supreme reign over our cultural, political, and economic attention.

However, of the hundreds (and hundreds and hundreds) of headlines, tweets, comments under comments on Reddit, newspaper articles, magazine articles, YouTube videos, podcast interviews, and discussions, one thing has become clear.

Some people have predicted that "Taylor has peaked!" every single year since *1989* came out.

Other people are predicting that "Taylor is just getting started!"

The chasm between these two predictions of Taylor's future trajectory grows with every album Taylor releases, public appearance she makes, and Easter egg she drops. One side rolls their eyes, while the other has another turn forced upon their already tightly wound spring.

And so, while reality tends to live somewhere between two extremes, I'd like to examine this question in more detail:

Where does Taylor Swift go from here?

*   *   *

Because I'm not enough of a moron to try to predict the future as many journalists, economists, financiers, and weather people do, I'm going to examine the future of Taylor Swift in the context of the hundreds of businesses I've examined that have risen and fallen in the capitalist system.

Very simply, there are three future scenarios for Taylor, Inc.

The first is the future in which Taylor, per the Swifties' current prediction, is just getting started. She continues on this insanely exponential growth trajectory to amass more success in the form of an increasingly large Swiftverse, higher numbers of Taylor "superusers" or die-hard fans, and continued financial success.

The second alternative future is the one in which she crashes and burns, per the headlines of many frustrated "but-I-just-don't-get-her" journalists and traditional industry analysts. It kind of feels like there may be two scenarios in this future that are real possibilities. In the first, she is villainized and crowds with pitchforks come for her. The second scenario is significantly less negative; while her market share of our time, attention, money, and influence decreases significantly, she is not regarded as public enemy number one, but merely remembered in a positive light as "Wow, that was a weird few years" in museum exhibitions and discarded friendship bracelets.

The third possible future is one in which she kinda just stays where she is, maintaining her current level of fame and being an It Girl in music, fashion, sports (hello NFL), and beyond.

I want to start by quickly throwing away that possible future I just mentioned, for the following reasons.

We live in a world that is increasingly binary: You love it, or you hate it. It's on, or it's off. This is driven by the ways in which our world has become algorithmically curated, and by winner-takes-all dynamics that force the concentration of power and money onto seemingly fewer people, products, and companies.

Stagnation is an incredibly hard thing to sustain when an entity has so much momentum behind it. Think about those crazy bobsled athletes who throw themselves down ice chutes at 95 miles per hour. They can either keep getting faster as they gain momentum, or they can crash off the side. It's nearly impossible for them, given the laws of physics, not to speed up at all and to remain in a perfect equilibrium where neither acceleration nor friction overcomes the other.

Like the laws of physics, the laws of business and finance dictate that "stillness" is a near impossibility, especially when media, tech platforms, and the attention economy only become profitable when someone is 100 percent on or 100 percent off. It's like the venture capitalist who only wants to invest in companies that are worth $1 billion or nothing. Somewhere in between is no good.

So let's imagine, for the sake of argument that gets us closer to reality, that Taylor can only really get a lot bigger or get a lot smaller.

TOO MUCH OF A GOOD THING

The reactions to Taylor Swift's *The Tortured Poets Department* were one of the most insightful ways to understand the trajectory that she and the Taylor, Inc. brand were on.

For her, *TTPD* represented the first album release that would portray her in a starkly different way from every single album that had come before it, for one very specific reason: Taylor Swift has made it very, very clear to the world that she is no longer the underdog.

This sudden change of narrative, in which she is a multibillion-dollar brand, tied into the fact that she is bigger than any single singer-songwriter has ever been, has led to a moment of possible weakness for Taylor.

This inflection point can be used to strengthen her offering and double down on her trajectory, or cause her castle to crumble overnight.

There are two mechanisms that could cause Taylor to crash and burn. The first is that she becomes a victim of her own success; the second is that somebody else replaces her.

Let's consider the first.

TAYLOR BECOMES TOO BIG, TOO SUCCESSFUL, TOO *MUCH*

This is actually a very common cause of many business downfalls, and it can be seen scattered throughout the recent history of business, innovation, and capitalism.

It is assumed that all big and successful businesses follow a similar growth trajectory, which is as follows: Initially, the company is young, scrappy, and determined. It's small and nimble, so it can go far on very little money and with very few employees. Because of its speed and low running costs, it can innovate quickly and try lots of new and different things to see what fits best with its consumers.

In many ways, this was Taylor when she was younger. She moved quickly through genres and experimented with lyrics, motifs, and visual imagery that went on to define her brand when she realized what resonated most with her audiences. In doing so, she was able to grow very quickly.

The second stage of a successful company is when it has found a good fit with its consumers, and so it can stop experimenting and double down on its core offering. This is a bit like when Facebook was rolled out to its billions of users all over the world. The company grew in size, going from tens of employees to tens of thousands. It is during this phase that a company makes concrete its vision of becoming the "biggest in the industry" and matures in how it operates.

Growth at this stage of a business's life cycle is nearly guaranteed as long as it doesn't do anything weird or bad. Therefore, doing anything risky becomes *too* risky; it is much better for the company to stick with what it knows.

In my mind, this is very much the *Lover* and *folklore* era. Taylor has established an extremely strong fan base and brand identity, and now she just needs to continue to maintain her core offering to her fans.

The final stage of a business life cycle is the one in which the company has made the complete transition from a light and fast speedboat to a full-on oil tanker. It is bureaucratic from layers and layers of middle management, and the organization is so large that it cannot do anything quickly. Indeed, it can't do anything remotely risky or innovative either, because it needs to get approval from its hundreds of complex stakeholders in order to proceed. So it just doesn't even bother trying. The company is predictable, has minimal growth, and is in constant danger of being wiped out by the very fact that its size and success have turned it into something that can no longer offer customers what they want.

This is, potentially, where we see Taylor Swift right now—nearing the completion of her transition from speedboat to oil tanker. Slow, unable to turn quickly in response to incoming threats, and bureaucratic.

In particular, you can look at the reviews of her *TTPD* to better understand the specific ways in which those with a critical eye are starting to position her, through two main complaints.

"*Taylor is not innovating*" is the first, which highlights the biggest, most widely recognized, and age-old problem that big and successful businesses battle with. They are just too big to be innovative.

And Taylor is not immune to this issue herself, as she faces exactly the same problems that face every CEO of a multibillion-dollar conglomerate I've ever met.

Something that you frequently hear about child stars is that they emotionally "freeze" at the age at which they became famous. I'll come back to this point in more detail shortly. Whether this actually happened to Taylor or not, one of the big reasons for the perception that she has frozen is the reality that when you become famous or successful the world becomes a very different place.

Extreme success or fame changes your life in two very specific ways. The first is that everybody wants to talk to you, all the time. I, personally, am obviously not anywhere close to this level of fame or success, yet I *still* find myself wondering every other weekend if it would be worth changing my phone number and cutting off contact with the world. I can't imagine how hard it must be to be famous and have so many people constantly emailing, calling, texting, Tik-Toking, WhatsApping, tweeting, and every other form of DMing you, 24-7.

The solution to this complex problem is surprisingly simple: Cut everybody out of your life apart from a very small number of people. The president of the United States wants to talk to Taylor Swift? Great, they can go through her publicist, Tree Paine.

I'm not kidding you. These Unicorns get really good at having no contact with the "outside world" and forgo any obsession with celebrities themselves, unless it's managed through the appropriate PR and branding people on their team as a business transaction. For example, I know an extremely famous sports person who was asked to join a former US president for a game of golf. By the time the request reached him through his management team, his wife had already said no. They were repainting their kitchen that weekend.

To preserve any sense of *I-am-still-a-functioning-human-being*-ness, these people have to literally isolate themselves from the outside noise.

The second way in which success and fame impact your life is that you begin to trust *nobody*, because you, yourself, have turned into a financial commodity about whom information—like your most personal details—can be bought and sold around you. In fact, the lengths that famous people go to in order to weed out the untrustworthy people around them are extreme, as the now infamous dispute between two high-profile soccer players' wives, Rebekah Vardy and Coleen Rooney, dubbed "Wagatha Christie," showed us.

If you don't have the time or inclination to go through such lengthy and complex ways to figure out whom you can trust or not, by far the easiest thing to do is to once again cut everybody out of your circle and make your world much, much smaller.

In fact, being surrounded by a tiny number of people is for most people at these high levels of success the *only way* in which you can function. And while this may solve two big problems that you face on an everyday basis in the short term, it leads to the creation of another much bigger, long-term problem: Successful people may become unable to innovate.

Being innovative requires constant exposure to new ideas, people, arts, cultures, ways of thinking and doing things, and risk-centered experiences. People like Taylor experience this level of success because they are so innovative. So what happens when the very thing that drove your success—innovation—is now the very thing that you can't figure out how to achieve?

This is the number one problem for the most important executives and corporations in the world.

We can see that this is a question that may start to haunt Taylor soon, as the reviews of her *TTPD* allude to her music as increasingly "boring," "similar to her last few albums," "unnecessary," "disappointing," "flat," "cringeworthy," and more.

In particular, it seems apparent that Taylor has come to rely on her small squad of friends to fulfill her future potential, with Jack Antonoff and Aaron Dessner producing familiar-sounding tracks, album after album, and persistent contributions from those friends very close to her and within her immediate group, such as Lana Del Rey, Phoebe Bridgers, the girl band HAIM, Zoë Kravitz, and now Post Malone, who happened to have a tattoo of Travis Kelce's name when the collaboration happened.

As your world gets smaller, your creativity diminishes at the same rate as the risk of venturing out into the real world becomes too great, and the trade-off is to settle into comfortable progression that may feel, at least to some music critics, "devoid of stylistic evolution."

"Taylor is losing authenticity" is the second way in which she could see her brand collapsing under the weight of her success, threatening to make a full departure from the very thing that fuels her central strategy in the first place—being authentic.

Given the extent to which she relies on authenticity as the very premise for the existence of the Swiftverse, Taylor's success has pushed her, unwillingly, into a new era in which she will begin to struggle to control the narrative on her authenticity.

If anything has become clear throughout her Eras Tour and *TTPD*'s release, it's that there's just no possible way to think of Taylor Swift as the BFF that you text when you're feeling down and out anymore, because while you're at home feeling miserable about the guy who ghosted you only a month after you exchanged I love yous, Taylor is on one of her private jets flying across the world to make an appearance at the Super Bowl with her very famous, very successful, very modelesque girlfriends.

While you're sitting at home in your pajamas, unable to eat from the nauseatedness of being lovesick (yet simultaneously getting over-full on ice cream), Taylor is feeling heartbroken onstage performing in front of hundreds of thousands of people.

We are simply no longer the same. My boyfriend isn't the biggest thing in the NFL. I'm not a billionaire. I don't threaten to sue climate activists for monitoring where my private jet is going.

Inauthenticity is a tough criticism to try to counter, because often when there are claims of its appearance, it's an irrefutable feeling that people allude to, rather than an irrefutable fact.

Let's take, for example, Taylor's seemingly rapid and very public relationship rebound with top NFL athlete Travis Kelce. The discussion around the time of their relationship debut focused on one key question:

Is this a publicity stunt?

It is one thing to authentically write about your feelings while you wear your heart on your sleeve. After all, this look inside Taylor's very real and very raw world is the exact underlying premise of the entirety of the Swiftverse.

It is another thing entirely to try to PR your way into mass media focus. When Swifties start asking, "Wait, is this real? Should we include this in our universe or not? I'm not sure I trust it," you're starting to lose the game.

And it's hard to know what is real and what's not. At the same time as the Swift–Kelce debut, Big Brand Collaborations™ were in overdrive. Barbie and Tiffany's. Actually, Barbie and just about anything. Marvel and just about anything. Louis Vuitton handbags and just about anything.

Celebrities, too, started to "collaborate" their brands through the guise of faux relationships. During the final filming and initial marketing stages of the movie *Anyone But You*, actor Glen Powell, thought to have been engaged at the time, started what was perceived as an off-screen affair with coleading actor Sydney Sweeney—the Next Big Thing in celebrity actors.

It turned out, after endless media hype, that Glen Powell had ended his engagement prior to the promotional tour and that the entire supposed relationship had been fake.

My point here is that it's hard to figure out what's real or not, in an age when brands—including individual actors and performers—are being forced to combine their multibillion-dollar brand values in the hope of reaching next-level sales of upcoming music, movie, or season ticket releases.

My goal here is not to speculate on whether or not Taylor is in fact truly in a relationship with Kelce, because it nearly doesn't matter. As she showed us through *TTPD*, she is incredibly good at keeping the parts of her life that she wants to keep secret, secret. I mean, she had a decade-long situationship with Matty Healy, which she only added as a dimension to the Swiftverse when she felt ready to.

But my goal here is to say that achieving long-held authenticity is hard, and maintaining it is even harder, especially when you reach superstar status in the age of sharp capitalism that requires bigger and bolder ways to maintain and even grow your market share.

And once there's even a whiff of inauthenticity, real or perceived, nearly everything can be seen through that light. Taylor has moved very rapidly from being the artist who was willing to take a massive cut on her *1989* album release numbers on Spotify when she withdrew her music in order to prove her point, to being the artist who is criticized for releasing a double album within a couple of hours to "play the numbers game" on Spotify to break any streaming record that may have existed.

There's an extremely fine line between coming across as authentic or not, especially when you're trying to balance artistry with consumer capitalism. However, when she has left some fans wondering whether the double album was necessary because of the extent of Taylor's heartbreak, or simply because she wanted to flood the market with content to win streaming records, Taylor Swift may be starting to lose at least some of the Swifties who have only one foot inside the Swiftverse.

Whether it's a lack of innovation or a lack of authenticity, managing a multibillion-dollar brand with extraordinarily high levels of emotional expectation from hundreds of millions of consumers across multiple products—music, tours, merchandise, brand partnerships—is next-level hard. And the more Taylor will try to manage each of these "fine lines," the more she will fall under the scrutiny of watchful eyes who claim her to be money hungry, power hungry, inauthentic, and boring.

Success is a double-edged sword, and often the success that makes a global business is the same thing that breaks a global business.

Now, let's consider the second way she could crash and burn.

TAYLOR IS REPLACED BY SOMEBODY ELSE

If you're an up-and-coming artist, you may be reading this and thinking: "There's absolutely no way anybody can replace her."

She has the global media behind her. She has every brand wanting to work with her. She practically owns Spotify. She has all the industry people in her back pocket. She has hundreds of millions of people waiting around for her to tell them what to buy. In fact, her distribution network is so good that there was one time she accidentally released an eight-second clip of white noise called "Track 3" on Spotify and it immediately became a number one hit. Everything this woman touches turns into gold.

You, on the other hand, have nothing. Nobody knows your name. You have a TikTok account with four hundred followers that hasn't grown in a month. You can't get agents to even open your emails, never mind respond to them. In what seems like a cruel joke, record labels have told you that they won't even consider signing you until you're very, very famous, making you think: "If I was already famous, I wouldn't need you!"

How on earth can someone—*anyone*—infiltrate and pop the Taylor Swift bubble? It's just not possible.

Well, believe it or not, this is exactly the question that business executives spend most of their time thinking about. "Our competitor has a $200 billion valuation, and we're only worth $1 million. How do we beat them?!" Most of the time, you don't. As people often correctly point out in such situations, power, money, and market share are far too concentrated for you to be able to penetrate what feels like has become a self-fulfilling prophecy of everlasting success.

However, history shows us that it is possible to dislocate even the biggest competitors after all. Consider that a company called Kodak used to be one of the leading multimedia technology companies in the world. Or even think about the fact that hundreds of thousands of words have been typed onto paper in books, policy papers, and antitrust journals about how on earth we're ever going to control Facebook's seemingly unending power and control.

Today, both Kodak and Facebook have lost their pioneering edge and market dominance, despite scholars, politicians, and financiers never thinking that it could be possible.

How, though, have competitors been able to come in and eat up their market share? The answer is simple and comes down to a theory created by a Harvard Business School innovation economist called Clayton Christensen, whom I was lucky enough to have worked with.

His framework for figuring out how to knuckle your way into the market, even when the space seems to have been taken up by a really enormous player already, is called the "theory of disruptive innovation." It works this way.

Every big company, as you now know, is extremely bureaucratic and slow. They don't innovate much, and they tend to double down on the offering they provide to their core customers. In fact, they dedicate nearly 100 percent of their resources to giving these customers increasingly complex, fancy, and savvy products and services that become, over time, growingly expensive to the end customer.

There are, however, customers who don't want all this fancy and expensive stuff. They just want something simple. For example, there are people who don't want to pay fifteen hundred dollars for an iPhone with an insane camera; they just want a hundred-dollar "dumb-phone" that they can use to text and call.

A new company can enter the market by deciding to serve the people who don't want the bells and whistles—by providing the hundred-dollar phones. Since Apple doesn't care about these people because they don't spend that much money, it's a win-win. The new company gets some customers, and the customers get exactly what they want.

Over time, however, the new company will start to innovate and create more products with higher complexity. They will release a four-hundred-dollar phone with better specifications, and so even more customers from Apple will decide they don't need the fifteen-hundred-dollar phone. After another couple of years, the new company, realizing it is smaller, faster, and cheaper for them to innovate than it is for Apple, will release a nine-hundred-dollar phone that will be nearly exactly the same as an iPhone. Now Apple has a real problem on its hands. Seemingly out of nowhere, a company started peeling off its customers without Apple noticing. And by the time this progression has been noticed, *it's too late* for Apple to do anything about it. The new company is seen as more innovative, fresher, and cheaper.

In other words, a new entrant into the market can very easily steal the customers who do not need all the fancy stuff that the dominant company is offering, and over time it can increase its offering to peel off more and more of the dominant company's core customers, making it seem like a much better offering than the status quo.

Taylor Swift is not immune to this theory of disruption. In fact, if I were on her management team, I would be looking around her right now, wondering exactly who is likely to be trying to disrupt her in this way.

Consider the fact that, while the Swiftverse is absolutely, monumentally massive, there are also a lot of people who are not in the Swiftverse. And *The Tortured Poets Department* made one thing painfully obvious: If you haven't followed Taylor's journey through the Swiftverse for the last few years, and if you're not up to date on the extreme intricacies of Swiftverse lore, then this album isn't going to make much sense to you. In fact, it's going to be pretty inaccessible. So much of the value of her music is now about mapping relationships, dimensions, and key characters in her world. To a large extent, this has become one of the prevailing mechanisms upon which the entire Swiftverse grows, perhaps even as much as the *music itself.*

This example becomes really relatable to even me, despite being a huge Swiftie, when I consider the fact that I never went to see any of the early Marvel movies, and the whole Marvel Cinematic Universe has been going on for so many years and feels so complex that by now it's easier not to engage with it at all rather than try to figure out where to start.

Should a new Marvelesque movie series be announced that had a considerably lower time and energy commitment, with an opportunity to start a fresh and uncomplicated relationship from the beginning, I'd certainly be interested in getting on board with it.

So there are a considerable number of people who are the Taylor equivalent of "give me something cheaper than an iPhone." And there are a lot of singer-songwriters who have good, catchy music. And you can turn on a song, understand it, and leave without having to do a PhD in "Who is Matty Healy?"

Someone, somewhere, is going to capture a large portion of this audience. And over time, it is likely that they will do exactly what Taylor Swift does, because it is obvious that her business model *works*. Eventually, this artist will make their music increasingly complex and bring this new set of fans on a narrative journey with them, just as Taylor did. And eventually, people will get excited about an interesting, complex, and mystical universe that is *not* the Swiftverse but that seems equally interesting.

Eventually, even Taylor's core fan base will start to peel off to something that is viewed as newer, shinier, and, dare I say it, *better.*

The two will go head-to-head to compete over who gets to "own" the fan base, in which case the newer artist, being the speedboat, will likely be able to easily outmaneuver Taylor, the slow, oil-tanker incumbent.

If you've ever wondered how companies that are "too big" to compete against or to ever disappear actually *do* disappear, this is exactly the playbook that is most often used to beat them.

And Taylor rightfully keeps a close watch on those who are around her, and what they are doing. In fact, her song "Clara Bow" is about exactly this phenomenon. In this song, Taylor describes how someone somewhere will be "chosen" to be the newer, better, hotter, smarter, cooler version of Taylor. And eventually, the music industry will back this new person.

However, her lyrics famously reference a constant set of struggles and bloody wars that she is engaged with, suggesting that Taylor does not intend to go down without a fight. And not just a fight, but war. A bloody, fleshy *war*.

So, being killed by her own success, or being killed by her new replacement.

Is Taylor Swift going to be around in five years' time? What about ten years' time? In interviews, she has said that she wants to leave before people get sick of her. She wants to know when it's time to move on. But as we're seeing, it's hard to predict when that moment may be from the outside, and much, much harder to sense the reality of the situation from the inside.

TAYLOR TO THE MOON

There is a nonzero chance that Taylor Swift, her music, and her brand could collapse under the weight of her own success and in the process be replaced by someone who is "better." Right?

I mean, I've just outlined the many sensible arguments for why a not-so-insignificant number of people have been predicting that Taylor has "peaked," that she is "over," or that she is "on the way out."

I've written a whole damn book on Taylor, so I can't exactly ignore the signs saying that, statistically, once a company or brand gets this big, it can still quite easily be disrupted.

However, being an inhabitant of the Swiftverse and having a

strong desire/bias for wanting Taylor's unequivocal success to continue, I find it rather easy to convince myself that those theories about why or how she may self-disrupt or be disrupted out of the world may not come to pass.

But these, too, are grounded in business history realism, and there is equally much evidence to point to the fact that she may, in fact, be on a trajectory that says, to her fans' joy: Taylor is just getting started.

I want to go back to "chaos theory," the field of physics and mathematics that attempts to explain complex disorder and randomness.

Remember that in Power Move Five I told you about the physicist-biologist-financier-polymath whose theory of antifragility changed the way we think about the world? Well, in Nassim Nicholas Taleb's book, there was another interesting theory that makes me strongly suspect that the Taylor Swift brand is going to be hanging around for quite a while longer, in some form or another.

This theory relates to the concept of "noise" and how to figure out which music, literature, and ideas are actually culturally important and relevant, versus what is just total nonsense being tossed around with hype and driven by oversize marketing budgets.

Taleb argues that every day we have to deal with hundreds of thousands of pieces of information, from texts and emails to ads, from people trying to move our opinion on ideas and to influence our very being. In the midst of this, Taleb says that *time* acts as a natural filter of what is valuable or not. For example, if a song is still being played fifty or one hundred years after it was written, it is a highly relevant piece. Likewise with books that are still being printed decades or hundreds of years after being written.

Taleb's theory then argues that the longer someone or something is around, the longer it will remain relevant in the public domain.

Thus, a band that has a searingly hot number one album in its first year of releasing music is more likely than not to be a one-hit wonder. A band that has a couple of albums is likely to hang around even longer.

Taylor Swift has been *cementing* banger tunes into our ears for *twenty freaking years.* That's a really, really, really long time. At this stage, she has more than just luck on her side. She has the backing of statistics in her favor that say: If she's been able to stick around for the first twenty years, there's very little reason to believe she won't be here for the *next* twenty years.

So, phew. If you also live in the Swiftverse, this is *great* news. But beyond just statistical reasoning, there are other reasons to believe that she is not only going to be hanging around but increasing her reach and the momentum with which she is scaling her brand, her business, and her influence.

And that is: She has absolutely enormous momentum behind her that is actually *very hard* to reduce, never mind eliminate entirely.

Assuming that she is not replaced by a younger, cooler, hotter, more whatever version of herself, there is actually good reason to believe that the criticisms I just outlined are the *wrong* way to think about her business and her growth.

I want to revisit the idea that she will be a victim of her own success, and in particular offer up counterarguments for the two reasons that her success could be her poison pill: her failure to innovate and her inauthenticity.

Firstly, I am always astounded when I come across the perspective that Taylor is not innovating, and her "creative zone" has turned into her "comfort zone." However, I am never *surprised* by this comment.

You see, her work, and in particular her latest, *TTPD*, serves as a strong Rorschach test that separates those who come across her music into two categories: those who listen to her music for the *music*, and those who listen to her music to derive further *meaning* from the *Swiftverse*.

The people in the former category—those who listen to her music for music—happen to be the same people who have predicted her downfall album after album and are always surprised (and even suspect foul play) when that does not actually come to pass. They see her music as being devoid of stylistic evolution, claiming that too many callbacks to the previous *Lover*, *folklore*, and *Midnights* hits make her unable to create something new or different or *innovative*.

These are the people who do not have the time or interest to commit themselves to PhD-level research for every album release. These are also the people who are looking for a cheaper iPhone, without the fancy camera.

On the other hand, understanding that even the music itself has become an Easter egg, the Swiftverse has come to contextualize the apparent "sameness" in *TTPD* as additional dimensionality to the messages. Taylor's "Guilty as Sin" was created as a lyrical overlay to The 1975's "About You," connecting two powerful pieces of a Swiftverse puzzle that makes it feel like the questions upon which Taylor's universe is built are suddenly closer to being solved. In the opening of "So Long, London," staunch fans can hear *Reputation* Era's "Call It What You Want," rather beautifully bookending the beginning and ending of a six-year relationship with Joe Alwyn.

What feels like similarity to critics is actually just Taylor Swift painting over the same walls of the house that she's built for her fans, in the hope that she can finally close the doors to rooms she wishes she had never opened.

Far from being boring, this has been viewed as extraordinarily innovative, more deeply meaningful than any other album release, and has served to activate new layers of intimacy and connection both among the Swifties in the Swiftverse and between the Swifties and Taylor.

It's not that the critics and those who predict Taylor's imminent decline are wrong; they're just looking for something entirely different than the fan universe that Taylor is offering up.

Time will tell, on this matter at least, which group of the two will become more powerful and eventually direct Taylor's brand into heightened success or eventual failure.

The issue of her perceived inauthenticity is a more curious, and ultimately more complex, issue.

As I mentioned, it's hard to nail down a definitive reason for somebody sensing a lack of authenticity; however, it's a feeling that is so strong that once it exists, it's hard to diminish it (as anybody who has been a sixteen-year-old girl in high school has learned the hard way).

But the reasons for her coming across as inauthentic are a little puzzling, given that they are, in fact, all *authentic for Taylor*.

"Taylor is a billionaire who flies on a private jet" is, indeed, a fact of life for her now. And while the underlying issue with Taylor's success is that she is no longer relatable as the girl next door, there is in fact a difference between somebody *having* billionaire status and somebody *acting* like they have billionaire status.

This goes back to what I suspect is Taylor's core goal throughout the last two decades, which was to become the most culturally iconic figure of our time. There were many times when Taylor chose cultural relevance and demonstrated an authentically good nature while doing so over twenty years; it's very possible that this is still her goal, her strategy, and who she is—*despite* having experienced financial success along the way.

Another set of criticisms I hear about her that relate to authenticity and relatability go something like this: "Taylor is immature, sing-ing about her relationships, and while she froze in time during her teenage years, I did grow up, and I have outgrown and outmatured her. She is just not *normal.*"

Well, goddamn. If you wanted to have a twenty-year pseudo-friendship with somebody who was normal, you certainly wouldn't go near Taylor Swift. She is absolutely the *furthest* thing from nor-mal, and that is exactly *why* she is so damn iconic.

"I want you to be enough of an extraordinary Unicorn to write this amazing music, but if you're not 'normal' at the end of it, I won't like you" is one hell of an expectation to place on a human being.

The reason I, personally, have been so drawn to Taylor Swift throughout my twenty-year, admittedly one-way friendship with her is precisely because I see in her the magical, glistening eyes that I see in the other Unicorns I actually do know in real life.

These people are more rare than diamonds in our society. And as I have pointed out in Power Move One of this book, Unicorns see and experience the world in a way that most "normal," "mature," and "grown-up" people never do—through the eyes of children who are brave enough to experience the awe that surrounds them, never mind courageous enough to translate it into a format that the rest of us can digest.

Is Taylor Swift "frozen" in time? Who knows? I certainly don't—although she has somewhat alluded to her desire to grow up herself through her music and in her *Miss Americana* documentary. But I suspect that what people feel when they use words like "immature" and "infantilizing" is the huge chasm between Taylor as a person who practices the dedicatory virtues and allows herself to see the world in an imaginative and creative way that we now exclusively associate with being "childlike," and her long-term fans who, as they have gotten older, have lost the skill of imagination under the burden of "life."

I would argue that her inauthenticity is actually misunderstood. Perhaps she is actually being more authentic in how she shows us her life, and perhaps we are realizing for the first time how different and insanely bizarre her life as a twenty-year celebrity has become.

One of my favorite quotes from the Netflix documentary is when she discusses her ability to remain unchanged in the face of feeling extreme hurt: "I want to still have a sharp pen and a thin skin and an open heart."

This, I believe, has served as a guiding principle for Taylor's commitment to authenticity that has long defined her. Here, she puts it on the table for us.

There is no denying that her life is extremely different from the lives that her Swifties live, but that's always been the case. Taylor never went to college and has never experienced life in a college dorm—the exact place where her music defined millions of students. She never had normal dating experiences, despite her music comforting millions of people who did. In the last decade, there hasn't been a single day when she couldn't have gone on a date with a male supermodel if she wanted to, yet we still connected to her many albums about feelings of inadequacy and being unwanted.

I don't believe that she's any less relatable today than she was twenty years ago, because her entire brand was built upon *who* she is (kind, talented, hardworking, and nice) instead of *what* she is (a billionaire, a private jet owner, an NFL girlfriend).

In particular, I find that labeling her unrelatable is confusing because, if anything, *TTPD* showed that not even Taylor Swift can *have it all*. Like millions of women in their mid-thirties, she is realizing that there may in fact be more to life than work. She might

want a family. She might want to settle down into a committed relationship. While she finds herself suddenly single on an eighteen-
month-long tour, she simultaneously finds herself surrounded by
friends who "*all smell like weed or little babies.*"

I am the same age as Taylor Swift, and I can confirm: Absolutely
none of my friends are self-made billionaires who are dating global
superstars. Yet all of my friends, married, dating, or single, are still
asking themselves exactly the same questions Taylor poses in her
music: What do I want, how do I get it, and why the hell do men still
ghost me?!

● ● ●

When you read predictions of the future, do yourself a favor and
throw them out. As Taylor says, "Toss it out, reject it, and resist it."
There are an insane number of people who speak bullshit as their
first language, and they love nothing more than to tell you exactly
what will happen to the Tesla share price, the rate of inflation, the
weather, and Taylor Swift's popularity.

However, that's not to say that "Where does Taylor go from
here?" isn't a legitimate question; it is. And it's especially important
because, as it so happens, she has amassed levels of fame, fortune,
and power that were previously considered unachievable for a single
singer-songwriter.

There is no doubt that she is one of the most, if not *the most*, powerful women in the world. But even Taylor Swift wakes up in the
morning, wondering: Is today going to be the day it all ends?

And if that's *not* what she's thinking, then the answer automatically becomes "yes."

If the history of the stock market and large companies has taught
us anything, it's that the bigger a company, brand, or person becomes,

the more exposed they become to being disrupted by the very mechanisms that made them successful in the first place.

And this isn't applicable to just Facebook, Tesla, or Taylor Swift. There's a reason that people find goal-setting such a useful activity in their own personal and professional lives—so that they can look back on their ambitions and determine whether or not they have slowed down, become less innovative, or stopped challenging themselves as much.

I mean, it's absolutely not surprising that Taylor Swift is so damn dogged in this way, given that she is known to be a serial diary-writer.

Learning how to deal with success is just as hard as learning how to become the best in any industry; and it's not uncommon for even the best Unicorns to fall under the pressure of one or both of these difficulties. Success breeds success, until a certain point when success becomes a thing to be carefully managed in and of itself, for fear that it may infect your ability to keep growing and innovating.

Maintaining speed and the ability to outmaneuver competitors is key. However, the path to becoming successful requires acknowledging that you're not always going to please everybody. There will always be the people who want a hundred-dollar dumbphone, in the same way that there are people who do not want Taylor's Swiftverse—they just want the damn music.

And that's fine. As your mom will have told you a hundred times, you can't be everything to everyone, lest you become nothing to nobody.

Taylor's ability to navigate the future relies on her being able to bring her core fan base with her as she transitions from being the traditional underdog, who used songs about punching up to build deep relationships with her fans, to knowing that anything she sings about others in a negative capacity will always mean that she's punching down. She's at the top now; everybody else is now the underdog in comparison to her. And there's *never* any glory in punching down.

Taylor has entered a new phase in which she will transition from being the "top music icon of our time" to potentially realizing her goal of being the "top cultural icon of our time" as she expands her Swiftverse into movies, books, poetry, and beyond.

Should she be able to outrun her up-and-coming competitors, who will inevitably try to replicate her model and her trajectory, her path will become binary: She will either perish and fall, having been the woman who nearly had it all, or her fans will have been just right—until now, she was only getting started.

Just like in *Jurassic Park*, the water is on the dashboard, vibrating.

The shape and form of the Taylor Swift that appears in the corner of our eyes are going to determine what may come next for this Unicorn and for the millions of fans who've followed her so far.

CONCLUSION

SO, WHAT NOW?

You've read about Taylor Swift's journey from being a teenage singer-songwriter to the CEO of a global business powerhouse as she attempts to become the most culturally iconic figure of our time. You've seen her fearless approach to challenges, her ability to adapt and innovate, to be antifragile when it matters most, and her unshakable commitment to her vision. Perhaps most important, you've learned how these lessons can be applied to your own life.

Much like Taylor's songs and lyrics and music, which might be a reflection of her own life, this book was never just about Taylor Swift. It's about *us*. It's about *you*.

Taylor's story isn't one of overnight success or unattainable genius. It's a story of deliberate choices, relentless hard work, and an unwavering belief in the power of having agency, and of believing in herself enough to use that agency. She has shown that success, no matter how outsize, is within reach for those who are willing to take risks, learn from setbacks, and stay true to their goals.

And yet we'll never truly know what's next for Taylor Swift.

That's the magic of her career. We know that she's always thinking years ahead of her Swifties, executing plans they can't even imagine (even if they can try to statistically reverse engineer what they may be!). She stays unpredictable, reinventing herself and consistently leaving the world in awe.

But while we can only speculate about Taylor's next move, there's one thing we can control: what's next for us.

I hope that as you've read this book you've started to recognize your own Power Moves. Just as I did throughout my career and life by watching Taylor, maybe you've identified the areas in your life where you can act fearlessly, where you can double down on your strengths, or where you can make the bold decision that others are too scared to try.

Maybe you've started to see yourself as the CEO of your own life, in charge of creating opportunities rather than waiting for them to come to you.

The truth is, as I learned early on, extraordinary achievements are not the result of extraordinary people. They're the result of ordinary people deciding to act extraordinarily. The NASA engineers I met as a teenager weren't superheroes; they were regular people who chose to follow their curiosity and channel their talents into something they believed in. The famous CEOs I've been fortunate to work with are people, just like you and me, who wake up every morning and put in the hard work. Taylor Swift isn't just a pop star; she's a strategist, a brand builder, and a master of reinvention.

And you? You can be whatever you decide to be.

There's one key lesson I hope you'll take away from this book: You have more agency than you think. The barriers that seem insurmountable are often illusions, reinforced by others who are too afraid to dream bigger. Trust me, and as Taylor Swift has shown us, this is nonsense. The path to success may not always be clear, but it's always there for those willing to carve it out, however easy or hard that may be.

The world needs more fearless people (and fewer dead fish)—people who are willing to take bold, strategic action to pursue what matters to them. Whether your dream is to start a business, become an artist, revolutionize an industry, or simply live a life that feels authentically yours, I hope you'll use Taylor's Power Moves as a blueprint for your own.

The people who achieve extraordinary things aren't waiting for permission. They're not sitting back, wondering if they're good enough, or if someone will hand them the opportunities they've been dreaming of. They're out there, making their moves, just like Taylor Swift.

And if she can do it, so can you.

The next era of your own story is unwritten. Be fearless. Be a *Unicorn.*

ACKNOWLEDGMENTS

O H. GOSH. there is an endless list of people for whom I am deeply grateful.

First, to Taylor, for providing such a rich tapestry of study-able material. It's been a wild twenty years!

Second, to the people who made this book possible: my agent, Mel, for pushing forward this idea; my editors, Emily and Geraldine, who are also this book's coconspirators; and the seemingly endless number of people who appeared out of nowhere along the way and who shaped this project into what it has become.

Finally, to Eoin, who has ever-so-patiently listened to over a decade of my Swiftisms, and particularly for enduring the daily, hours-long walks to listen to me discussing the frameworks contained within these pages.

ACKNOWLEDGMENTS

There is a much longer list of people who would be impossible to include here in full, but suffice to say: This book and I are a product of your kindness, talents, and generosity of time and ideas.

Thank you!